Text processing and document manipulation

THE BRITISH COMPUTER SOCIETY WORKSHOP SERIES

Editor: P. HAMMERSLEY

The BCS Workshop Series aims to report developments of an advanced technical standard undertaken by members of The British Computer Society through the Society's study groups and conference organisation. The Series should be compulsive reading for all whose work or interest involves computing technology and for both undergraduate and post-graduate students. Volumes in this Series will mirror the quality of papers published in the BCS's technical periodical *The Computer Journal* and range widely across topics in computer hardware, software, application and management.

Some current titles:

Current Perspectives in Health Computing
Ed. B. Kostrewski

Research and Development in Information Retrieval
Ed. C. J. van Rijsbergen

Proceedings of the Third British National Conference on Databases (BNCOD 3)
Ed. J. Longstaff

Research and Development in Expert Systems
Ed. M. A. Bramer

Proceedings of the Fourth British National Conference on Databases (BNCOD 4)
Ed. A. F. Grundy

People and Computers: Designing the Interface
Ed. P. Johnson and S. Cook

Expert Systems 85
Ed. M. Merry

Text Processing and Document Manipulation
Ed. J. C. van Vliet

Text processing and document manipulation

Proceedings of the International Conference
University of Nottingham, 14-16 April 1986

Edited by J. C. van VLIET

Centrum voor Wiskunde en Informatica, Amsterdam

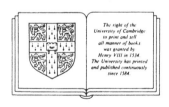

Published by
CAMBRIDGE UNIVERSITY PRESS
on behalf of
THE BRITISH COMPUTER SOCIETY
Cambridge
London   New York   New Rochelle
Melbourne   Sydney

CAMBRIDGE UNIVERSITY PRESS
Cambridge, New York, Melbourne, Madrid, Cape Town, Singapore, São Paulo

Cambridge University Press
The Edinburgh Building, Cambridge CB2 8RU, UK

Published in the United States of America by Cambridge University Press, New York

www.cambridge.org
Information on this title: www.cambridge.org/9780521325929

First published 1986

A catalogue record for this publication is available from the British Library

ISBN 978-0-521-32592-9 hardback

Transferred to digital printing 2007

Contents

Preface

For many years text preparation and document manipulation have been poor relations in the computing world, and it is only recently that they have taken their rightful place in the mainstream of computer research and development. Everyone has their own favourite reason for this change: word processors, workstations with graphics screens, non-impact printers, or authors preparing their own manuscripts.

Whatever the reason, people in computing have suddenly found themselves using the same equipment and fighting the same problems as those in printing and publishing. It would be nice to say that we are all working happily together, but there are still plenty of disputes (which is healthy) and plenty of indifference (which is not). There is no doubt, however, that this coming together of different disciplines has brought new life and enthusiasm with it.

The international conference on *Text Processing and Document Manipulation* at Nottingham, is not the first conference to focus on this field of computing. It follows in the footsteps of *Research and Trends in Document Preparation Systems* at Lausanne in 1981, the *Symposium on Text Manipulation* at Portland in 1981, *La Manipulation de Documents* at Rennes in 1983, and the recent *PROTEXT* conferences in Dublin. We hope, however, that it marks the beginning of a regular series of international conferences that will bring top researchers and practitioners together to exchange ideas and share their enthusiasm with a wide audience.

As the papers for this conference started to come in, a number of themes began to emerge. The dominant theme (in number of papers) was document structures for interactive editing. Other well-represented themes were page description languages, document retrieval, design considerations, techniques for handling and presenting electronic documents, and standards.

The three keynote papers, *Procedural Page Description Languages* by Brian Reid, *Trends and Standards in Document Representation* by Vania Joloboff, and *The Design of Lucida: an Integrated Family of Types for Electronic Literacy* by Charles Bigelow and Kris Holmes, all fall within these themes. The dominant theme of document structures and interactive document editing is addressed in several papers, including *Formatting Structured Documents: Batch versus Interactive?* by G. Coray, R. Ingold and C. Vanoirbeek, *An Integrated, but not Exact-Representation, Editor/Formatter* by Richard Furuta, *A Disciplined Text-Formatting Environment* by Dick Hamlet, and *Grif: An Interactive System for Structured Document Manipulation* by Vincent Quint and Irene Vatton. The other themes are all represented, too, as can be seen from the titles.

We believe the papers in this book provide a valuable state-of-the-art presentation of work in computer-assisted document production and manipulation, and would like to take this opportunity to thank all the authors and organisers for their help in making the conference possible.

Finally, a few words about the appearance of the book. Having the Proceedings available at the conference imposes a stringent timetable on production. Typically this results in a messy looking book, which may be an initial source of pride and relief, but is a reproach ever after. An ideal solution is for authors to submit electronic manuscripts which are then processed by the editor or publisher into a uniform style. This method was considered but abandoned, reluctantly, in favour of the more usual method where authors were asked to provide camera-ready copy. We felt, however, that authors for a conference on text processing should be able to produce good-looking papers if given proper guidelines. So, as an experiment, the editor (with advice from the Cambridge University Press) has supplied authors with detailed *Guidelines for Authors* which assume access to high-quality formatting and printing facilities.

At the time of writing, the result of this experiment is unknown. (This Preface has to be in the hands of the editor, in camera-ready form, at the same time as all the other contributions — I, too, am working from the *Guidelines*!) Readers are invited to judge the success or failure of the experiment for themselves.

Heather Brown
Canterbury, January 1986

The Design of Lucida®: an Integrated Family of Types for Electronic Literacy

CHARLES BIGELOW* & KRIS HOLMES**
*Stanford University
**Bigelow & Holmes

ABSTRACT
Electronic printing and publishing transform traditional analog letter-forms into digital pixel patterns. At medium and low resolutions, aliasing degrades the legibility of digital types. To maintain typographic quality in an aliased image environment, the design of readable digital typefaces requires rational, technical considerations as well as intuitive, artistic processes. The graphic functions of typefaces in electronic publishing also require rational structuring. Documents can be more effectively designed when typographic variations of weight and style are integrated into a systematic design family.

OMAGGIO A GRIFFO
One by one, each seriffed black figure
is transfixed in the luminous white field.
As the gaze travels across the page,
it goes like the wind on a summer night,
Blowing the clouds in their atmosphere,
Light in the face of the full moon,
and dark in the depths of the starry sky.

In designing the Lucida typefaces for laser printers, digital typesetters, and CRT screens, we found inspiration in the work of Francesco Griffo, a Renaissance typeface designer who flourished at the end of the 15th century during an era of profound change in the technology of literacy.

At a time when other type-founders were attempting in vain to copy manuscript writing hands, Griffo was the first punch-cutter to actively explore the design possibilities of the engraved, typographic letter. He created letterforms that were no longer handwriting, but that nevertheless stemmed naturally from principles inherent in the alphabet. The types he cut for the Venetian printer Aldus Manutius profoundly influenced the history of typography [Mardersteig69] [Morison73].

The fundamental problem that Griffo faced was how to maintain clarity and vivacity of the text image in a radically changed imaging technology. We face the same problem today.

1. Transformations of Letterforms.

1.1 From Ductal to Sculptal to Pictal.

Griffo helped transform the ductal handwritten letter of the scribe into the sculptal typographic letter of the printer. The analog typographic letter became the publishing standard for five centuries, but it is now being replaced by the pictal electronic letter in digital printing and electronic publishing. From the reader's point of view, the main flaw of digital typography is the degraded appearance of the typefaces [Bigelow81, 82].

1.2 Aliasing.

Current digital screens and printers lack resolution sufficient to render traditional analog letterforms adequately. A digital letter is typically produced by sampling an analog letter. Low and medium resolution devices like CRT screens and laser printers do not provide enough samples in a letter image to reproduce all the information in the original design. "Undersampling" causes loss of high-frequency information and "aliasing", a form of digital noise. The contours of an aliased letter are disrupted by "jaggies"; its proportions, weight, and spacing are distorted, and its fine details obscured [Bigelow,Day83].

To understand how to design letters for rasterized reproduction in the one bit per pixel technologies common today, it is helpful to consider the common ad hoc methods of ameliorating aliasing in letterforms. These are bitmap editing and outline deformation.

1.3 Bitmap Editing.

A letter is first scan-converted to a raster from an analog image or a digital outline. Then a designer "edits" the resulting raster image by adding, deleting, or rearranging pixels. In this process, the designer's intuitive, internalized model of what the letter image should be is mapped onto the actual raster image, modifying the arbitrary output of an electro-optical or algorithmic process. This is often effective because the designer actually *sees* what she is doing, and thus intuitively tunes the image to the characteristics of the human visual system in accordance with knowledge of canonical letter shapes.

Bitmap editing has the disadvantage of being a low-level, local manipulation of the letter image. An alphabet design also contains global information that bitmap editing cannot directly address. The alphabet structure remains a concept in the mind of the designer, but it is not a part of the data representation.

1.4 Outline Deformation.

A higher-level method of ameliorating aliasing is to deform letter images globally throughout an alphabet before scan-conversion. When letters are represented as outlines, the points defining the outlines can be adjusted in relation to the output raster so that certain letter features will fall nicely on raster values. For example, the edges of all vertical stems in an alphabet could be deformed to fall on integer values of the raster, and constrained to have the same pixel thickness [Karow83].

1.5 Noise & Signal.

Bitmap editing and outline deformation can have similar results, and it is possible that they are related in an abstract way.

Bitmap editing appears to be a way of rearranging the aliasing noise in the rasterized letter image. Because editing does not increase resolution, aliases remain from under-sampling, but their spatial positions in the image have been moved.

In the frequency domain, bitmap editing may be a way to shift the frequencies of the aliasing noise further from the fundamental frequencies of the signal. The noise would then mask perception of the signal to a lesser degree. The letters remain distorted, but appear less so because certain lower frequency components (e.g. stems) have a more regular relationship to the raster.

These are merely conjectures, but efforts to optimize digital type could benefit from a rigorous analysis of the effects of scanning, editing, and deformation on the frequency spectra of letterforms at various resolutions. Typefaces are a special kind of image that could benefit from refined methods of anti-aliasing, especially on displays with multiple bits per pixel [Kajiya,Ullner81] [Dippe,Wold85].

Deformation of outlines appears to accomplish the same thing as bitmap editing, though prior to scan-conversion, by deforming the original image to match more closely the periodicity of the sampling grid. Major letter features become aligned with the raster, and thereby exhibit less obvious distortion.

In both cases, important information about the structure of the alphabet is missing from the basic font data, whether raster or outline, and must be supplied from an external source (a designer). An explicit model of alphabetic structure could support automatic identification of letter features and their parameterized deformation to optimize scan-conversion of letterforms.

It may be that such a model could take the form of a more elaborate data structure for each outline font, or perhaps canonical models could be developed for the kinds of alphabet design: either by style, i.e. seriffed, sans-serif, etc.; or by class, i.e. Latin, Greek, etc. Much of the research in this area is currently embedded in proprietary research or commercial systems [Plass] [Sheridan] [Warnock].

1.6 Rationalization.

To facilitate digitization and enhance image quality, alphabet designs for electronic printing and publishing should be more explicit and more rationalized than traditional analog typefaces. A *structural model* of the alphabets should be communicable both to designers editing bitmap fonts, and to algorithms performing automatic transformations on digital outlines.

An outline representation with precise specifications of proportions, parameters, letter parts, and other design features is one way to implement alphabetic structure. Philippe Coueignoux has described one approach to a "syntactic" font description [Coueignoux75]. A different approach to a parameterized, structured alphabet design, based on a "pen-drawing" model rather than outlines, is described by Donald Knuth [Knuth80].

1.7 Tuned Features.

The features of letterforms intended for digital printing and display should in general be tuned to the marking characteristics of digital devices. This is difficult because different devices may have contradictory effects, and new kinds of technologies are continually being developed.

1.8 Systematic Typography.

Typeface design is not isolated from the literate culture that uses printing systems. Electronic document production has certain typographic requirements that are different from those of traditional publishing; these will proliferate as the digital technology becomes more prevalent. Among the present needs are simplicity and clarity in typeface families, so that authors and editors may achieve greater fluency in the symbolic language of typographic signs, without protracted study. Typographic variation should be coherent and systematic.

2. The Design Concepts of Lucida

Following these observations and conclusions, we designed the Lucida family of typefaces to provide, at the perceptual level, acceptable legibility in an aliased image environment, and, at the semiological level, a functional system of typographic variations.

Although types are designed at a large size (the master outline characters of Lucida are digitized at an em square of 168 x 168 mm), text is read at small sizes. In designing Lucida, we worked at several levels of the letter image.

2.1 Form, Pattern, & Texture.

At the large size of the master design, a letter form is comprised of sculpted contours delineating dark forms and light counterforms. At a middle size of headlines, letters in combination make patterns out of the quasi-symmetries of repeated forms. At the small size of text, a complex texture emerges from the interaction of the letter features en masse.

We design the features of a typeface at the level of forms, but the character of the face emerges at the level of texture. For the designers, there are often surprises when a type design is first proofed: rational decisions about formal properties turn out to have irrational effects when the texture is perceived. This is part of the excitement of typeface design.

In its features, Lucida is intended to be a font-independent design. This is not the same as a device-independent font. A type design is a visual concept, whereas a font is an implementation of that concept in software or hardware. Traditional type-faces were tuned to the typefounding and printing processes. We sought to tune the letterforms of Lucida to digital image processing and reconstruction.

2.2 Weight.

An index of the weight of a normally proportioned typeface is the ratio of the thickness of a straight stem to the height of the lower-case 'x'. The shade of the gray texture of a face is termed "color". Our survey of several traditional and popular text typefaces showed a variation of stem to x-height ratios from 5:1 to 6:1. Types with ratios toward 5:1 are darker; those with ratios toward 6:1, lighter.

In laser-printing, the polarity of the marking engine becomes an important factor. White-writing engines tend to erode the contours of the letterforms, lightening the color of the text. Black-writing engines tend to spread the contours, darkening the text.

Another factor is the use of laser-printer output as masters for offset-lithography or photocopying. These processes further darken or lighten the text image.

On screens, the writing spot which reconstructs the bitmap letterforms also changes the weight of the text image. The perceived weight of screen text is influenced by the intensity contour of the spot and the size of the spot in relation to the resolution of the raster. The reconstruction filter effects are strongest at the pixels along the contour of a letterform. Small sizes and lower resolutions, where the contour is a greater part of the total image, are more strongly affected.

Numerically, the weight ratio of a face necessarily varies from size to size because stems and x-heights are rounded-off to integer pixel values at each raster size. We examined the amounts of error in ideal weight ratios caused by round-off at common sizes and resolutions.

These observations led us to estimate that the weight of the text image seen by the reader would on the average vary about 10% from the original design, and in the worst cases by as much as 25%. To make the typeface resistant to extreme variations in color, we designed the normal weight of Lucida with a stem to x-height ratio of 5.5 to 1.

2.3 Contrast.

Contrast is the ratio between the thick and thin parts of letters. Serifs, hairlines, and joins are thins; vertical stems, curved bowls, and main diagonals are thicks. The contrast of traditional text types ranges from a high of 5:1 to a low of 2:1. The high-contrast faces appear delicate and brilliant; the low-contrast faces, sturdy and solid.

High contrast faces are believed to be more difficult to read than medium and low-contrast designs. Moreover, thin hairlines and serifs are more susceptible to breakage and erosion by printing processes. Text degraded by broken thins is especially objectionable because the letterforms lose connectivity and become more difficult to discriminate. Marking effects that change weight change contrast even more, because erosion or expansion of thin hairlines is proportionally greater than for thick stems.

To prevent of loss of hairlines and serifs on white-writing engines and bitmap screens displaying black text on an illuminated background, we chose a low contrast of 2:1 for the basic Lucida seriffed designs. This decision in favor of robustness also influenced the design of joins and serifs.

2.4 Joins.

Black-writing printers and reverse-video displays increase the thickness of thin elements. In particular, the white triangular counter-forms produced where an arch joins a straight stem, as in an 'n', tend to be filled in when letter contours are emboldened. Therefore, when joins are kept sturdy to prevent erosion by white-writing printers, counters are susceptible to clogging by black-writing printers.

Our solution to this antinomy was to branch the joins relatively deep on the stems, so that the triangular counter-form of the master design has a generous area. Hence, even when the counter is filled to some degree, it remains open enough to be acceptable. After we had designed this feature in Lucida, we discovered that Fleischman, an 18th century punch-cutter, used a similar technique in cutting small sizes of types intended for journal publishing [Carter37] [Enschede08].

To further prevent clogging, we reduced the thickness of the stem close to the join by making the segment of the stem edge closest to the join cut into the stem at a slight angle. The amount

[1]   Outline of Lucida Roman 'n' showing details of the simplified polygonal serif structure and enlargement of the counter area where the arch joins the left stem. The chamfered serifs and tapered stems can be resolved at high resolutions, but the underlying slab serifs and straight stems result at low resolutions. The stem is narrowed at the join, to prevent the counter from clogging with toner at lower resolutions on black-writing printers. The gap can be narrowed for white-writing printers and higher resolutions. These details are seen here at a large size at the level of form, but they are intended to be seen at a small size at the level of texture.

Hanov Honav Hvano Hnova Oanov Oonav Ovano Onova
Vanov Vonav Vvano Vnova Ranov Ronav Rvano Rnova
Hanov Honav Hvano Hnova Oanov Oonav Ovano Onova
Vanov Vonav Vvano Vnova Ranov Ronav Rvano Rnova
Hanov Honav Hvano Hnova Oanov Oonav Ovano Onova
Vanov Vonav Vvano Vnova Ranov Ronav Rvano Rnova
Hanov Honav Hvano Hnova Oanov Oonav Ovano Onova
Vanov Vonav Vvano Vnova Ranov Ronav Rvano Rnova
Hanov Honav Hvano Hnova Oanov Oonav Ovano Onova
Vanov Vonav Vvano Vnova Ranov Ronav Rvano Rnova
Hanov Honav Hvano Hnova Oanov Oonav Ovano Onova
Vanov Vonav Vvano Vnova Ranov Ronav Rvano Rnova
Hanov Honav Hvano Hnova Oanov Oonav Ovano Onova
Vanov Vonav Vvano Vnova Ranov Ronav Rvano Rnova
Hanov Honav Hvano Hnova Oanov Oonav Ovano Onova
Vanov Vonav Vvano Vnova Ranov Ronav Rvano Rnova

[2]   The eight basic styles of Lucida, composed in "key-words" made up of round, straight, diagonal, and composite letterforms: Roman, Italic, Bold, Bold Italic in seriffed and sans-serif styles. At a small size, in this case 8 point at 300 lines per inch (= 33 pixels per em square), the formal details become invisible and the textural qualities of the design dominate the image. The relationships between roman and italic, normal and bold, seriffed and sans-serif become subtle but significant.

of cut is determined by the position of a single point. When the join is in danger of clogging at small sizes, this point can be shifted toward the interior of the stem and the cut widened. When the stem should appear straight at large sizes, the cut can be narrowed.

2.5 Serifs.

Our design experiments showed that long, thick serifs give a typeface a stolid appearance and a dark color. We wanted thick serifs to resist erosion, but we didn't want too dark a color. Accordingly, we reduced the total area of the serifs by abbreviating their lengths to one-half of the stem thickness.

Serif shapes also posed problems. When letters are reduced to coarse bitmaps at low and medium digital resolutions, bracketed serifs are reduced to slab serifs. When letters are represented as outlines, curved brackets are complex details that can require extra time to digitize, more space in storage, and more time to scan convert.

A slab serif would have simplified the alphabet design without appreciable loss of elegance at low resolution, but at high resolution, the slabs would have seemed monotonous. We chose a middle path, chamfering the serif and stem with slight diagonal taperings. At low resolutions, these serifs can be rounded-off to simple slabs, but as resolution increases, the chamferings provide variations in weight and thickness that enliven the printed texture.

These polygonal serifs can be compactly and precisely represented by vectors. In a font format that provides for adjustment or deformation of letter features to enhance scan-conversion, the polygonal serifs are more diagrammatic than absolute, because the points on the vertices can be moved by algorithm or by designer specification to enhance the appearance of the resultant bit image.

2.6 X-height.

The x-height (height of lower-case 'x') of a typeface is an index of the apparent size of a typeface. Most of the shape information in the lower-case alphabet is carried by those parts of the letters that lie between the baseline and the x-line. Typefaces with large x-heights look bigger than those with small x-heights, even when the actual body sizes (total cell height from bottom

[3] Lucida seriffed lower-case 'a' at three resolutions corresponding to 8, 10, and 24 point fonts on a 300 line per inch laser printer. The effects of under-sampling are plainly evident. At left, the lowest resolution shows a strongly aliased image with "jaggies" that disrupt the curved and diagonal letter elements. At right, the highest resolution still shows noise along the contours. When these idealized bitmaps are reconstructed as actual images by a laser printer, the sharp images of the stair-steps are smoothed, but some distortion of the forms remains.

abcdefghijklmnopqrstuvwxyz ABCDEFGHIJKLMNOPQRSTUVWXYZ
0123456789 #$%@&.,;:!¡?¿'"'"/|*(){}[]↑−∞+−=~∧<>_—−‐ fffiflffiffl硭˘˙¨˝˚˜ .

abcdefghijklmnopqrstuvwxyz ABCDEFGHIJKLMNOPQRSTUVWXYZ
0123456789 #$%@&.,;:!¡?¿'"'"/|*(){}[]↑−∞+−=~∧<>_—−‐ fffiflffiffl硭˘˙¨˝˚˜ .

abcdefghijklmnopqrstuvwxyz ABCDEFGHIJKLMNOPQRSTUVWXYZ
0123456789 #$%@&.,;:!¡?¿'"'"/|*(){}[]↑−∞+−=~∧<>_—−‐ fffiflffiffl硭˘˙¨˝˚˜ .

abcdefghijklmnopqrstuvwxyz ABCDEFGHIJKLMNOPQRSTUVWXYZ
0123456789 #$%@&.,;:!¡?¿'"'"/|*(){}[]↑−∞+−=~∧<>_—−‐ fffiflffiffl硭˘˙¨˝˚˜ .

abcdefghijklmnopqrstuvwxyz ABCDEFGHIJKLMNOPQRSTUVWXYZ
0123456789 #$%@&.,;:!¡?¿'"'"/|*(){}[]↑−∞+−=~∧<>_—−‐ fffiflffiffl硭˘˙¨˝˚˜ .

abcdefghijklmnopqrstuvwxyz ABCDEFGHIJKLMNOPQRSTUVWXYZ
0123456789 #$%@&.,;:!¡?¿'"'"/|*(){}[]↑−∞+−=~∧<>_—−‐ fffiflffiffl硭˘˙¨˝˚˜ .

abcdefghijklmnopqrstuvwxyz ABCDEFGHIJKLMNOPQRSTUVWXYZ
0123456789 #$%@&.,;:!¡?¿'"'"/|*(){}[]↑−∞+−=~∧<>_—−‐ fffiflffiffl硭˘˙¨˝˚˜ .

abcdefghijklmnopqrstuvwxyz ABCDEFGHIJKLMNOPQRSTUVWXYZ
0123456789 #$%@&.,;:!¡?¿'"'"/|*(){}[]↑−∞+−=~∧<>_—−‐ fffiflffiffl硭˘˙¨˝˚˜ .

[4] ASCII character sets for the eight basic styles of Lucida, augmented with ligatures and diacritics. The stylistic variations also apply to the non-alphabetic characters, so that the semiological contrasts are consistent throughout a given typeface. Note that the sans-serif italic is a true cursive style, rather than an oblique distortion of the roman. This gives the sans-serif italic greater vivacity, and maintains its relationship to the seriffed italic.

of descender to top of ascender) are the same.

Low-resolution systems entice the designer toward large x-heights because the complex middle portions of the lower-case need more resolution than the relatively simple ascenders and descenders. However, if the ascenders and descenders are reduced too far, the complex lower loop of the humanistic 'g' will be distorted, and the shapes of other letters ('h' - 'n', 'b' - 'p') will become indistinguishable from each other, destroying the legibility of the face. Thus, there is an upper bound to the size of the x-height.

The x-height of Lucida is 52% of the body. This allows more detail to be devoted to the lower-case letter shapes, and permits Lucida to pack a relatively large amount of legible text information into a relatively small area. Lucida set at 9 point seems as large as many other faces at 10 or 11 point. Where page space is limited and text economy important, this increase in apparent size is a definite advantge. However, where economy of space is not crucial, we prefer to see Lucida composed with extra points of "leading" (white space) between lines, to give the page a more open and relaxed texture.

2.7 Fitting.

The positive (black) and negative (white) shapes in a letterform are equally important. Traditional typefaces are fitted so that the spaces between letters are visually equivalent and harmonized with the white counters inside the letters. Aliasing distorts the interletter white spaces as much as the black shapes of the letters, causing an irregular texture with dark collisions of some characters and empty voids between others.

In advertising typography, tightly kerned letter spacing draws attention to texts that are otherwise empty of content. However, when this kind of spacing is attempted on low resolution printing systems, round-off error of letter widths creates an objectionable, splotchy texture.

The best printed books of the last 500 years have typefaces that are regularly, harmoniously, and often openly spaced [Tschichold66]. We followed these models when fitting the Lucida designs for laser printer resolutions. At typesetter resolutions, where tighter fitting can be accomplished without losing a regular rhythm, Lucida can be more closely spaced.

2.8 *Capital Height.*

Our traditional capital forms were developed by the Romans, and our lower-case (minuscules) by Carolingian scribes. Capitals and lower-case were separate alphabets until the early 15th century, when they were first amalgamated into a single duplex alphabet by the Florentine humanist and scribe, Poggio Bracciolini. At the end of that century, Francesco Griffo fine-tuned the relationship between typographic capitals and lower-case by reducing the relative size of the capitals.

Documents printed by laser printers often are dominated by capitals, usually for retrograde reasons left over from monocase terminals and printers. Following Griffo's lead, we made the Lucida capitals slightly shorter than the ascenders of the lower-case so that capitals would not be too emphatic and distracting when used heavily in a text. As well as reducing their height, we also gave the capitals slightly narrow proportions to provide even greater space economy when capitals are used extensively in a document.

We also observed that weight differences between capitals and lower-case are often exaggerated at low resolutions, when a one pixel increase in stem thickness will make the capitals seem much darker than the lower-case. Therefore, we made the capitals similar in weight to the lower-case to keep the alphabets harmonious at lower resolutions.

The design of capitals is also affected by the orthographies of different languages. De-emphasized capitals are often preferred for German language texts that make extensive use of capitals. However, we also anticipated that some French and English typographers would request more robust capitals, in keeping with certain national printing traditions and cultural views. We therefore designed an alternate set of capitals that are heavier in weight, especially for use on higher-resolution devices.

3. The Structure of an Extended Family

3.1 *Teleology.*

The history of typography shows a tendency for typeface designs to become united into families. Capitals and minuscules (lower-case) were united in the early 15th century; roman and italic in the 16th century; normal and bold weights in the 19th century. The first typeface family to include both seriffed and sans-serif alphabets was Romulus, designed by Jan van Krimpen in the 1930s.

3.2 Dimensions of Typographic Space

Lucida continues the historical trend toward extended design families by structuring several letterform styles in one family: roman vs. italic; normal vs. bold; seriffed vs. sans-serif; proportional vs. mono-spaced; Latin vs. Greek. The family is thus a system of oppositions which can be thought of as defining a multi-dimensional space of typographic variation.

These contrasting variations are precisely aligned in their vertical letter proportions and standardized in weights. A change along one dimension leaves most other characteristics of the typeface unaltered, with the exception of letter widths. Widths are similar, though not quite identical between roman and italic, and seriffed and sans. The bold weights are proportionally wider than the normal weights.

3.3 Semiology of Type Styles.

Each graphic typeface variation can be used to signify or *mark* some semantic aspect of the text. Roman may be used for normal text, italic for differentiation, bold for emphasis, bold italic for emphatic differentiation, sans-serif for technical text, script for casual notes, and so forth.

Type styles used as signifiers are part of the "passive vocabulary" of typographic literacy; readers understand them, but type variations are not necessarily part of the "active vocabulary" of every author. Like other languages, a graphic language of formal variations requires practice for the user to become fluent. Initially, one follows conventional styles of typography, but more imaginative expression becomes possible as one becomes more familiar with the medium.

The harmonization and simplification of the Lucida family is intended to make the Lucida typefaces easier for authors to use intuitively. When typographic documents are formatted with systems like TROFF, TeX, and Scribe, graphic variations should be clear and comprehensible to the author as well as to the reader. Clarity and simplicity of variation makes it easier for an author to use typefaces expressively and powerfully.

3.4 Modularization.

Another effect of harmonization is to make typefaces easier to implement. Within each Lucida face, many elements such as stems, serifs, and bowls are repeated. Should it be necessary to save space in a font implementation, characters can be represented as assemblages of component parts rather than separate characers. Across the family, different designs may also share certain features. Seriffed and Sans-serif faces of the same weight and stress share the same stems and outer contours of bowls. The entire Lucida family could be further compacted by exploiting these similarities.

Modularization of design also made it easier to produce the faces, both in outline and in raster format. More often than not, the principal advantage of rationalization and modularization was simply a precise understanding of the design parameters. This was often reasurring when we were caught in the coils of the magnitude of the actual production. The Lucida family currently includes 1,500 outline masters and 12,000 raster characters, with more in production. In the midst of this daunting multiplicity, a coherent design structure that could be expressed in logical and numerical relationships made it easier to remember, communicate, and record what a given letter image or group of images was supposed to look like at any given size on a variety of displays.

3.5 Screen Fonts.

The principles that shaped the Lucida designs for printers similarly influenced the design of bitmap versions of Lucida for CRT displays. At screen resolutions of 75 and 100 lines per inch, all sizes of the Lucida fonts required bitmap editing.

From 6 to 22 pixels per body, the fonts were mainly constructed by hand, using a bitmap editing system. At these low resolutions, there are so few pixels in each letterform, and the position of each pixel is so crucial, that only the experienced eye of the designer can make an optimal judgement. For sizes of 24 pixels per body size and greater, the fonts were produced in two stages. Digital spline outlines were first deformed to the given raster, using the Ikarus software system. This provided a general idea of the charactristics of the font at a given size. The resulting rasters were then hand-edited to optimize the fonts on the screen.

Because of their low resolution, screen fonts cannot be exact reproductions of their higher resolution counterparts. We wanted the screen fonts to be usable in "WYSIWYG" systems along with Lucida on printers, but also to be useful on their own, when optimized for legibility on the screen without the procrustean distortion to match spacing values of higher resolution devices that the simple-minded WYSIWYG systems usually demand. To emphasize that the screen fonts can exist as independent entities, we christened them with the name Pellucida, which connotes that the designs are related to Lucida, but optimized for "pel" based screen displays.

4. Conclusion
Typography holds a particular fascination for the inquiring mind, and this is nowhere more evident than in the realm of electronic printing and publishing. Typography is abstract, achromatic, and two-dimensional, yet it constitutes a complete aesthetic microcosm accessible to the literate intellect. Typefaces exist only to serve language, yet their art is as subtle as music or painting. The forms of the letters are intuitive and mystical, yet they are ruled by numerical principles and systems of measurement and proportion. The patterns of the alphabet are arbitrary and historical, yet they reveal a complex symmetry and an intricate evolution. The texture of a page is completely visible, yet how it emerges from the interaction of its myriad components remains obscure.

We designed Lucida to meet the practical needs of contemporary electronic publishing, but it was for us also an exploration of that aesthetic realm at the intersection of science and art. Because Lucida was, to our knowledge, the first original typeface family produced for digital printers and displays, we necessarily based much of its design on principles more than on precedents. Some of those principles had to be invented as we worked on the design and encountered puzzles for which there were no ready answers. Yet the design is not completely novel, nor can it be wholly reduced to logic, for many of the principles were distilled from alphabets created in previous eras by visionary artists who bequeathed us their letterforms but not their reasoning.

References

[1] Mardersteig, G. (1969).
Petri Bembi De Aetna Liber & Pietro Bembo, On Etna,
Verona, Italy: Officina Bodoni.

[2]Morison, S. (1973).
A Tally of Types,
Cambridge, England: Cambridge University Press.

[3] Bigelow, C. (1981).
Technology and the aesthetics of type, *The Seybold
Report on Publishing Systems,* **10**, 24, 3-16.

[4] Bigelow, C. (1982).
The principles of digital type, *The Seybold
Report on Publishing Systems,* **11**, 11, 3-22;
11, 12, 10-19.

[5] Bigelow, C. & Day, D. (1983).
Digital typography,
Scientific American, **249**, 2, 106-119.

[6] Karow, P. (1983).
IKARUS: for typefaces in digital form,
Hamburg, West Germany: URW Unternehmensberatung.

[7] Michael Plass, Xerox PARC, personal communication.

[8] Michael Sheridan, Imagen Corporation, personal communication.

[9] John Warnock, Adobe Systems, Inc., personal communication.

[10] Kajiya, J. & Ullner, B. (1981).
Filtering high quality text for display on raster scan devices.
Computer Graphics, **15**, 3, 7-15.

[11] Dippe, M. & Wold, E. (1985).
Antialiasing through stochastic sampling.
Computer Graphics, **19**, 3, 69-78.

[12] Coueignoux, P. (1975).
Generation of Roman Printed Fonts,
unpublished Phd. Dissertation,
Massachusetts Institute of Technology.

[13] Knuth, D. (1980).
The Computer Modern Family of Typefaces,
Computer Science Department Report,
Stanford University.
(A new version to appear as volume E of
Computers and Typesetting,
Reading, Massachusetts: Addison Wesley.)

[15] Carter, H. (1937).
The Optical Scale in Typefounding.
Typography, **4**, 2-6.

[16] Enschede, C. (1908).
Fonderies de Caracteres,
Haarlem, Holland: Enschede en Zonen.

[17] Tschichold, J. (1966).
Treasury of Alphabets and Lettering,
New York, New York: Reinhold.

Tabular Typography

RICHARD J. BEACH

Computer Science Laboratory, Xerox PARC

ABSTRACT

This paper presents a comprehensive survey of the typographic issues for laying out information within two-dimensional tables. Early typesetting systems formatted tables by coding the table style and layout into the program, and later systems provided a limited range of typographic features. The typographic issues include table structure, alignment of rows and columns simultaneously, formatting styles, treatment of whitespace within a table, graphical embellishments, placement of footnotes, various readability issues, and the problems of breaking large tables. Extending the table formatting problem to both page layout and arrangement of mathematical notation is highlighted, as is the need for interactive design tools for table layout.

1. Introduction

This paper presents a comprehensive survey of the typographic issues for laying out information within a two-dimensional table. Tables are a concentrated form of the more general layout problem; one can find table formatting analogies in both the larger-scale problem of page makeup, and the smaller-scale problem of aligning notation within a mathematical equation.

Few table formatting tools have addressed all the issues raised by this paper. In fact, it was a challenge to identify the various issues that typographers, compositors, and graphic designers have managed with great skill through the traditional graphic arts processes. Thus this paper provides a checklist for the designs and implementations of new table formatting tools, algorithms, and structures. The ultimate goal is to pursue general mechanisms that solve the table formatting problem and extend gracefully to both the larger- and smaller-scale layout problems of page and notation formatting, as well as apply to the more general layout problems with graphical information.

Additional references for tabular formatting in the graphic arts may be found in Phillip's article "Tabular Composition" published in *The Seybold Report* [Phillips79], and the U.S. Government Printing Office Style Manual [GPO73], which is replete with detailed guidelines suited to tables published in government documents. This paper is an excerpt of a dissertation on table formatting and graphical style [Beach85].

2. What is a table?

A table is an orderly arrangement of information. Tables are defined to be 'rectangular arrays exhibiting one or more characteristics of designated entities or categories' [Morris78]. Tables may be less structured than this, simply serving to present a list of entries. However in most cases, tables have some structure that is relevant to the presentation of information. We will take a fairly general view of tables to encompass a broad range of layout possibilities.

Designing table typography is a hard problem. There are many formatting details to get right and there is only a small amount of space with which to work. The two-dimensional nature of tables requires alignment of information in both directions at the same time. It is very important to maintain control over placement because the organization of information in tables is part of the message. Juxtaposition and other spatial relationships within tables have an important impact on the way in which tables convey information.

"The principles of table making involve matters of taste, convention, typography, aesthetics, and honesty, in addition to the principles of quantification." [Davis68]

The sources and purposes of tables in documents span a broad range of information. Some examples include computed data from mathematical algorithms, statistical data from scientific experiments, financial data and spreadsheets, taxonomies of observed data, extracts from databases of information, or just about anything else an author might wish to convey to a reader.

Tables also serve as a concentrated form of a more general layout problem. Two extremes of this general problem are page makeup at the large-scale end and mathematical notation at the small-scale end. Page layout might be viewed as a multipage table with entries that flow between the breaks and headings that are continued on successive pages. Mathematical notation contains many internal alignment requirements, such as aligning entries within matrices or the limits of summations.

Keeping in mind these more general applications of table formatting may prompt a unifying solution to all of these layout problems.

3. Early Table Formatting Systems

Several very early composition systems could typeset tables. Computers were primarily involved in numeric computations at that time. Because photomechanical typesetting devices used electronic input data that were compatible with computer systems, it was natural to conceive of a computer program that would convert the numeric data directly to the formatting commands suitable for driving the typesetting devices.

Several reviewers [Barnett65] [Stevens67] [Phillips80] have reported that the earliest book of computer typeset tables was the monograph produced at the National Bureau of Standards by Corliss and Bozman in 1962 [Corliss62]. Another pioneering effort in typesetting tables was TABPRINT [Barnett65] developed by Barnett at MIT in the early 1960's. These programs for formatting tables of numeric data were relatively simple. "The significance of this early work in tabular composition is that all the typographic parameters were defined by program." [Phillips80]

To format the more general table designs required in technical publications, we need effective interactive design tools that can handle a wide range of typographic requirements because many table designs are unique. The variety of table designs limits the amortization period for the time invested in programming a table formatter with sufficient specifications to accomplish each arrangement.

The rest of the paper investigates these complications and the typographic requirements for formatting aesthetic tables.

4. Tables as Two-Dimensional Structures

Tables have a two-dimensional structure because of the organization of a table into rows and columns. These row and column structures intersect to identify the characteristics of the table entry at each intersection. The layout of a table must simultaneously align table entries horizontally in a row and vertically in a column. The table width is determined by accumulating the widths of each column. In turn, column widths are determined by the widths of the entries in the column. Similarly, the table and row depths are determined by the depths of the entries in each row. It is important to realize that the arrangement of table entries within rows or columns can be expressed independently from the actual widths of the entries or the rows and

Stub Head	Spanning Head				Col. Head
	Col. Head	Spanning Subhead		Col. Head	
		Col. Head	Col. Head		
Row Head	xxx	xxx	xxx	xxx	xxx
Row Head	xxx	xxx	xxx	xxx	xxx
Total line	xxx	xxx	xxx	xxx	xxx

Figure 1: The two-dimensional structure of a table includes the arrangement of its entries into rows and columns. Here the parts of a table have been shaded for easy identification. The light grey area is the *box head* that contains all of the column headings. The dark grey area is the *stub* that contains all of the row identifications. The remaining white area is the *panel* containing the actual table entries.

columns. Therefore we can use automatic means to determine the widths and actual alignment positions.

The two-dimensional nature of tables differentiates table formatting from simpler text formatting. Tables deal with areas and graphical relationships, both of which have two degrees of freedom. Lines and paragraphs of text have only one degree of freedom (where to break the line), although even then a complex algorithm may be necessary to produce aesthetic line breaks [Knuth81].

The conventional two-dimensional structure of tables is illustrated in Figure 1. The rows and columns intersect to form the table entries in the *panel* which is the main body of the table. The area with row identifications at the left of the panel is called the *stub*. The column headings in the area along the top of the panel are called the *box head* because when a table is fully outlined the column heads are completely boxed. Some headings group several columns together and are referred to as *spanning heads* or *spanning subheads*, depending on the depth at which they occur in the box head. Spanning row headings for several rows are also possible.

As an example, the box head in the table of Figure 1 has completely determined the width of each column because the headings themselves are wider than the information in the columns. In other tables, the table entries may be wider than the headings above them, and therefore the entries would then determine the column widths.

Various graphic embellishments to the basic row and column structures help convey the table information. Dividing lines called *rules* help separate dissimilar parts of the table. The box head and stub in

Figure 1 are completely outlined by rules; all possible horizontal and vertical rules are present in the headings. Some table designers prefer to use only horizontal rules (see below for more discussion of table rules).

The word 'rules' will appear frequently in this paper in relation to the typographic lines (rulings) drawn in a table to separate rows or columns. This use of the word is traditional in the graphic arts. However, it may be confused with the notion of 'style rules.' Throughout paper, the word 'rule' by itself refers to a typographic line and terms 'style rule' and 'formatting rule' refer to a way of doing things.

The content of table entries may vary considerably. Certainly textual and numeric information are commonly organized into tables. However, other types of information often organized into tables are pictures, illustrations, mathematical equations, and even other tables.

In most table designs, the table entries are fully contained within the row and column intersection. Furthermore, tables are often structured as hierarchical subdivisions of rows and columns. More general table designs permit a table entry to cross these hierarchical divisions, and thus allow the content of one table entry to flow into another. Connected entries would be necessary when folding a long table entry of text into two column entries, or when flowing a caption around several illustration entries. This capability is necessary to extend table formatting to full page-layout requirements.

5. Typographic Treatment of Tables

This section discusses the wide range of typographic details required to format tables. Careful text placement is an obvious requirement coming directly from the two-dimensional structure of tables. Alignment choices to guide the placement are also needed. Formatting attributes can be applied to different parts of the table structure. The treatment of whitespace, typographic rules, and rows of dots between table entries are all devices for guiding the eye along rows or columns. Footnotes on table entries must be referenced and positioned appropriately. Finally, readability concerns in table formatting are important.

5.1 Fine Resolution Placement

Compared to the line lengths in normal text, table entries are formatted within a relatively short line length in each column. These short line lengths force more hyphenation and line breaks in text entries. Placing several narrow columns side-by-side requires inserting a small amount of whitespace between each column to improve readability. Centering table entries or balancing space between entries also requires fine control of their position. These small distances must be chosen carefully since the human visual system perceives patterns and groupings, whether intentional or not, and bad choices may dramatically affect the way the table is interpreted by a reader.

Typesetting devices often provide resolutions in very small units, a common one being 1/10 of a printer's point (about 1/720 of an inch). However, formatting a table with the coarse positioning typical of a fixed-pitch printer or typewriter is a much easier task. The results are normally not very aesthetic, since the fixed-size units are quite large, but they eliminate many choices and simplify decisions:

"Tabular material is always difficult to typeset – much more so than to compose on the typewriter. This is true even though figures have a 'monospaced' value. Letters do not, and therefore it is more difficult to align material or even to determine what will fit in a given space . . . The monospaced typewriter – where you can actually visualize what you are setting – is certainly the simplest way for the novice to proceed. And it will not be an easy task for the typesetter to imitate what the typist has done." [Seybold79]

5.2 Alignment within Tables

The alignment choices within tables correspond to the two-dimensional nature of table layouts. Horizontal row and vertical column alignments predominate. However, other alignments for spanned headings, equal width rows or columns, and balancing the extra whitespace between columns are common.

Column entries are *vertically aligned* with each other in various ways, as seen in Figure 2. (Note that one must adjust an entry horizontally in order to align it vertically with another above or below it; such distinctions are made carefully in the remainder of the paper.) The three most frequent choices for vertical alignment are flush to the left (generally for textual material), flush to the right (generally for numeric material), or centered within the column (generally for headings and textual material).

FlushLeft	Center	FlushRight	Decimal.Align
xxxxxx	xxxxxx	xxxxxx	000000
xxxxxxxxxx	xxxxxxxxxx	xxxxxxxxxx	00.000000
xxxx	xxxx	xxxx	.000
xxxxxxxx	xxxxxxxx	xxxxxxxx	0000.0

Figure 2: Vertical alignment within a column of table entries is commonly flush left, flush right, centered, or decimal aligned.

Numeric data with a varying number of decimal digits require another type of vertical alignment where the data items align on the decimal point. Numeric entries without decimal points must have one inferred, usually after the last decimal digit. The alignment on decimal points can be generalized to alignment on any character. For example, mathematical equations are often aligned on their equality signs. More complex alignment possibilities arise when multiple alignment points are needed, such as aligning the terms of polynomials in a system of equations where each of the additive and subtractive operations requires alignment (although the unary minus sign does not):

$$10x_1 - 7x_2 \qquad\qquad = 7,$$
$$-3x_1 \qquad\qquad + 6x_3 = 4,$$
$$5x_1 - x_2 + 5x_3 = 6.$$

Just as for columns, row entries are *horizontally aligned* with each other in various ways, as shown in Figure 3, again with three frequent choices, flush to the top, flush to the bottom, or centered. (Again, note that an item is adjusted vertically to accomplish horizontal alignment.)

Row entries possess an additional characteristic similar to decimal-point alignment of column entries: the baseline on which successive characters are aligned. The rightmost column of the table in Figure 3 contains entries with baselines different from the other three columns. Without a horizontal alignment choice for baseline alignment, table entries with different baselines will not be arranged in a visually pleasing manner.

Spanned headings are aligned within a set of columns, or set of rows if the heading spans several rows. The set of columns spanned by the heading determines the aggregate dimensions of the spanned heading. Should the heading exceed this size, perhaps because it is longer than the narrow columns it spans, then the heading may be folded to make it shorter, or the columns spaced out to accommodate the long heading

Flush Top	xxx xxxxxxxx xxxx	xxxxxxx xxxxxx	$xx^x + yy_y + zz$
Center	xxx xxxxxxxx xxxx	xxxxxxx xxxxxx	$xx^x + yy_y + zz$
Flush Bottom	xxx xxxxxxxx xxxx	xxxxxxx xxxxxx	$xx^x + yy_y + zz$

Figure 3: Horizontal alignment within a row of table entries is commonly flush top, centered, and flush bottom as indicated by the stub labels on each row. The entries in the second and third columns have multiple lines of text. The last column contains entries with superscripts and subscripts that affect the height and depth of the text entry. Alignment without regard to baselines produces unaesthetic results, especially when centering an even and an odd number of lines in the middle of the table, and when aligning entries with different heights and depths. A fine point: note that the capitalization of the stub labels affects their position when aligned, especially 'Flush Top' and 'xxx' in the top row, and 'Center' which is not on the same baseline as the x's.

(see the treatment of whitespace section following). Spanned row headings have similar needs.

Equal widths of columns (or equal heights of rows) may be called for. In some cases the precise size will be specified by the designer and applied to the table. In other cases, the size can be determined automatically by finding the largest entry in the set of rows or columns.

5.3 Formatting Styles

Tables are often formatted with a different (but related) set of attributes from those used for normal text. Frequently tables are typeset in the same typeface but in a smaller point size than the body text, both to attract less attention to the table and to include more information. These changes in formatting attributes promote the use of a separate formatting environment or set of style rules for tables.

Further specification of formatting attributes is necessary when rows or columns are to be distinguished. For instance, a row of totals may be the most important aspect of the table and therefore should be set in a bolder type face, or one column of information may be exceptional and thus be distinguished in an italic type face. Finally, individual table entries may be distinguished with special formatting attributes such as highlights. Figure 4 contains a table with an example of these specifications.

Stub Head	Spanning Column Head				
	Col Head	*Col Head*			Col Head
		Col	*Col*	*Col*	
Row	value	*value*	*value*	*value*	value
Row	**value**	***value***	***value***	***value***	**value**
Row	value	*value*	*value*	*value*	value

Figure 4: Style attributes for a table entry are determined by several style rules specified for the entire table, a single row, a column or an individual table entry. This table was typeset with a Helvetica type family. One row has a style attribute for bold face. The spanned subcolumn has a style attribute for italic face. One of the three table entries in the intersection of the bold row and italic column has a Times Roman type family attribute, which overrides the global specification. The style attributes for a particular entry are determined by accumulating all the style attributes according to a natural search order: table, row or column (according to a preference choice), then table entry.

5.4 Whitespace Treatment

The treatment of whitespace between table entries is more complicated than between paragraphs of text because there are more relationships for each table entry. The space between two columns of text is called the *gutter* in normal formatting, while the space between table entries is generally referred to as the *bearoff* or a *bearoff distance*. The separation of rows or columns with whitespace helps to establish the apparent grouping of data. The introduction of rules into a table permits the physical separation to be reduced or eliminated since the grouping is provided by the rule.

Some strategies for compacting large tables to fit a page (discussed later) involve shrinking the bearoff space. The bearoff may provide a place for a footnote reference or *gloss* marker to intrude between table entries without expanding the column width. These markers do not participate in the alignment of table entries and therefore need not be separated with the same bearoff distance.

Excess whitespace due to a large spanned heading requires apportioning the space among bearoffs for the spanned rows or columns, for example, the columns in Figure 5.

5.5 Rules and Decorations

The use of dividing rules within tables to separate rows or columns is a traditional practice. Rules run along the row or column boundaries in either the horizontal or vertical direction. In large tables with narrow columns, vertical rules are often indispensible in maintaining order among the vast quantity of data. The preference for horizontal rules is a recent phenomenon due in part to faddish design preference and

Short Head			Very Long Column Head Over Narrow Entries	
54.321	54.321	54.321	54.321	54.321
654.32	654.32	654.32	654.32	654.32
54.321	54.321	54.321	54.321	54.321

Figure 5: Specifying position within a column as well as aligning table entries may be necessary when there is excess whitespace to disperse among the row or column entries. All the numeric table entries are aligned on decimal points. The last two columns have excess whitespace due to the very long column head; the first set of aligned column entries is positioned flush right within the column and the second is flush left. Similar specifications are necessary for rows.

in part to harsh economic reality. Consider the experience of the University of Chicago Press by comparing the statements from the 1969 and 1982 editions of *The Chicago Manual of Style:*

"Ruled tables, for example, are usual in the publications of this press, in part because Monotype composition has always been readily available. For a publisher who is restricted to Linotype, open tables or tables with horizontal rules alone may be the only practical way tabular matter can be arranged." [Chicago69]

"In line with a nearly universal trend among scholarly and commercial publishers, the University of Chicago Press has given up vertical rules as a standard feature of tables in the books and journals that it publishes. The handwork necessitated by including vertical rules is costly no matter what mode of composition is used, and in the Press's view the expense can no longer be justified by the additional refinement it brings." [Chicago82]

The difficulty with inserting vertical rules stems from the mechanical properties of photocomposition devices. With manual makeup of pages from metal type, inserting rules involved laying down a thin metal strip. High-speed phototypesetting devices that have only a narrow aperture across the page are strongly biased towards the horizontal, both for typesetting text and for drawing typographic rules. This same bias towards the horizontal is reflected in the composition software that supports these devices. Newer typesetting devices with more accurate positioning of raster-scanning laser beams can print in both horizontal and vertical orientations with equal ease and eliminate this restriction.

There are several distinguished rules that frequently occur in tables: the *head rule* above the box head, the *cutoff rule* below the box head, the *spanner rule* below a spanning head, the *foot rule* below the table, and the *total rule* above the total row. These rules may be of different thicknesses, with the outermost head and foot rules generally drawn thicker than rules inside the table.

Rules come in a variety of shapes, sizes, and patterns. Different thicknesses or *weights* of rules provide appropriate emphasis. A common design is to use medium-weight rules for the head and foot rules above and below the table, and fine *hairline* rules for the cutoff rules between the column headings and the table entries [Williamson66]. Double rules or combinations of thick and thin rules are sometimes used to provide emphasis and closure to a table. The intersection of these patterned rules is a complicated affair.

Braces that group table entries are sometimes required within tables. The brace is placed in the space between two rows or columns, sometimes requiring extra space to accommodate its curly shape. Braces are frequently added by hand from transfer lettering sheets because they are not supported by table formatters and their positions are awkward to specify and align properly.

Ornaments, such as flowers or other interesting designs, are inserted at the corners or along the outer border of a table. They are old fashioned and used mainly as a decoration for the purpose of catching the reader's attention.

Background tints were used in Figure 1 to highlight the different parts of the table. Traditionally, tints would be added by hand at the page makeup or camera stage since they involved halftone screens. Phototypesetters and laser printers can produce screens automatically by shading the area of the table before the content is typeset.

5.6 Leaders

Various graphic techniques, such as *dot leaders*, help the reader capture the content and meaning of the table.

Leaders are the dot patterns that guide your eye from an item at one side of a table to the related item at the other side of a table. Headings in tables of contents are often connected with dot leaders to the page numbers on the right. Typically, leaders are formed from dots although dashes or rules are sometimes used. Dot leaders are positioned congruently so that successive rows of leaders all have the dots in the same horizontal position. The harmony of the aligned dots enhances their purpose of guiding the reader without distraction. Leaders cross through column gutters and possibly vertical rules, although rules are ill-advised when leaders are used.

5.7 Footnotes within Tables

Footnotes within tables pose an interesting layout problem. As in page layout, footnotes for table entries are collected and placed at the bottom of the table within the page area allocated to the table. This means that for the table formatter to accommodate footnotes, it must be at least as powerful as the page formatter. Most table formatters only handle footnotes placed manually within the table.

By convention, footnote references are separately marked or numbered for each table. Typically, footnote references within tables use letters or symbols rather than superscript numbers to avoid confusion with numeric exponents in the data. Should footnote references be numbered, they usually are sequenced independently from any text footnotes.

5.8 Readability Issues

Tables of numeric information have been published for many years and there are classic methods for making tables more readable [Knott15]. For example, long columns of numbers are separated with extra whitespace or with thin rules every 5 or 10 entries to provide 'chunks' that help the human visual system scan the long columns. Background tints behind rows of a table are another technique to improve readability in long tables. Grouping digits in threes by introducing commas or extra whitespace provides the same chunking for long decimal expansions of logarithms or huge sums of money.

6. Large Tables are Awkward

Tables tend to be awkward to handle in page composition. They must be treated separately from the running text because they contain separate information. However, the tables may be too wide for the page width or too long for the remaining space on the page, or even too long for the page height.

6.1 Common Strategies for Large Tables

Tables are commonly formatted in a smaller type size to reduce the impact of the table on the reader. This choice also helps fit more information in a table. Reducing the point size to 70% or 80% of the text size reduces the character height and width proportionately. Common sizes for text are 10-point type on 12-point leading. Tables often use 8-point type on 9-point leading or even 7-point on 8-point. Compressed type faces have the same height but reduced width that permits more text to be typeset in the same horizontal space.   For example, Helvetica Light Condensed is a narrow font commonly used in tables.

The bearoff distances between table entries can be reduced to eliminate whitespace and thereby reduce the width of a large table.

Transposing rows into columns and vice versa [Williamson66] may make a large table fit the page.   Wide tables with many columns are transposed into longer tables with fewer columns, and long tables with few columns are transposed into wider tables with many columns.   A table and its transpose are shown in Figure 6.   Note that the stub and boxheads have been transposed in a nontrivial matrix transposition that preserves the boxhead structure of the table.   One must be careful about transposing statistical tables that might imply an incorrect cause and effect relationship [Zeisel57].

6.2 Long Tables

Some tables can be made shorter by folding a long column into multiple columns.   For instance, one long list of names in a single column would become two or more columns of names.   This folding trades off shorter table length with increased table width.

Long tables that exceed the page height must be broken into smaller tables.   Breaking a table is similar to breaking lines of text at page boundaries, and similar algorithms [Plass81] can be applied.   However, broken tables must introduce continuation headings in the second and subsequent parts of the table.   The continuation headings may be very complicated functions of the table entries:

"It would be asking rather a lot of a page make-up program to insert carried-forward and brought-forward totals automatically at a table break, and indeed these were often omitted when tables were made-up by the hand compositor." [Phillips79]

The continuation headings can be supplied in the table input as variants of the regular headings.   When a table is broken then these variations can be used.   Brought-forward totals could be supplied automatically when the table structure and content is recognized within the formatting program, for example, in financial spreadsheet programs. This is an instance of a particular table entry (a total) that might compute itself on behalf of the table formatter (for the current total of all formatted entries) when required.

Stub Head	Spanning Head				
	Col. Head	Col. Head	Col. Head	Col. Head	Col. Head
Row Head	xxx	xxx	xxx	xxx	xxx
Row Head	xxx	xxx	xxx	xxx	xxx
Row Head	xxx	xxx	xxx	xxx	xxx

Spanning Head	Stub Head		
	Row Head	Row Head	Row Head
Col. Head	xxx	xxx	xxx
Col. Head	xxx	xxx	xxx
Col. Head	xxx	xxx	xxx
Col. Head	xxx	xxx	xxx
Col. Head	xxx	xxx	xxx

Figure 6: Transposing a table may help make a table fit on the page. The top table is wide with more columns than rows. The bottom table is the transpose of the top table and is narrower with fewer columns than rows.

6.3 Wide Tables

Wide tables with a few wide columns can be made narrower by folding column entries to fit shorter line lengths. Usually, table formatters require the line lengths or column widths to be explicitly stated by the table designer. The automatic calculation of column widths is a difficult optimization problem that has not yet been discussed or solved.

A wide table may be made to fit the page by rotating the table and printing it *broadside*. A broadside table has the long dimension of the table along the long dimension of the page, that is, rotated 90° so the rows read up the page and the columns read from left to right. Right-hand pages are preferred for such tables since a turned book will present the broadside table closer to the reader [Williamson66]. Broadside tables (or illustrations) impact page composition, because these pages are typically designed with page numbers in a different position and without running heads (otherwise the page numbers would appear in a different orientation to the broadside table and detract from the readability of the facing page).

Instead of rotating the entire table to make a wide table fit the page, it may be sufficient to rotate the text of column headings to read vertically. Especially when the column headings are much wider than the column entries, turning the text so that it reads upwards with successive heading lines to the right reduces the column width. If column headings in a broadside table are turned, they should instead have the descenders to the left, otherwise the text would appear upside down on the page [Williamson66].

Wide tables may be formatted as a two-page spread across two facing pages. A two-page *upright* table would appear with the box head spread across the *binding gutter*. A two-page broadside table is possible with the rows split across the gutter. Continuation headings may not be needed in a two-page broadside table, but would be if the table continued onto subsequent pages.

Extremely wide tables may be printed on a foldout plate. This requires special-sized paper to be folded and inserted into the book at the binding stage. The extra manual handling makes this alternative very expensive and rarely used.

Otherwise, wide tables are broken into smaller table parts with continuation stub headings. Any spanning headings in the box head will have to be continued across the break. Some reference columns, such as sequence numbers, may be repeated to assist in finding information in the continued table parts.

7. Conclusions
The survey of tabular typography has highlighted the difficulties in accommodating the aesthetic decisions employed by the craftspeople who work as compositors and typesetters. The table formatting problem is a difficult one with few automatic solutions available. The typographic issues of alignment, spacing, typographic rules, decorations, and leaders require careful attention to detail. The general structure of tables with subdivided rows and columns, with repeated rows or columns required when breaking large tables, and with general alignment relationships, implies that more general solutions similar to grid design layouts will be necessary. The difficulty of composing large tables and breaking them into page-sized components is an added dimension to the table formatting problem.

These issues motivate the need for a continuum of design tools for table layouts. At one extreme are interactive design tools for those few tables with unique requirements which require considerable individual attention. At the other extreme design tools for the series of tables with very similar requirements which require style mechanisms to enforce a consistent appearance. The development of these formatting techniques must address the typography issues surveyed here in this paper.

References

[1] −. *A Manual of Style*. The University of Chicago Press, 12th edition, 1969.

[2] −. *The Chicago Manual of Style*. The University of Chicago Press, 13th Edition, 1982.

[3] −. *U.S. Government Printing Office Style Manual*. Government Printing Office, 1973.

[4] Barnett, Michael P. *Computer Typesetting: Experiments and Prospects*. MIT Press, 1965.

[5] Beach, Richard J. (1985) *Setting Tables and Illustrations with Style*, PhD thesis, University of Waterloo. Also published as Xerox PARC Technical Report CSL-85-3, May 1985.

[6] Corliss, C.H. and Bozman, W.R. "Experimental Probabilities for Spectral Lines of Seventy Elements," *NBS Monograph* **53**. July 20, 1962.

[7] Davis, James A. and Jacobs, Ann M. "Tabular Presentation," *International Encyclopedia of the Social Sciences*. 1968, 497-509.

[8] Knott, Cargill Gilston, editor. *Napier Tercentenary Memorial Volume*, Published for the Royal Society of Edinburough by Longmans Green and Co., London, 1915.

[9] Knuth, Donald E. and Plass, Michael F. "Breaking Paragraphs into Lines," *Software − Practice and Experience* **11**. 1981, 1119-1184.

[10] Morris, Willam, editor. *The American Heritage Dictionary of the English Language*. Houghton Mifflin, 1978.

[11] Phillips, Arthur H. "Tabular Composition," *The Seybold Report* **8** *23*. August 13, 1979.

[12] Phillips, Arthur H. *Handbook of Computer-Aided Composition*. Marcel Dekker, 1980.

[13] Plass, Michael F. *Optimal Pagination Techniques for Automatic Typesetting Systems*. Xerox PARC Technical Report, ISL-81-1, August, 1981.

[14] Seybold John W. *Fundamentals of Modern Photocomposition*. Seybold Publications, 1979.

[15] Stevens, Mary Elizabeth and Little John L. "Automatic Typographic-Quality Typesetting Techniques: A State-of-the-Art Review," *NBS Monograph* **99**. April 7, 1967.

[16] Williamson, Hugh. *Methods of Book Design*. Oxford University Press, 1966.

[17] Zeisel, Hans. *Say It With Figures*. Harper & Row, Fourth edition, 1957.

A Simple Mechanism for Authorship of Dynamic Documents

P.J. Brown

University of Kent at Canterbury

ABSTRACT

It is difficult to make dynamic documents easy to use, but even more difficult to make authorship of dynamic documents simple. This paper outlines a system called GUIDE, which provides users with a modest yet powerful set of facilities for viewing documents on screens. GUIDE aims at a close integration of the author's view with the reader's view. The paper discusses the advantages of this approach, and the problems of adding functionality to a conceptually simple system.

1. Introduction

Writing good documentation is hard. Hardest of all, perhaps, is to write good user manuals for computer software. The reason why this is so difficult is that there is a great diversity of possible readers, and of modes of perusal. Readers will range from the naive to the expert, and in between there are important special cases of readers with expertise in a related area, such as a FORTRAN expert learning BASIC. Furthermore readers, whatever their background, will want to peruse the user manual in different ways at different stages in their learning process. Early on they will want summaries and tutorial information; later they may want to browse; finally they will want a reference manual. In order to cover this spectrum properly you need a huge range of user manuals. In a few spheres this range exists: there is, for example, a big range of manuals — mostly books — on Pascal and many of these are aimed at specific niches in the market of possible readers. For most software, however, there is just one user manual, and this aims to cover all possible readers and all possible types of perusal. Not surprisingly the aim is rarely realised. This applies even when the 'user manual' is just a page or two of text, like many UNIX manual pages.

2. On-line Documentation

Recently there has been an increasing trend to make documentation available on-line, to be read from a terminal rather than from paper. In some cases, such as the UNIX manual pages, this on-line documentation is simply a reproduction of the paper-based documentation. More ambitious systems, however, try to take advantage of the interactive environment provided by the computer in order to tailor the material displayed to the needs of the reader. Many such systems are based on glass teletype interfaces, and require the user to navigate round some tree structure. Such systems are rarely pleasant to use — the reader simply gets lost in the tree. (See [Apperley & Spence83] for a discussion of this.)

Recently the availability of graphics workstations with a pointing device such as a mouse has enabled much more pleasant user interfaces to be created. Such workstations present an opportunity to provide more flexible on-line documentation. As a result many ambitious document display systems have been proposed or implemented. These include ZOG [Robertson, McCracken & Newell81], which is ambitious in that it caters for huge volumes of documentation and is designed to be used by all members of the crew of an aircraft carrier, the electronic document systems at Brown University [Feiner, Nagy & van Dam82] and [Yankelovich, Meyrowitz & van Dam85], which are remarkable for their graphics, and the encyclopedia system of [Weyer & Borning85], which is remarkable for its scope.

This paper is concerned with a much more modest system, called GUIDE, which is designed to support a few simple facilities which are easy to use, both by readers and — the main concern of the paper — by authors. GUIDE runs on the MacIntosh and, under UNIX, on the ICL PERQ. The Figures in this paper came from the PERQ implementation.

Unfortunately interactive on-line documentation inevitably makes the author's job harder still. Not only must he write well, but he must also organise his material to be readable in a dynamic way. In particular he must provide navigational aids for the reader, and he must organise the material so that, whatever path the reader takes, the material is still coherent. Worst of all, perhaps, he has a problem of entering material into the document display system: he may have to master a new 'authoring language' for the particular system he is using.

Given these huge problems that authors have, a documentation display system must do everything it can to ease the author's lot. If not, there will be no authors and thus, even though the system may have the best reader interface in the world, it will be useless.

Although the thrust of this paper is concerned with authoring facilities, we shall start by outlining the reader's view of GUIDE, since this leads into the author's view.

GUIDE is designed to be useful for any kind of on-line documentation. For example, it is used to display material on office procedures or material on how to get from X airport to Y hotel, as well as documentation about software. Thus authors are not necessarily computer scientists, and may well be as naive in computer terms as the potential readers.

3. Features of GUIDE

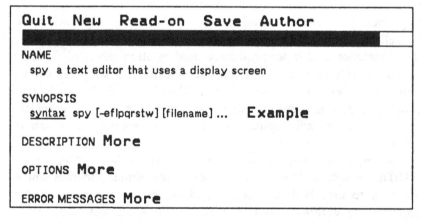

Figure 1: GUIDE displaying documentation about an editor

Figure 1 shows GUIDE in action. At the top of the display is a menu and beneath that a *thumb-bar* which is used for scrolling the document. The black part of the thumb-bar represents the currently displayed part of the document and the white part the rest of the document. In Figure 1 most of the document is on the screen and therefore most of the thumb-bar is black. Below the thumb-bar is the document itself. In Figure 1 this document is a 'user manual' for an editor called *spy*. The document consists of ordinary text plus embedded *buttons*, which are active and can be selected using the mouse. Buttons are of one of two types:

● *replace-buttons*: these are shown in bold — the same font as the menu at the top. If the user selects one of these buttons, it is replaced by a body of text associated with the button. The name of the button and the body of text associated with it have, of course, been previously defined by the author of the document. Figure 2 shows the effect of selecting the **More** replace-button that follows the word 'DESCRIPTION' in Figure 1.

```
Quit  New  Read-on  Save  Author

NAME
  spy  a text editor that uses a display screen

SYNOPSIS
  syntax  spy [-eflpqrstw] [filename] ...   Example

DESCRIPTION
  IMPORTANT: if you want to try any Examples in this DESCRIPTION, you
  should expand the introductory example that follows. Example

The principles behind the spy editor are as follows.
```

*Figure 2: the result of selecting the **More** button in Figure 1*

● *glossary-buttons*: these are underlined. If the user selects a glossary-button, then GUIDE searches some pre-defined glossary files for a definition of that button. When the definition has been found, it is added to a sub-window reserved for the glossary. Figure 3 shows what results from Figure 1 when the syntax glossary-button is selected.

The replacement of a button can itself involve further buttons, and this can be carried to any desired depth. Buttons can be selected in any order the reader wishes. If, at any time, the reader wants to get rid of the text associated with a button he can undo it: this returns the document to its state when the button was selected.

This ends our overview of GUIDE as the reader sees it; further details can be found in [Brown84].

4. How the Author Presents Documents
It is not the philosophy of GUIDE to impose a style upon authors: we know so little about the best ways to display documents interactively that it would be foolish to constrain experimentation.

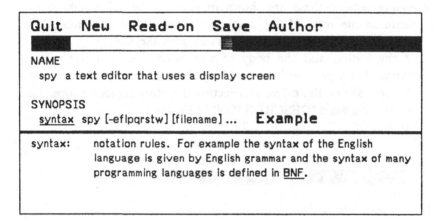

Figure 3: the result of selecting the 'syntax' glossary-button in Figure 1

Instead GUIDE aims to provide a few simple facilities that authors can exploit in whatever way they wish.

Most authors choose to present documents so that the reader first sees an overall summary; he can then select replace-buttons to expand the pieces that interest him. Figure 1 is an example of this. The reader expands just enough buttons to provide the level of detail that he wants. Typically this process includes an element of experimentation — selecting buttons and then undoing them if the replacement turns out to be unwanted.

If the reader is using GUIDE simply to find out some information then, when he has found it, GUIDE will have served its purpose and the reader will quit. If, on the other hand, the reader is using GUIDE to read some tutorial information — which, we hope, contains replace-buttons that allows him to tailor the information to his own needs — then, when he has generated a document suited to these needs he may want to save it for future reference. He may, indeed, wish to print the saved document on paper. GUIDE supports such facilities.

5. Editing

GUIDE also allows the reader to edit his document; indeed GUIDE is also a screen editor. Thus the reader may add personal comments (e.g. 'This works in a similar way to the X facility on my home computer') or even delete some of the fine words written by the author and replace them with his own. The reader then becomes an author.

This leads on to a fundamental principle of GUIDE: *the author is a reader and the reader is an author.* Readers, as we have just explained, can act as authors; on the other side, the *only* way an author can prepare a document is to act as a reader does. The author therefore has the same simple user interface as the reader, albeit with an additional menu for creating new buttons and the like. The author either starts from scratch with a null document, or takes an existing purely textual document and adds GUIDE structure to it.

The most important quality in an author is to see the world as his reader wants to see it. In GUIDE the author is forced, at every stage of document creation, to see the document in the same way as the reader sees it, and this is a good start; it would, of course, be wrong to extrapolate from this and say that GUIDE authors will always create good documents. GUIDE only puts the author in the environment of the reader; it does not give the author access to the reader's mental processes. Thus the author can still write a lot of appalling jargon that will baffle any reader.

GUIDE readers navigate through a document by expanding and undoing buttons (and also by scrolling through the currently expanded document). If the author provides a good structure of buttons, with coherent and sensible replacements, then he has catered for these navigation needs.

6. The Extra Menu for Authoring

Figure 4 shows what results from Figure 2 when the user (we now use the neutral term 'user' rather than 'author' or 'reader') selects the **AUTHOR** menu command. An extended menu is presented, and we shall explain this later. Within the document in Figure 4 several extra white-on-black *control characters* have appeared in the document; these help indicate its structure. In particular ▉ indicates the start of a button and ▉ indicates its end. ▉ and ▉ are used in a similar way to delimit the beginning and end of the replacement of a button, and ▉ and ▉ at the start of a document are concerned with certain global options (which are null in Figure 4).

Arguably this flattened view of the document structure is not ideal, and a more graphical representation such as a tree might be easier to follow. However the GUIDE principle that the author should view the document as the reader does was felt to be overriding.

The six items in the extended menu that begin with a '+' are used to create new GUIDE constructs. These all create null objects, such

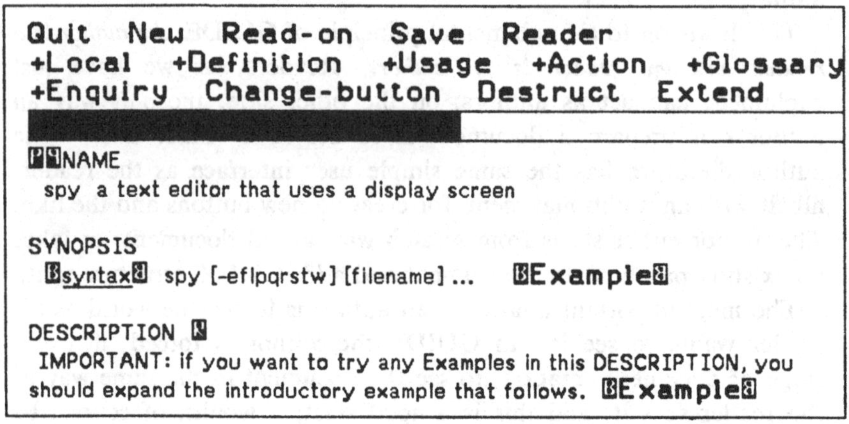

```
Quit  New  Read-on  Save  Reader
+Local  +Definition  +Usage  +Action  +Glossary
+Enquiry  Change-button  Destruct  Extend
```

▨▨NAME
  spy a text editor that uses a display screen

SYNOPSIS
  ▨syntax▨ spy [-eflpqrstw] [filename] ...   ▨Example▨

DESCRIPTION ▨
  IMPORTANT: if you want to try any Examples in this DESCRIPTION, you
  should expand the introductory example that follows. ▨Example▨

Figure 4: Figure 2 with the authorship menu

as a button with a null name and a null replacement. Having
created a button the user then edits in the name he wants to use for
it. He then selects the button, just as a reader would do, and edits
the null replacement. The **Extend** menu command can be used to
extend a construct to include some existing text. It is specially useful
when adding buttons to an existing document: the replacement of
new buttons can embody sections of the original text. The **Destruct**
menu command removes components of the structuring and allows a
user to undo a document structure; he can then build a new one.
The **Change-button** menu command is concerned with changing the
properties of a button.

Originally GUIDE only had three commands for creating new
structures: these created new glossary-buttons (+**Glossary**), replace-
buttons (now done with +**Local**) and definitions of glossary-buttons
(+**Definition**). Since then, for better or for worse, GUIDE has been
embellished. There are two further types of replace-buttons, called
Usages and **Actions**. Usages are like glossary-buttons, but involve
the in-line replacement of buttons using a global definition; actions
allow an arbitrary shell command to be executed, the replacement of
the button being the output from the command. There is also a new
construct called an *enquiry*, which allows a multi-way replacement.
A sample enquiry is

  Is it **Red, Green** or **Blue?**

A further embellishment is the 'ask-level' associated with each replace-button; this allows buttons to be automatically replaced for certain kinds of user.

These embellishments add considerably to GUIDE's functionality, though it still remains a modest system, and meet real user needs. The users are clamouring for further embellishments.

On the other side, each new facility added to a document display system inevitably makes authoring more difficult. Even the author who does not use the new facilities is presented with extra choices in the menu: he needs to make and to understand more decisions, and to know more about the properties of the buttons he has created. Some of these extra problems can be alleviated on a graphics display — for example the properties of a button can be indicated as the cursor passes over it — but nevertheless the problems cannot be eliminated.

In spite of this, most of the GUIDE embellishments can probably be justified on balance. Nevertheless, as document display systems are extended they soon pass a point where the bulk of potential authors are driven away. No warning bells are rung when this happens — instead the designer goes on blithely adding more and more goodies to his system and comes to reflect on how perverse the world is in not using his superb product. GUIDE has probably already reached the critical point.

7. Document Structure

Over the centuries, many techniques have been developed for showing the structure of paper documents. Documents are divided into sections, perhaps with numbered headings, sections are divided into subsections, and so on. Typographical conventions have been refined so that section headings stand out to an appropriate degree.

These techniques generally carry over to on-line documents and are just as necessary. The GUIDE author imposes a further structure on documents as a result of the hierarchy of replace-buttons. There are thus two structures: the *section structure* carried over from the genre of paper documents and the *button-structure* of GUIDE. Should the author make the two structures coincide so that each section and sub-section of the document corresponds to a GUIDE button? The answer is that doing so is a safe approach, but it is worth experimenting with authoring approaches where the two structures are complementary rather than coinciding. For example a section might be displayed by GUIDE as

3.4 CAPITAL GAINS TAX

> If you make profits from buying and selling
> shares, antiques, houses, etc., you need to
> know about capital gains tax or to discuss it
> with your accountant. **More**

Here the initial text of the section gives a flavour of its content and
the **More** replace-button is used to bring in the bulk of the text of the
section.

There is no one 'best' way of structuring a document, and,
hopefully GUIDE authors will gradually refine an array of good
techniques.

8. Summary

This paper has shown a simple and flexible document display system,
and, it is hoped, a relatively simple and flexible authoring system. If
document display systems are to become widely used it is vital that
authoring of documents be made simpler. If this means less
functionality then that is a necessary cost.

9. Acknowledgements

I am grateful to my colleagues for many useful suggestions about
GUIDE and its use, and to the Science and Engineering Research
Council for some financial support.

References

[1] Apperley, M.D. & Spence, R. (1983). Hierarchical dialogue structures
in interactive computer systems, *Software—Practice and Experience*, 13, 9,
pp. 777-790.

[2] Brown, P.J. (1984). *GUIDE user manual*, Computing Laboratory,
University of Kent at Canterbury.

[3] Feiner, S., Nagy, S. & van Dam, A. (1982). An experimental system
for creating and presenting interactive graphical documents, *ACM
Transactions on Graphics*, 1, *1*, pp. 59-77.

[4] Robertson, G., McCracken, D. & Newell, A. (1981). The ZOG
approach to man-machine communication, *International Journal of Man-
Machine Studies*, Vol. 14, pp. 461-488.

[5] Weyer, S.A. & Borning, A.H. (1985). A prototype electronic
encyclopedia, *ACM transactions on office information systems*, 3, pp. 63-85.

[6] Yankelovich, N., Meyrowitz, N. & van Dam, A. (1985). Reading and
writing the electronic book, *IEEE Computer*, 18, 10, pp. 15-30.

VORTEXT: VictORias TEXT reading and authoring system

VICTORIA A. BURRILL

The University of Reading

ABSTRACT

As the cost of paper and library space increases, so does the necessity for alternative forms of book storage. Computers seem the obvious answer and already much work has been done into various on-line text reading and writing systems. These systems are very effective within their own domains, yet remain essentially for computer users, rather than the ordinary man-in-the-street.

Real paper books may not actually be the best way of presenting information, but they are certainly the most familiar. It seems logical therefore to design a reading system that can be made more widely accessible because it resembles a real book as much as possible both in appearance and use - a sort of generic *advance organiser* [Ausubel60].

The system described here - VORTEXT - is an attempt to do precisely that.

1. How people read books

Books are rarely read completely linearly; mystery novels almost are, but how many people let their curiosity get the better of them and sneak a look at the last page to see *who dunnit?*. A text book is more likely to be *dipped-into* looking for a particular section, and a journal article tends to be read in full only if the reader considers it useful and relevant after having read the title, then the abstract, conclusion and finally the references [Maude85, Line82].

"The printed article is well-adapted to speedy rejection - an inestimable virtue"[Line82]

These reading methods depend on three main recognition methods:

1. *Recognition of text from the text itself*: For example, searching specifically for a section concerning screen editors

2. *Recognition of text from its physical position*: For example, the final pages of a text book must be the index, while those of a mystery novel must be where the villain is identified

3. *Recognition of text from typographical factors*: For example, if a large, simple font is used this must be a childrens book; if a small, dense font is used, a technical (and boring?) book

1.1. Recognition of text from the text itself

A **hypertext document** is defined as: *"The combination of natural language text with the computer's capacities for interactive branching or display... a non-linear text..."* [Nelson67].

Current hypertext systems such as GUIDE [Brown84], ZOG [McCracken84], FRESS [vanDam71] and the electronic book [Feiner82] concentrate on recognition from the text itself, relying heavily upon the author to anticipate the needs of the reader. If the various functions of the book were not foreseen accurately or the readers expectations and knowledge do not match the information provided, then the reader rapidly becomes confused. Also, as the number of hierarchical levels of information increases, so do the chances of the reader, especially a novice to the system, making unintentionally incorrect choices and getting hopelessly lost [vanNes82]. Now the reader requires alternative search strategies:

Solution 1: Give up
Solution 2: Rely on the system to provide helpful hints
Solution 3: Reformulate the question

Obviously, solution 1 should be avoided! Solution 2 is feasible but can still produce surprise results if the "helpful" hints are based on past pages read (some of which may have been selected by mistake anyway), or if the reader's original request was outside the scope of the document. Solution 3 appears to be the most satisfactory, but assumes that the reader is sufficiently familiar with either the subject matter or the mechanics of asking and rephrasing questions in order to be successful. Since it is incorrect to assume that a reader will always be familiar with the subject matter of any and every book, care must be taken to ensure that the latter assumption holds.

> *"Telephone books are like dictionaries - if you know the answer before you look it up, you can eventually reaffirm what you thought you knew but weren't sure. But if you're searching for something you don't already know, your fingers could walk themselves to death"* [Bombeck81]

1.2. Recognition of text from its physical position

Recognition of text from its physical position occurs in two forms:

1. **Current page → Document**: Determine the position of the current page in relation to the document as a whole and in relation to the subject

2. **Document → Required page**: Determine the position of the required page within the document

The first form is the *orientation* or *Where am I now?* form. GUIDE orientates the reader by using a scrollbar to represent the size and position of the current screenful in relation to the document as a whole. The electronic book uses small system diagrams as orientation in relation to the subject.

The second form is the *I know it's there somewhere* form. A page may be found because it always appears in a particular position (for example, the introduction at the beginning of a book, the index at the end), or because the reader remembers its position in conjunction with the layout of the page as being *Somewhere in the middle of the book, second paragraph down, just above a large table of numbers.*

The **What, Where and Whence system** [Engel83] goes part-way towards solving the text and physical recognition problems by enabling the user to ask:

WHAT is the overall structure of information in the book?
WHERE am I in relation to that?
from WHENCE did I get to this page?

1.3. Recognition of text from typographical factors

Every individual develops mental frameworks or
schemata of observations and deductions in order to
recognise objects and situations [Schumacher81]. A
schema for identifying journal articles might include:

Sheets of paper attached along one side	☛	notebook, book
Pages are filled with handwriting	☛	notebook
Pages are filled with print	☛	book
Very few headings	☛	novel
Many headings and emphasised words	☛	text book, journal
Major headings of a few lines	☛	text book
Major headings of several lines	☛	journal article

Diagram 1: Simple schema for identifying journal articles

Note that this is a very simple example and no attempt
is made to describe the schemata for recognising
handwriting, print, headings and so on. It does however
indicate the complexities of recognising different types
of documents without actually understanding the text of
them. These subjective typographical aspects are very
important in the comprehension of both paper and
computer texts, and could usefully be incorporated as
default layout suggestions within the VORTEXT authors
documentation.

But both readers and authors alike must already be
aware, if only subconsciously, of these conventions of
document layout from past experience. It therefore
seems unnecessary to *teach grandmothers to suck eggs*
and include such rigorous typographical guidelines as
part of VORTEXT itself - at least for the present.

2. Description of VORTEXT

Introduction

The underlying philosophy of VORTEXT is to try to map the design of a paper book onto the computer screen in such a way that the reader takes advantage of the power of a computer without losing the familiarity of the presentation and use of conventional books. As computer technology advances so do the facilities for authors themselves to write, design and produce their own camera-ready documents. In company with many other systems, VORTEXT authors will have much to learn about the typographical aspects of their documents in order for the new technology to be as aesthetically acceptable as the old.

VORTEXT is seen typically as being used:

1. In a library for reading and reference, especially for highly volatile information such as short-loan books

2. By authors, especially as the trend towards using computers to produce camera-ready (or almost) documents increases

3. For on-line help and documentation in local situations such as a university computer department

A smaller, read-only version could be used:

4. For distance-learning situations such as the Open University

5. Home reference manuals such as gardening, DIY and recipe books

6. Helping disabled people read a variety of books

Note that none of the text systems described in the previous section claim to be ideally suited to very large documents or to the various library-type environments. Because of their highly-structured approach they are perhaps better suited-to reference documents for non-novice users. In contrast, VORTEXT tries to cater for the complete subject- and computer-beginner as would be found in these situations. The ways in which it does this are described below, based on categories of text display suggested by Bork [Bork83].

2.1. Environment

The two main groups of VORTEXT users are (obviously) the authors and the readers.

For the reader, control is almost exclusively via a mouse because it is the easiest of currently-available devices to use [Card78], although the keyboard might be necessary for initially logging-into the system.

For the author, the keyboard is used for text entry and editing, but control may be via either of the two devices. This physical separation and redundancy between input devices has been found to be the most successful method of helping the author mentally differentiate between the modes in which each should be used. (For example, always using the keyboard when graphics are switched-on for editing, but otherwise reverting to the mouse) [Burrill84].

2.2. Screen design

Screen 1 is the title page of an article as seen by the reader. Note how it looks like an open book, with **closed pages** down each side. The distribution of these closed pages and the text of the headings within them alters according to the current page. This simple concept provides essential **perceptual landmarks** to the reader [Woods84], indicating not only the readers position *physically* within the book, but also their position *in relation to the subject matter.*

In this example, the contents page is selected by moving the mouse to point to the required closed page and then clicking the mouse button.

2.3. User control

Initially the contents page displays only the highest-level section headings. By selecting one of these headings, its corresponding subsections can be displayed too, (**Screen 2**), and so on until the lowest level is reached when a subsequent selection will turn directly to that page.

This *windowed* presentation of the contents is in effect a hierarchical map of the subjects and sibling-subjects within the document, and so helps reduce the users memory load by successively refining the subject area to

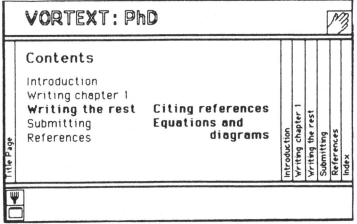

Screen 1: VORTEXT title page showing closed pages

Screen 2: VORTEXT contents page showing highest-level headings and a set of subsection headings

the desired level [Brooke83]. Since the contents page is (obviously) confined to a single screenfull and the current pathway is always visible, the reader cannot get lost.

Note also that the author need not arrange the headings in rows or columns, but may distribute them anywhere on the page. This augments the *symbolic clues* of the actual text of the headings, adding the *spatial clues* of its position on the screen [Fields77]. (This is equivalent to saying *The bookshop opposite the cinema* rather than *G Blackmans' shop*).

Screen 3 is a typical text page as seen by the reader. Only the author can select the paint-brush icon in the lower left-hand corner of the screen to display the page in its internal, authoring form (**Screen 4**).

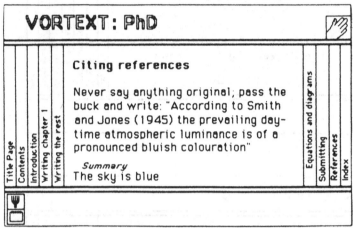

Screen 3: VORTEXT text page as seen by the reader

Screen 4: VORTEXT text page as seen by the author, showing named-boxes and graphics icons

Note the **named-boxes** containing various kinds of text. The names of these boxes are set-up by the author, who also specifies whether or not the box is:

Concorded: The text inside is added to the index so it is then searchable

Indexed: The box name itself is added to the index, so for example the reader could browse through the document reading all the abstracts or summaries

The actual editing is done on a **direct manipulation WYSIWYG** (What You See Is What You Get) basis [Shneiderman83]. Thus boxes of text can be moved around the screen by selecting and then dragging them to the required position. Similarly, by dragging on the closed pages readers may flick through the document to *visually* search for a particular page or feature.

2.4. Aids to browsing

By selecting the word *sky* on **Screen 3**, the user can request the glossary entry for the word (**Screen 5**). Note that this **glossary panel** contains a brief definition of that word and is associated with three **Mmi icons** - Major, minor and illustration icons. If the reader requires further information, one of these three icons may be selected in order to retrieve specific types of reference.

Major references are those in which the selected word occurs in the heading of a page, implying that the section concerns that item in particular.

minor references are those in which the selected word occurs in the main body of (concorded) text anywhere within the document, implying that the item is referred-to in passing.

illustration references are those in which the selected word occurs as the caption to a diagram, implying (probably correctly) that a picture is worth a thousand words.

By selecting the minor references icon, other references to *sky* can be found (**Screen 6**). Note the **bookmark** in the top right-hand corner which displays the current search term and uses blank closed pages to reflect the number of references found. By selecting these closed pages the reader can browse through the *sky* references. In a similar way to the main screen, the bookmark closed pages alter according to the position of the currently-displayed reference page in relation to the other referenced pages.

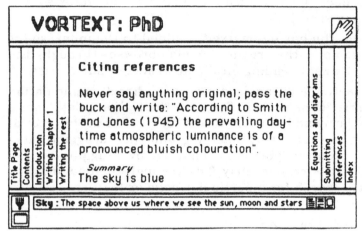

Screen 5: VORTEXT text page showing a glossary panel with Mmi icons

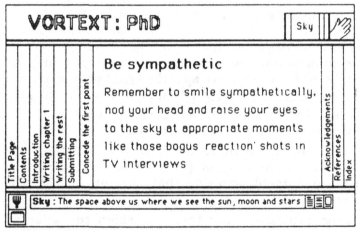

Screen 6: VORTEXT text page after a minor references request, showing bookmark

Note that any word in the document may be associated with one of several glossary definitions as set-up by the author, so confusion over the correct glossary entry for *rabbits* in the contexts of *Small furry animals with long ears* and *Chatters incessantly* may be avoided.

By selecting the glossary panel of a second word and then one of the *combined* Mmi icons, references to pages on which *both* these words occur may be found. If the glossary panels have been set-up appropriately, the reader can select words from within the panel itself to specify the request further (**Screen 7**).

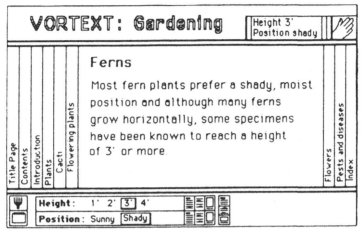

Screen 7: VORTEXT gardening book text page after a minor references request for suggestions as to what plants would grow behind the garage - up to 3' in height and in a shady position

Note that these **ordinary glossaries** may be used in a variety of ways, the most obvious being to provide the actual definition of a word and then to find other occurrences of that word within the (concorded) text of the document. In addition, they could easily be used to provide a form of footnotes, for example by expanding on a reference to give an article and journal name, and then as a form of citation index to find other references to a particular work.

In addition to the ordinary glossaries, VORTEXT implements **historical glossaries** which may be used for temporal definitions. Historical glossaries have closed pages instead of Mmi icons and the reader can browse them in the usual way.

Historical glossaries have a variety of uses. The time aspect may be applied to the document as a whole, for example by giving a résumé of the life of a particular character in a novel (**Screens 8 - 10**), or may be applied to smaller sections as an additional summary-level of information, for example describing the operating instructions of a particular piece of equipment (**Screens 11 - 13**).

As in paper books, VORTEXT documents usually include an index. Unlike paper documents however, the VORTEXT

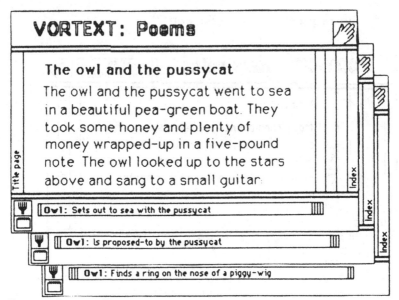

Screens 8 to 10: The first page of a VORTEXT novel, showing successive historical glossaries of a biography of the Owl

index will contain a list of all the unique (concorded) words used in the document, their various alternative definitions and the names of any indexed named-boxes. As usual, clicking on a word displays its glossary panel and Mmi icons.

The VORTEXT index is effectively acting like a large menu-selection system instead of requiring the more conventional free-form command-driven retrieval. Although somewhat pedantic from the reader's point of view, this menu approach does help in the choice of search terms especially when combined with a subject index and the glossary feature to determine the intended context before the retrieval is performed [Burrill86].

2.5. Marginalia and cross-referencing

In addition to the system-determined browsing features of the glossaries, Mmi references and bookmarks, VORTEXT includes some user-determined features, converting an essentially static document into a dynamic one [Weyer82].

The readers of conventional paper documents can use their fingers to keep several places in the book; the VORTEXT **fingers icon** in the top right-hand corner of the

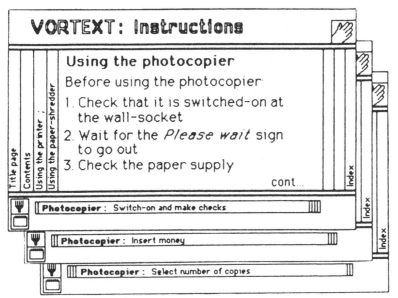

Before using the photocopier

1. Check that it is switched-on at the wall-socket
2. Wait for the *Please wait* sign to go out
3. Check the paper supply

Screens 11 to 13: Part of a VORTEXT technical manual, showing historical glossaries used as brief instructions

screen may be used in much the same way. Fingers may be added or removed, and the next kept page is found by clicking on the fingers bookmark in the usual way.

2.6. Time domain

One additional dimension that computers can add to documents is that of time.

This may include altering the overall rate of output of text (slowly for novices, faster for experts more familiar with the subject) [Bevan81], or altering the relative rate of output (slowing before and after a keyword) [Heckel83].

Finally, in the same way that a lecturer would modify a diagram on the blackboard in stages according to what was being described at the time, different parts of the screen may be output at different times, *leading* the readers attention as the subject progresses.

Summary

The main strength of VORTEXT would appear to be its book-likeness, especially in the very simple but obvious concept of the closed pages. The information retrieval aspect seems primitive but it is anticipated that the use of glossaries, Mmi icons and the index should more than compensate for this, providing novel (pardon the pun) and highly effective tools for a wide variety of retrieval tasks.

From the author's point of view, the VORTEXT *wysiwyg* approach vastly simplifies the writing of a document, and by exploiting the graphics features to the full can incorporate quite sophisticated word-processing capabilities.

It is emphasised that this description as of August 1985 is based on theory alone; the real work began a few months ago implementing VORTEXT on a VAX-11/750 with a VT220 terminal.

Acknowledgements

The screen diagrams are mock-ups of the intended displays and were produced using *MacPaint* on an Apple *Macintosh* computer. The rest of this document was produced using TROFF on a PDP-11/44 and Versatec V-80 phototypesetter. Many thanks to John for proof-reading.

References

[Ausubel60] Ausubel DD "The use of advance organisers in the learning and retention of meaningful verbal material" *Journal of Educational Psychology 51* p.267-272 1960

[Bevan81] Bevan N "Is there an optimum speed for presenting text on a VDU?" *International Journal of Man-Machine Studies 4(1)* p.59-76 1981

[Bombeck81] Bombeck E "At wits' end" *The Peninsula Times Tribune* Palo Alto, CA 22nd. September 1981

[Bork83] Bork A "A preliminary taxonomy of ways of displaying text on screens" *Information Design Journal 3(3)* p.206-214 1983

[Brooke83] Brooke JB, Duncan KD "A comparison of hierarchical pages and scrolling displays for fault-finding" *Ergonomics 26(5)* p.465-477 1983

[Brown84] Brown PJ "Interactive documentation: GUIDE" *Computing Laboratory, Kent University, Canterbury* 1984

[Burrill84] Burrill VA, Unpublished conversations 1984

[Burrill86] Burrill VA "Indexing in VORTEXT: a short note on the problems of searching for 'canned', 'worms' and 'canned worms'" *To be submitted for publication* 1986

[Card78] Card SK, English WK, Burr BJ "Evaluation of mouse, rate-controlled, isometric joystick, step keys and text keys for text selection on a CRT" *Ergonomics 21* p.601-613 1978

[Engel83] Engel FL, Andriessen JJ, Schmitz HJR "What, where and whence: means for improving electronic data access" *International Journal of Man-Machine Studies 18* p.145-160 1983

[Feiner82] Feiner S, Nagy S, vanDam A "A graphical system for creating and presenting interactive graphical documents" *ACM Transactions on Graphics 1(1)* p.59-77 1982

[Fields77] Fields C, Negroponte N "Using new clues to find data" Proceedings of the Third International Conference on Very Large Databases" p.156-158 1977

[Heckel83] Heckel P "Walt Disney and user-oriented software" *Byte 8(12)* p.143-150 1983

[Line82] Line MB "Redesigning journal articles for on-line viewing" *Trends in information technology* ed. PJ Hills 1982

[Maude85] Maude TI, Pullinger DJ "Software for reading, refereeing and browsing in the BLEND system" *Computer Journal 28(1)* p.1-4 1985

[McCracken84] McCracken DL, Akscyn RM "Experience with the ZOG human-computer interface system" *International Journal of Man-Machine Studies 21(4)* p.293-310 1984

[Nelson67] Nelson TH "Getting it out of our system" *Information retrieval: a critical review* ed. G Schecter p.191-210 1967

[Schumacher81] Schumacher GM "Schemata in text processing and design" *Information Design Journal 2(1)* p.17-27 1981

[Shneiderman83] Shneiderman B "Direct manipulation: a step beyond programming languages" *Computer 16(8)* p.57-69 1983

[vanDam71] vanDam A "FRESS: file retrieval and editing system" *Text Systems* 1971

[vanNes82] van Nes FL, van der Heijden J "Data retrieval by inexperienced users" *Ergonomics* 1982

[Weyer82] Weyer SA "The design of a dynamic book for information search" *International Journal of Man-Machine Studies 17* p.87-107 1982

[Woods84] Woods DD "Visual momentum: a concept to improve the cognitive coupling of person and computer" *International Journal of Man-Machine Studies 21* p.229-244 1984

An Approach to the Design of a Page Description Language

DAVID J. HARRIS
Chelgraph Limited

ABSTRACT

With the recent development of cheap highly functional laser printers and Raster Image Processors, there has been an upsurge of interest in languages for interfacing to these devices. An approach to the design of such a Page Description Language is described, the primary design requirement being a clean interface which is an easy target for translators from various front-end systems. The design of an actual PDL, the Chelgraph ACE language, based on these principles is described. Finally the ACE language is reviewed in the light of experience gained in its use.

1. Introduction

This paper discusses some issues relevant to the design of a Page Description Language (PDL). A PDL is a type of language commonly used for communicating page information from a composition system to an intelligent page printer. These languages are usually specified by the printer manufacturer as an input language, but device-independent outputs from some composition packages, for example DI-TROFF, are also PDLs. I also present a particular PDL, the ACE language, which has been designed by us at Chelgraph and implemented on our Raster Image Processor, the features of ACE itself have been described elsewhere [Chel84, Harris84].

2. What Is a PDL ?

There have always been languages for communicating page information to typesetters and printers. Until recently the capabilities of computer output printers have been very limited, so their input languages have been simple ASCII formats modified by escape codes. Typesetters such as the Autologic APS 5, on the other hand, have quite complex input languages with a syntax and tens of commands.

With the recent advent of laser printers and raster typesetters the issue of PDLs has received much attention, and a number of languages have been invented and often promulgated as industry standards. Laser printers and modern typesetters usually consist of two parts, a raster marking engine whose task it is to make marks on the paper, and a Raster Image Processor (RIP) which takes in some description of a page (i.e. a PDL) and generates a bit-image of the page for the marking engine. The facilities incorporated in the typical modern RIP, which can usually scale and rotate characters and generate other graphics, together with the need to interface these printers to a wide variety of composition packages and other 'front ends', make the specification of a good PDL a real challenge.

3. Design Aims
The principal reason for having a PDL is to provide a clean interface to a typesetter or other printing machine, other secondary aims can include the provision of device-independence and the use of the PDL as a 'metafile' to transfer page descriptions between sites. Although the secondary, and grander, aims are sometimes seen as important, the provision of a good composer/printer interface must remain paramount.

It is desirable that the PDL should be easy to implement, mainly for those whose task it is to generate it from a front end system, but it must also be easy to implement at the printer end if it is to become widely accepted (i.e. an 'industry standard'). In order to provide this ease of interfacing the language must be designed with the needs of the front-end systems in mind, drawing on existing standards, both formal and informal, used in the field.

A further requirement, from the point of view of the printer supplier, is that the PDL provides full access to the facilities of the printer and presents a logical, and easily understandable model of the printer to the user of the language.

Additional aims, good for the design of any language, include Consistency, Orthogonality, Simplicity and Efficiency (these are of course, usually incompatible). Readability of the language by humans is not a prime concern as PDLs are normally generated and interpreted by programs, readability does greatly help the writers of such programs, however.

4. The Three Layers of Language
Document content can be defined at several levels, these seem to break most naturally into three layers, each layer having its own characteristic ways of defining a document.

On the highest layer, we have Abstract languages. These are often declarative in tone (for example 'this is a paragraph'), and are very portable, both between output devices and even different composition systems. A good example of this type of language is the SGML (Standard Generalised Markup Language). Another, more accessible, example is the TBL table description language used with the TROFF documentation programs.

On the medium layer are the Procedural languages, which tend to have a command and parameter structure (for example 'at depth X change margin to Y'). They are seldom portable, but can offer output-device independence. An example from this layer is CORA V, the Linotype composition language.

The lowest layer contains the Slave languages. On this layer all abstract information is gone (for example 'goto X,Y'). All decisions, such as kerning, line breaks, and footnote placement have been made, although general coordinate transformations are still possible (for example rotation and scaling of the whole page). An example of a Slave language is the TeX DVI output format.

Document composition is often seen as being analogous to compilation [Reid80]. Using this model the higher two layers parallel various types of high level languages, and the Slave level the compiler intermediate code or the machine code.

The most appropriate layer for PDLs is the Slave layer. The reason for this is to provide the maximum ease of interfacing. It is impossible to translate from a low layer to a higher layer, and usually difficult to translate between languages on the same layer. On the other hand it is straightforward to translate from a high layer to a low layer, a low layer language thus provides the easiest 'target' for the output routines from composition programs.

Using the slave layer can, although aiding one of the primary design aims (ease of interface), work against one of the secondary aims (portability). When documents must be ported between printers and systems, formatting decisions may need to be re-interpreted in the light of the facilities of the target printer (for example available fonts). Such portability can best be provided by a language on the Abstract layer, where style tags can be redefined at will. The question of portability must not be allowed to confuse the design of a Slave PDL, as it can be dealt with far better in the higher layers.

5. The Design of ACE

The reason for developing ACE was to provide an interface language for the Chelgraph Modular RIP. This is a flexible Raster Image Processor whose modular design allows it to be easily configured to drive almost any raster device, from an A4 300 dot per inch laser printer to a 2000+ dot per inch double broadsheet laser platemaker. This flexibility, coupled with the RIPs advanced functions combining versatile (typesetter-quality) text and computer graphics meant that the RIP must be interfaced to a wide variety of driving front end systems, ranging from newspaper editorial systems, to PC based graphics packages.

The starting point for the design, under the guidance rules developed above, was to consider existing standards formal and de facto. In the case of computer-generated graphics there was in existence a very suitable formalised standard in the proposed ANSI Virtual Device Metafile (VDM). This standard (which has now been taken up by ISO as CGM, Computer Graphics Metafile) is part of the GKS family of standards for graphics. It specifies content at a level equivalent with the Slave PDL, thus making it suitable. CGM is an evolving standard which specifies line and area drawing functions such as :

> Polyline
> Arc
> Elliptical Arc
> Polygon
> Circle
> Circular Arc Close
> Elliptical Arc Close

All these commands can be modified by a set of modal variables to produce different effects (such as tinted or cross-hatched circles). CGM also provides a model for specifying text attributes and the interaction of text with graphical objects. For example text rotation angle is specified by the text vector, which is a vector running along the text baseline in the direction of travel of the text. In the corresponding ACE command 'tv 0 1' (being a horizontal vector) is the default, this means that the baseline of text runs horizontally from left to right. By specifying 'tv 1 1' the text would be rotated so that the baseline runs at 45 degrees to the horizontal. Rotation can be combined with shearing, reflection and scaling to create a wide range of effects.

When it comes to the lay-down of text however, CGM with its background in graphics systems labelling pie diagrams and graphs is not really suitable for bulk text formatted by a typesetter. There are also no helpful formal or industry standards in the typesetting field. In the specification of this area of ACE we drew on experience gained in typesetter interfacing. This suggested that the important point in order to provide a clean, trouble-free interface was that ACE should itself specify the position of each character on the page, thus the reader of the ACE does not need access to width tables in order to interpret it. This kind of output can always be generated easily from a composition system's model of the page and helps to reduce the number of copies of a width table that need to exist within a system (hopefully to one). We were further influenced in this direction by the DI-TROFF intermediate device independent code specification [Kern82].

As in the DI-TROFF code system, ACE uses a scheme whereby escapements (or relative motions) are included in the file along with the text characters. Absolute positioning commands are also available, but are seldom used. So, to set the line 'The ACE language' the code could be :

M "T28h23e38A28C28E47l11a21n24g19u24a21g19e. G
V 48

The 'M' and 'G' commands save and restore the current position and the 'V' command applies a relative motion at 90 degrees from the text vector (i.e. in the correct direction for inter-line spacing). Each character of text is followed by, in this case, two digits of escapement information. ACE provides a means whereby this may be reduced to one in most cases, by using offsets and number bases greater than 10. The units of measurement need not be device pixels.

A further boon of this way of positioning characters is that the composition system does all the justification, kerning and letterspacing, and other aesthetic positioning calculations. There are an innumerable number of ways of doing these and to provide for them efficiently in the Slave PDL requires a number of fairly complex command facilities. These things really are done much better in the front-end system or its output driver. Of course, a charge of inefficiency can be made against this approach but it is greatly mitigated the relative positioning and escapement encoding schemes. Any remaining inefficiency is a small price to pay for simplicity.

6. Implemented ACE processors

As mentioned above the first receiver of ACE was the Chelgraph RIP, this has become a successful product and is being designed in to laser printing and typesetting equipment.

On the side of generating ACE the simplicity of its approach has proved itself again and again. Chelgraph and its associates, with only a small development team, have already implemented drivers for ACE from typesetting languages : Linotype's CORA V, Autologic's APS 5 ICL and Monotype's Lasercomp; microcomputer packages : Digital Research GSX and GEM, and Microsoft Word; and DI-TROFF (including PIC, EQN and TBL).

The adherence of ACE to graphics standards often helps (e.g in the case of GSX, which is also derived from VDM), and the similarity with DI-TROFF made that driver easy. Where neither of these holds ACE generation is still straightforward due to its simple model of character positioning and page construction.

7. Conclusions

Our experience has shown that, in general, the right decisions were made in the design as borne out by the ease of development of the ACE drivers. As further testimony to the design, when the APS 5 emulator was developed it was desired to provide a 'wrong reading' (reflected output) facility in the emulator. This was implemented simply by the emulator modifying the setting of the ACE text vector and up vector values, no new commands had to be added to ACE.

To draw some conclusions on the form of the resulting language I will compare it with PostScript [Adobe84], which is certainly the most discussed PDL at the moment. A comparison of output functions available in the two languages (ACE and PostScript) certainly shows that there are some functions in PostScript, for example the ability to image bitmap graphics, which are not present in ACE. Such a comparison does not, however, reach the heart of the difference between the two languages, as it would be easy to add commands to ACE to make such output functions possible.

The real difference lies in the number of 'high level' functions included in the language. The aim of ACE is to provide a simple, but sufficient, set of tools to make page images, rather like a machine instruction set. PostScript on the other hand provides programming language features such as functions, loops and variables. At first sight the PostScript approach may seem obviously the more desirable - Have not programmers progressed over the years from machine code, through assembler to 'C', LISP and Ada ? To use this analogy, attractive though it may seem, is to forget that the 'programmer' that generates the PDL is almost invariably a computer program and not a person.

Thus we come back to the analogy of PDL as a machine instruction set with document formatter or other composition software as the compiler. Those who design complex PDLs are effectively following the same road as mainframe and mini computer designers who built machines with large and complex instruction sets containing 'high-level' instructions. In the case of machine architectures it turned out that many of these instructions were little used by the compilers, a discovery that lead to today's movement towards simpler RISC instruction sets. As is the case with instruction sets, a larger, more complex PDL tends to require more computer hardware (memory, processing power) to implement, at the same performance level and moment in time, than a simpler language, thus one should not ignore the benefits of simplicity.

To conclude, then, ACE provides (like the RISC machine) a simple set of basic operations which allow the higher layers of document preparation software to access device facilities through a consistent interface. These higher layers incorporate programming features and add the bulk of the device independence into the document structure. To build such features in at the PDL level, I believe is unnecessary and leads to an uncalled for increase in the size and complexity of the language.

Acknowledgements

I would like to thank the referees, and in particular Heather Brown, for their comments on this paper.

References

[1] Adobe Systems (1984). *PostScript Language Manual* (first edition), Adobe Systems, Palo Alto, California, 1984. PostScript is a trademark of Adobe Systems.

[2] Chelgraph Ltd. *ACE (ASCII Coded Escapement Language) Specification*, obtainable from Chelgraph in Cheltenham by post at the price of ten pounds sterling (plus VAT for UK orders).

[3] Harris, D. J. (1984). ACE - A Device Independent Lay Down Language for Text and Graphics. In *PROTEXT I*, ed. J.J.H. Miller. Dublin, Ireland: Boole Press.

[4] Kernighan B. W. (1982) *A Typesetter-independent TROFF*, Bell Laboratories, Murray Hill, New Jersey.

[5] Reid B. K. (1980). *Scribe: a document specification language and its compiler*, Ph.D. Thesis, Computer Science Dept., Carnegie-Mellon University.

Intelligent Matching and Retrieval for Electronic Document Manipulation

Dr E J Yannakoudakis

Postgraduate School of Computer Science
Bradford University, Bradford, BD7 1DP

ABSTRACT
The paper presents a new system for automatic matching of bibliographic data corresponding to items of full textual electronic documents. The problem can otherwise be expressed as the identification of similar or duplicate items existing in different bibliographic databases. A primary objective is the design of an interactive system where matches and near misses are displayed on the user's terminal so that he can confirm or reject the identification before the associated full electronic versions are located and processed further.

Introduction

There is no doubt that 'electronic publishing' and other computer based tools for the production and dissemination of printed material open up new horizons for efficient communication. The problems currently faced by the designers of such systems are enormous. One problem area is the identification of duplicate material especially when there is more than one source generating similar documents. Abstracting is a good example here. Another problem area is the linkage between full text and bibliographic databases.

As part of its attempt to establish collaboration between different countries, the European Economic Community initiated the DOCDEL programme of research and a series of studies such as DOCOLSYS which investigate the present situation in Europe regarding document identification, location and ordering with particular reference to electronic ordering and delivery of documents.

The majority of DOCDEL systems likely to be developed fall under one of the following areas:

(a) Delivery from computer-based systems
(b) Delivery from non-computer based systems
(c) Electronic publishing
(d) On-demand publishing

DOCMATCH is another programme of research of the EEC which addresses a more general case in which there is no direct and obvious link between cited reference and full text, for example, when references and texts are identified by the same accession number. The University of Bradford together with the British Library are involved in the first stage of DOCMATCH. This paper presents an outline of the methodology and the current state of the project.

The planned work is based on the hypothesis that it is possible to transform the Universal Standard Book Code (USBC) into a Universal Standard Bibliographic Code [1] which could be applied to on-line databases for bibliographic and document manipulation.

The generation of the USBC is based on information-theoretic considerations and utilises discriminating attributes of documents to create 'finger print' codes. The principle is that, given an adequate probability space, the items with a low probability carry maximum self-information. These are then selected from pertinent bibliographic fields for the creation of codes used as primary or secondary keys. The codes themselves are fixed in length, regenerable, verifiable, and can be applied retrospectively.

Our initial work will concentrate on two types of literature which in general are considered to form the most important part of many databases; these are citations of references to periodicals, and papers from conferences. Recommendations will also be made for the elements that will require coding for patents, government publications, reports, theses and miscellaneous pamphlets, monographs and trade literature.

The 'intelligent system' planned will be able to establish the necessary link by probabilistic means and to measure the degree of connectivity between different citations. It is envisaged that different modes of operation will allow the user to (a) match, (b) link, (c) isolate, and (d) process full electronic documents on request.

1. The Problem

Current information retrieval systems operate on databases which have a predefined and fixed format offering limited access by means of indexes. The problems arise when the retrieved references are to be matched to the actual electronic version. In many cases, and where different hosts are involved, the bibliographic attributes will be similar but not necessarily identical. Therefore, while it is possible for a standard cataloguing system to be accepted, and for standard indexes to be agreed, the problem that documents are not coded and catalogued identically on different databases still remains.

It can be argued, unsuccessfully, that current systems such as the ISBN and ISSN can form the basis of the linkage, but these do not go as far down as the individual article of a Journal. Extension of current systems to cope with this would not, in any case, be able to cope with grey literature, conference proceedings, theses, etc.

Evidently, the problem is complicated further by the need to vary the degree of connectivity or similarity between documents, as well as the need for strict and unique identification of documents where the bibliographic attributes are verifiable and consistently defined.

It is difficult to see how any generalised standard algorithm could be developed to deal with the variety of formats likely to be found. In selecting fields to be used in the matching process it may be advisable to use those least susceptible to variation, or those easily brought into a standard form. The present work is not concerned with this problem, although substantial software has been developed to read tapes and to identify fields from dozens of different hosts.

Finally, an ideal system would be able to utilise information from the citation and proceed to carry out a number of tasks besides intelligent matching. Examples are, free format identification, hashing and automatic calculation of physical addresses, resolution of collisions. For it is only with these tasks that a truly machine- independent system can be established to enable true international collaboration and exchange of scientific and cultural information.

2. The Matching Process

Given that the fields of request citations can be identified and reduced to a standard form to allow for different cataloguing practices, the problem of automatically matching items with the full text document is still not insignificant. The problems that have arisen in the related area of eliminating duplicates from monographic databases already in standard MARC format, are evidence of this [2].

The DOCMATCH problem is a special case of retrieval where the request may consist of a complete citation, and where ideally there is a complete match between all the attributes of the request and those in the citation describing the document. Generally, it is impractical and unnecessary to carry out a complete match between the whole citation and the index, and it is necessary to select a combination of fields or parts of fields, in compressed or uncompressed form, to be used in matching. Besides, the citation may not comprise of all the descriptive attributes of the associated document. An example here is the issue 'Number' within a Volume of a Journal.

Therefore, it becomes necessary to select a set of fields which provide enough discriminatory power but the matching criteria must not be so narrowly defined that small variations between citations describing the same document cause a failure of the matching process.

Once pertinent fields have been decided upon, there would appear to be three main approaches to the mechanisation of the process:

(1)   To search on these fields, either singly or in boolean combinations, as a single step or as separate steps, in indexes organised under a traditional bibliographic information retrieval system.

(2)   To produce a matching key be concatenation of these fields in uncompressed form and to use this as before.

(3)   To produce a matching key by compressing pertinent fields and by deriving a fixed length code which is regenerable.

It is a matter of common experience that suggests the exclusion of any approaches which make use of the full citation especially with large databases holding millions of records. Besides, extensive experimentation has proved that codes of less than 18 bytes, generated from pertinent bibliographic fields, can identify uniquely over 99% of the records in a bibliographic database [1], [2], [3]. The present work thus adopts the last option and attempts to apply it on monograph material.

The index to the full document database would effectively be a bibliographic database made up of short citations, with fields independently searchable. The index to the ADONIS system was planned to be of this type, although with manual searching for documents to match requests.

If we approach the problem from the point of view of primary and secondary keys, as is the case with relational database techniques and in conjunction with the above considerations, we see that a document identifier can be:

A.   Assigned to the document
    (i)   At source or by the publisher, and printed on the document as is the case with the proposals for BIBLID and SISAC identifiers for serial articles.
    (ii) By the document store or reference database as a unique ordering number as is the case with TRANSDOC practice.
B.   Generated from pertinent characteristics of the document itself to act as a unique key for matching and retrieval as is the case with USBC.

Under both (A) and (B) above the primary key of the document would be the unique identifier and it could be argued that no other elements would be required in the index.   However, it might be useful if the primary key was associated with a short citation in order to confirm the identity of items retrieved and with fields to be available as supplementary keys.

3. Generation of Document Identifiers
If a unique identifier is to be used, the question arises as to where it is to be generated, and how reference databases and document stores keep in step if this is ncessary. There appear to be five possibilities here:

(a)   Unique identifiers assigned at source or by the publisher: This would avoid problems in coordinating numbering of documents by the reference database and document store. Requests could consist of the unique identifier only.

(b)   Unique identifiers assigned by the document store or reference database: This option requires communication between the two organisations so that the correct number is assigned to the same document.   This may be satisfactory where the document is passed from a single reference database to a single store, but would be more difficult in the case of many reference databases communicating with many stores. Requests could consist of the unique identifier only.

(c)   Unique identifiers generated from characteristics of the documents themselves at the document store: Here requests would be received in the form of citations. The unique key, for example USBC, would be generated from the request citations and matched against this key in the index.

(d) Unique identifiers generated as in (c) at both document store and reference database: This would allow requests to be received in the form of the unique identifier only.

(e) Document store generates unique identifiers for its holdings as in (c), and sends details of holdings to each reference database: The identifier is added only to those records which correspond to document store holdings. Note that a matching process is necessary at the reference database to identify these records.

In order to assess the effectiveness of USBC with monograph material, an INSPEC file of 14,998 records was analysed. A total of 505 records were found to be defective; 181 without pagination, 284 without authors and 40 had neither. Besides, a PASCAL file of 5,278 records was analysed where 501 defective records were detected; 249 without pagination, 80 without authors, 22 had neither, and 10 had no title.

USBCs were generated by selecting 8 bytes from the title with maximum self-information [4], 2 or 3 bytes from the least significant digits of the first page number, and the first 2 or 3 consecutive bytes of the first author. The results are presented on Tables 1 and 2. It is clear that the USBC is capable of differentiating between records and that a combination of title, pagination and author can produce matching with 100% unique retrievals.

Because USBC comprises of fixed length elements, it is possible to isolate these for use in matching along the lines of secondary key retrieval with relational databases. The difference here is that a single, corporate, master USBC index can perform the role of a number of isolated indexes as is the case with ordinary information retrieval systems today. Its effectiveness can thus be demonstrated by matching on a secondary key comprising of 3 bytes from pagination and 3 from the author on the INSPEC file. Experiments implementing this produced the following results:

INSPEC NO./ USBC	Title	Pagination/ Author
1157459 BDMPWCGH*01NEC	Analytic method for investigating the availability factor of power stations	1-6 of no.1 Nechaev...
1169785 BCDMWFGH*01NEC	An analytical method for investigating the availability factor of power stations	1-6 Nechaev...
1157539 CILMUWYG*11KIL	Large synchronous generators with smooth stator	11-16 of no.1 Kil'dishev
1170083 CIUWYGLH*11KIL	Large synchronous generators with a tothless stator	11-16 of no.1 Kildishev
1157351 HMVWSFGP*41KRU	Allowing for the arc of current-limiting protective apparatus in calculating fault currents	41-5 of no.2 Kruglianskii
1169761 HMVFSGOP*41KRU	Allowing for the arc of current limiting protective apparatus in calculating fault currents	41-5 Kruglianskii

We are not here attempting to define what constitutes a duplicate entry and what may be classed as a collision on the part of the USBC. The retrieval of what may be classed as 'putative duplicates' can in many cases be in the interests of the user, especially where new research is being initiated, or in educational establishments in general. At the end of it all it should be the user who decides what is relevant and what is not.

Matched code elements		Number of n-plicates			
(type, No. of bytes)	Unique	2-plicates	3-plicates	4-plicates	5-plicates
Title, 1-5	10248	1018	248	94	46
Title, 1-6	13097	498	63	25	9
Title, 1-7	14148	154	7	4	0
Title, 1-8	14374	58	1	0	0
Title, 1-5Pagn(2)	14322	81	3	0	0
Title, 1-6Pagn(2)	14473	10	0	0	0
Title, 1-7Pagn(2)	14491	1	0	0	0
Title, 1-8Pagn(2)	14493	0	0	0	0
Title, 1-6Auth(2)	14413	40	0	0	0
Title, 1-7Auth(2)	14443	25	0	0	0
Title, 1-8Auth(2)	14447	23	0	0	0
Title, 1-6Pagn(2) Auth(2)	14493	0	0	0	0

Table 1 - USBC matches from 14493 INSPEC records

Matched code elements		Number of n-plicates			
(type, No. of bytes)	Unique	2-plicates	3-plicates	4-plicates	5-plicates
Title, 1-6	4634	62	5	1	0
Title, 1-7	4755	11	0	0	0
Title, 1-8	4769	4	0	0	0
Title, 1-7Pagn(2) Auth(2)	4776	1	0	0	0

Table 2 - USBC matches from 4777 PASCAL records

4. Outline of Implementation Environments

In existing systems such as DIALORDER, the user of the reference database chooses which document supplier should be used for the request. DOCMATCH should plan for a situation where many reference databases might be used for requests to many document stores. It would of course be useful if requests could automatically be routed to the correct supplier either at the reference database, at a central union catalogue facility, or at the document stores.

Availability of a universally-used unique document identifier would greatly simplify the production of such a union catalogue, although it would no doubt be possible to link citations to each document supplier's own ordering number for a particular document.

If we therefore consider the various system components of: (a) Different host computers, (b) Different files similar information, (c) Automatic routing and Direct requests, (d) The availability of short citations, (e) The document store with full text, and (f) The document suppliers, we can establish two working outline solutions as follows:

4.1 Environment (A)

The primary key of the document store is a unique document identifier along the lines of the USBC (see Figure 1). The index includes a short citation used (i) to generate the USBC, and (ii) with fields available as supplementary keys.

Requests are received from reference databases or as typed-in messages in the form of bibliographic citations.

The matching process occurs at the document store. Where a unique key was available in the citation (e.g. a Report Number) it would be matched with the supplementary keys/fields. Otherwise the USBC would be generated from the citation and used for matching with the primary key.

4.2 Environment (B)

Requests are routed from the reference database to document suppliers via a central union catalogue facility (see Figure 2).

The central facility has the capability to match citations and produce a unique document identifier as described in Environment (A) for the document supplier.

Requests from reference databases are in the form of citations. Requests are forwarded to document suppliers in the form of unique USBCs.

Conclusions

Most work on document matching is currently concerned with the merging of MARC files to produce union catalogues of monographs. There appears to be little recent work on matching at the level of individual articles as required in the DOCMATCH 1 programme of the EEC. A variety of methods of selecting elements from records and of producing matching has been reviewed. However, the performance of such methods depends very much on the nature of the material - for material at the article level statistics will be required as a basis for the design of an algorithm.

The matching algorithm proposed is based on the USBC which can provide a unique and flexible identifier for non-monographic material including journal articles, conference proceedings, patents, reports, theses, etc. It is proposed that the USBC also be used as the primary key to the index at the document store.

The USBC has a number of advantages over other adhoc identifiers:

(a) It is generated by computer from the attributes of the citation.
(b) It can be regenerated at any time in any computer environment, either from documents being indexed for the document store or from incoming requests, or even at source by the publisher.
(c) The algorithm is machine-independent, simple, compact, based on theoretic considerations.
(d) The components of the USBC are discrete, and can be isolated for use in retrieval functions. This facility would allow for approximate matching with weights assigned to different elements.
(e) The discriminatory power of individual elements of the USBC can vary according to the retrieval needs without affecting its standard format or universal application.
(f) Since the code is generated from the citation it can be applied and used retrospectively.

Results of current tests suggest that the title is the most discriminating element, but requires back-up by elements derived from pagination, authors and date. The final code thus consists of 7 bytes from the title, 2 bytes from pagination, 2 bytes from authors, and 2 bytes from the date.

References

[1]   F.H. Ayres, D. Ellis, J.A.W. Huggill and E.J. Yannakoudakis (1984), Universal Standard Bibliographic Code (USBC): Its development and use as a method of bibliographic control.   British Library R & D Report No. 5817, (Available from the JBP Library, University of Bradford, BD7 1DP, U.K.).

[2]   F.H. Ayres, D. Ellis, J.A.W. Huggill and E.J. Yannakoudakis (1984), Universal Standard Book Code (USBC): Its use for union file creation. British Library Bibliographic Services Division.

[3]   E.J. Yannakoudakis, F.H. Ayres and J.A.W. Huggill (1980), Character coding for bibliographic record control, *COMPUTER JOURNAL*, Vol. 23, No. 1, pp 53-60.

[4]   E.J. Yannakoudakis (1979), Towards a universal record identification and retrieval scheme. *JOURNAL OF INFORMATICS*, Vol. 3, No. 1, pp 7-11.

Acknowledgements

The following are all members of the research team involved in the DOCMATCH 1 programme of the EEC: D.R. Millson and M.B. Line from the Lending Division. C.J. Dance, A.B. Long and A.A. Mullis from the Bibliographic Services Division. F.H. Ayres and J.A.W. Huggill from the University of Bradford.   Without their help this paper would not have been written.

76

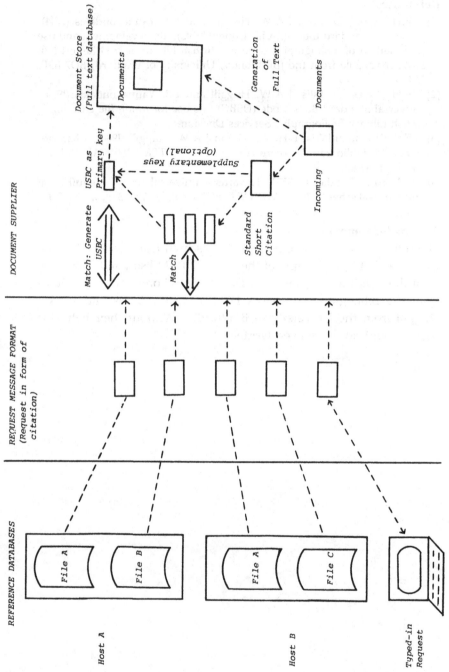

Figure 1. Environment (A)

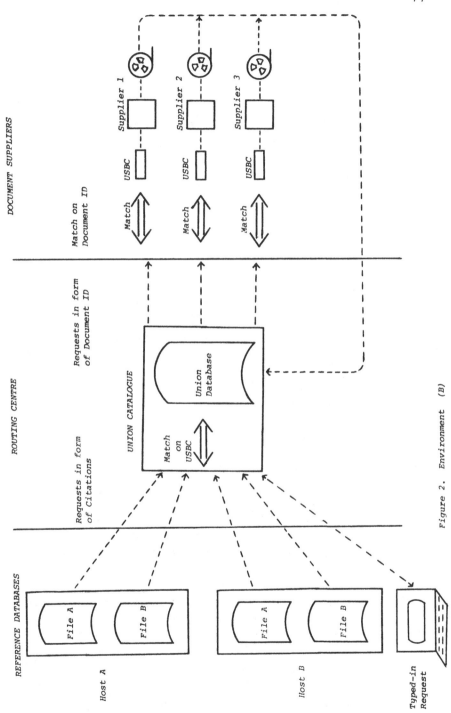

Figure 2. Environment (B)

A Disciplined Text Environment

RICHARD HAMLET

Oregon Graduate Center

ABSTRACT

Computer text processing is still in the assembly-language era, to use an analogy to program development. The low-level tools available have sufficient power, but control is lacking. The result is that documents produced with computer assistance are often of lower quality than those produced by hand: they *look* beautiful, but the content and organization suffer. Two promising ideas for correcting this situation are explored: (1) adapting methods of modern, high-level program development (stepwise refinement and iterative enhancement) to document preparation; (2) using a writing environment controlled by a rule-based editor, in which structure is enforced and mistakes more difficult to make.

1. Wonderful Appearance—Wretched Content

With the advent of relatively inexpensive laser printers, computer output is being routinely typeset. It can be expected that there will be a revolution in the way business and technical documents are created, based on the use of low-cost typesetters. Easy typesetting and graphics is an extension of word-processing capability, which is already widespread. The essential feature of word processing is its ability to quickly reproduce a changed document with mechanical perfection. However, as the appearance improves, the quality of writing seems to fall in proportion. These forces are probably at work: (1) More people can (attempt to) write using better technology, and because writing is hard, novices often produce poor work. (2) With improved technology, projects are attempted that were previously avoided; now they are done, badly. These factors are familiar from programming, and suggest an analogy between creating a document and developing a program. The current word-processing situation corresponds to the undisciplined use of programming languages that preceded so-called "modern programming practices."

Technology can help solve problems that arise from the use of technology itself, but it is all too easy to compound a problem with a technological "fix." The lesson that programming method teaches is that progress comes through discipline. Methods must be found that are difficult to misuse, in which the discipline lifts many routine decisions from its user. The analogy between writing and programming suggests that techniques and tools valuable in controlling software development be investigated for improving document preparation. The most promising are the methods of stepwise refinement and interated enhancement, and the use of an integrated environment.

2. Current Text Processing Methods and Tools

Writing well is a difficult task, and there are many methods intended to help people do it better. For example, one scheme suggests outlining the complete document, then filling in details at each level of the outline, never going too deeply under one heading until all other headings have reached the same level of completion. Another scheme suggests completing a central section first, then working outward. At present there is no computer support for any such method, and it is misleading to say even that one *may* use a desired method with a computer. For example, it is hard to keep to a level of outlining if the growing outline cannot be kept on an editor's screen. In a similar way it was difficult to do structured programming in FORTRAN 66, for lack of the necessary control constructs.

2.1 Commands vs. WYSIWYG

Existing text-processing tools are of two competing types: command-oriented, and WYSIWYG (for "What You See is What You Get"). Examples are **troff** [Ossanna83] and the Macintosh programs like MacWrite, respectively. In both cases files contain explicit format-control information. A command-oriented processor translates the file into codes to drive an offline printer; a WYSIWYG processor also attempts to first give an accurate screen presentation. There are many arguments for the superiority of each system for different tasks, reminiscent of the controversy between advocates of batch and interactive programming styles. For creating a document, both kinds of system miss the point. Any kind of controls, displayed or hidden, are a distraction in a field of view that is already woefully small.

Human beings can work with printed materials spread out over a desk. In organizing a document, even this space is often insufficient. It is impossible to display a desktop of text pages on a screen 20 times smaller. Clever use of a powerful (and expensive) workstation is a great improvement over a "dumb" terminal, but still falls far short of looking directly at the pages being prepared.

The laser printer is a device with exactly the right characteristics to solve the problem of examining text: it is inexpensive because it can be shared, easy to operate, fast, and it gives an almost perfect simulation of the final appearance of text. Above all, a printer produces output that can be marked, spread out, etc., in the time-honored manner.

2.2 The Analogy to Assembly-language Programming

Existing formatting programs are analogous to assemblers, and the analogy shows two reasons why they are difficult to use well.

Local format details. The inexperienced writer does not know how to control the considerable abilities of a typesetting device. It is not that software is deficient—most formatters have provision for footnotes, subscripts, indentation, etc. and WYSIWYG systems are particularly good. Rather, users are not interested in mastering the details. The result is documents that fall below a minimum standard for manual typing, where a human typist would be expected to take care of such matters. In the analogy, beginners do not use assemblers well because they have not mastered all the options and bits, and most never will.

Document content. The very things that are easy to do with an editor and a document processor—move text, justify margins, check spelling, etc., have a pernicious effect on expository writing. For example, the ability to move text encourages word-for-word duplication, say an Abstract repeated as the first paragraph of the Introduction. Similarly, a spelling checker eliminates some typos, but subtle ones (e.g., "text" for "test") are more detrimental to sense. The very power of a processor can cause trouble: drastic deletions made (and not noticed even on a WYSIWYG screen) because a complex operation was misused or is badly implemented, etc. In the analogy, large assembly programs go wrong because the programmer loses sight of the overall structure while busy saving just the right registers.

The essential paradox of word processing is that perfect form hides organizational and conceptual flaws, especially from the writer.

Auxiliary tools for text processing seldom work together. For example, indices, word-frequency charts, style measures, etc., must be creatively used by the writer. This situation is again similar to the support for early assembly languages. For example, it is often a mistake to use a symbol only once in an assembly program, but cross-reference programs just list the single reference. Statistical measures are more useful for text than in programs. For example, a word-frequency graph (as used in Zipf's law) can be used to determine technical key words, and to eliminate jargon. The writer needs help integrating such information with the text.

The power and generality of low-level tools make them good targets for computer-generated output, as in the analogy an assembler can be the target for compiler output. Existing low-level processors are ideal for use in an experimental prototype system.

3. Text-processing Paradigms
Two methods from program development appear the most promising.

3.1 Top-down Stepwise Refinement [Wirth76]
Text is viewed as a hierarchy of small, self-contained units, with only a handful of units at each level. For a short technical paper, the units might be numbered subsections and figures. An example is described by the tree:

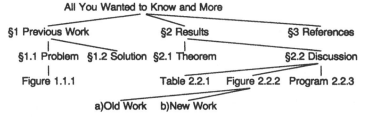

The organizing principle of the stepwise-refinement hierarchy is understanding and intellectual control. At each level the collection of units must be easy to comprehend. In the example above, §2 as composed of §2.1 and §2.2 (but without considering the content of §2.2) must be an obvious division of that section. The textual order of the section hierarchy is always important because the reader will encounter it directly. Other organizations can also be useful, for example in the above to control actions for special units:

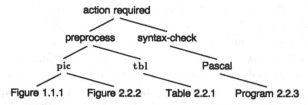

Figure 1.1.1   Figure 2.2.2   Table 2.2.1   Program 2.2.3

Another hierarchy could be used to cull appendices or summaries from text without duplicating material.

The choice of hierarchies is the writer's, but the system must keep them consistent with one another in the light of changes, and must be able to follow them on command. Access to the text of the document may use an hierarchy, and the textual-sections one should be the default. That is, to work on Figure 2.2.2 a) in the example above, the writer would have to go from the paper to §2 to §2.2 to Figure 2.2.2 to a). This chain can be circumvented, but it should be easiest to follow it. If the writer must look at the organization on the way, a change that is wrong in the context of the whole is less likely.

In many cases it is sufficient to display hierarchical structures of a document on the screen. But it is also useful to keep these in hardcopy form, and make them document units, too. Just as a screen is less good than a desk top for displaying text, so the multiple views of text provided by hierarchical descriptions may be best spread out on that same desk.

3.2 Iterative Enhancement [Basili75].

This programming technique seeks to create a prototype as soon as possible, by stripping the problem to a small subset. The omitted parts are then added incrementally, with whatever modifications in the existing structure they may require. When a problem has many autonomous parts, enhancement works well.

A document is a good candidate for iterative enhancement if its sections are loosely coupled. For example, a technical paper presenting several results may be tied together by a set of definitions common to them all, but it might benefit from being written as a definitional base combined with the main result for the "prototype." Iterative enhancement complements stepwise refinement, because the hierarchy used for the prototype can be modified to start each addition, and stepwise refinement then directs the addition.

It is a major problem in writing to maintain context when material is inserted or changed in a complex structure. Analogs of the techniques of revision-control [Tichy82] can keep inappropriate changes from being inserted. As a simple example, text can be checked for spelling, style, etc., before insertion; this avoids rechecking the same text over and over. It is a research question whether or not successive enhancements to a document can be maintained separately and merged when the final version is printed. (This question is also open for programs.) If enhancements can be kept separate, it is possible to automatically produce new organizations the author would like to try. If an instruction manual initially has the structure:

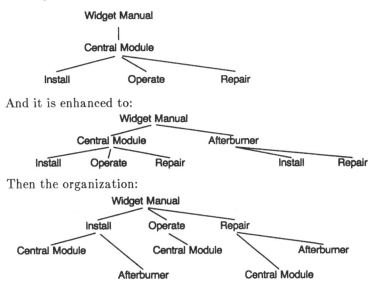

can be tried automatically. Similarly, successive enhancements can be isolated for printing as self-contained documents, perhaps in combinations that never occurred in the writing.

Revision-control techniques can also be used for partial printing. What has not changed should not be reprinted. Many people remember the "shape" of an idea on the page, and a marked up sheet with the same shape is better than a clean copy. For drafts, only part of a large document should be redone, leaving a ragged connection with the parts before and after.

4. Proposal for a Writing Environment

In a programming environment, the program syntax tree plays a central role. A writing environment based on stepwise refinement can use a document's hierarchical descriptions in the same way. An environment can be implemented as three integrated tools: an input editor, a copy editor, and a proof editor.

The *input editor* controls the entire process of creating and printing a document; it is analogous to the grammar-driven structured editor of a programming environment. It keeps the hierarchical structures imposed on the document, which give access to text. Existing low-level processors with a local nature (for example, spelling checkers) will be used by the input editor.

Once a document has been organized in one or more hierarchies, and entered or changed via the input editor, it may be passed to the *copy editor*. This component combines the traditional operations of copy editing a manuscript and typesetting it. The copy editor can be considered a "soft" expert system. It will be rule driven, with the form and organizational information of the text as input data. For different output devices, the processing parts of these rules may be different. "Soft" means that human checking will allow rules that fail. Rather than attempt to make no mistakes, the copy editor will seek opportunities for communication with the writer. Human copy editors work in just this way: an editor "queries" something dubious, and the author must answer. The copy editor will make use of existing low-level tools that apply across large blocks of text; for example, statistical style measures.

The copy-editor output will be queries and a proof copy of the document expressed in a low-level text-formatting language. The final component of the system is a *proof editor* that puts the document into final form. Using the proof editor, the writer makes changes to cover queries, and changes needed to obtain the proper format. Information supplied to the proof editor must be recorded in the original text and its structure, not in the version that drives the typesetter. To make changes in the latter would be like patching a machine-language program instead of the source. Changes recorded by the proof editor will be different than those entered by the input editor. It will insert explicit control information to correct local problems. A conflict between implicit rules and explicit controls would normally be subject to query by the copy editor; when the conflict is traced to the proof editor this query will be suppressed.

4.1 Input Editor

The input editor should be usable with a dumb terminal. Most of the screen must then be devoted to displaying text and no special input device like a mouse is available. Thus a single hierarchy and the text it controls can be displayed. Motion within the text is controlled by cursor keys in the way pioneered by the Rand editor; operations in the hierarchy require special keys or command sequences. With a workstation, the hierarchy can be a menu, and there may be room for more than one unit of text in windows.

Existing editors can perform most of the needed functions. The TEXTNET [Trigg83] and Mentor [Donzeau-Gouge84] systems provide hierarchy control that earlier editors [Walker81, Allen81] lack.

4.1.1 Explicit vs. Rule-defined Format Controls

The most important design decisions for the input editor concern the balance between controls directly attached to the document, and controls calculated from its text. Implicit controls defined by rules based on text features are preferred because they are easy to alter experimentally. For example, consider the location of paragraphs in text. An implicit definition is:

A paragraph break occurs at a sentence break at least five sentences after the previous break, where no noun of the accumulated paragraph occurs in the following two sentences.

This paragraph rule is probably not a good one, but it might be empirically improved. It is much easier to correctly define a sentence break, and a noun.

Given a document without paragraph marks, the editor can use a rule to insert them. If the calculation is made each time an alteration occurs in the text, paragraphs will shift in an apparently unpredictable way, for example when a noun is changed. It is a matter for experimentation whether this recalculation is a good idea or not. For an almost perfect implicit rule, recalculation notifies the writer that an apparently innocent change has mucked up the paragraph structure; when the rule is poor, it is better to use it only to insert initial explicit marks, and then maintain those. In any case, explicit marks have the virtue that they can themselves be used in style measures. For example, it is reasonable to query very short or very long paragraphs, but this makes no sense if the rule determining paragraph breaks depends on the length.

Both explicit marks and implicit rules can make the input editor easier to use. For example, punctuation, spacing, and capitalization rules can be preserved when changes are made near a sentence break. The input editor can show a facsimile of explicit and implicit textual features, but the display should not be recalculated too often. When a user causes a radical change, it may be better to issue a warning than to redo the screen.

4.1.2 Describing Hierarchies

Individual blocks of text, the units involved in stepwise refinement and iterative enhancement, have a structure that is fixed by simple rules about words, lines, paragraphs, text fonts, and layout. The controls for this structure are either calculated from the text itself, or maintained within it—no more complex format is warranted. The organizational structure of text is an ordered collection of directed acyclic graphs, with overlapping nodes. Each graph describes one of the hierarchies through which the text is viewed, the nodes representing text units, the arcs the hierarchy. (For example, in the textual-section hierarchy, if node A is the parent of node B it means that B is a subsection of A.) The ordering among hierarchies reflects the writer's idea of their importance. The natural screen representation of an uncomplicated directed graph is a menu with indentation and highlighting. Grammars might also be used to describe the graphs and their display either as menu or text; syntax-directed translation techniques can be used to make the correspondence between a graph and the screen.

Perhaps the most important issue in structure description is that of existing documents. When text exists only as a monolithic block (perhaps with explicit formatting controls), how can it be given a structure and painlessly incorporated into the text-processing system? Once again, calculation from the text itself (and the explicit controls, if present) is the answer. The structure can be obtained from the document using imperfect but all-inclusive rules, and the writer can then edit the structure in the normal system-supported way to get it right.

4.1.3 Incremental Operations

With the usual syntax-directed programming-environment editor, it is impossible to enter a syntactically incorrect program. The editor can also perform compilation incrementally, overlapping thinking and typing time to reduce later waiting. Both more and less than this is possible for natural-language text.

The difficulty of writing natural-language grammars, their inefficient parsing, and the low quality of any writing that could benefit from complete grammatical help, argue against a strict analog of the syntax-driven editor. But agreement between subject and verb, parallel clause construction, etc., can be described grammatically. For a weak grammar it is appropriate that input be questioned rather than rejected. Any kind of bracket construction— parenthetical remarks, quotations, font changes, even sentences and paragraphs—can be shown on the screen just as a structured editor marks BEGIN - END pairs.

Natural-language text has some grammatical structure that lends itself to techniques used in error-correcting compilers. For example, sentence and paragraph breaks can be adjusted or queried if deletions occur near the break. Changes at the character level should not cause words to run together. Attribute grammars can be used to describe these active aspects of syntax.

Semantic checking is not part of programming-language editors, but for a natural language some semantic checks are possible. Incremental spelling checking overlaps well with typing/thinking time, and style analysis based on statistical features of the language is also a possibility. Certain typos (e.g., "It is now possible..." for "It is not possible..."), can be exposed using the techniques of mutation testing [Hamlet77]. Semantic analysis should work better on changes, because a change can be compared to the body of existing text. For example, using the word frequencies of a text, an inserted sentence can be queried if it falls too far toward either often-used words, or seldom-used ones. Similarly, it is probably a mistake to delete the sole occurrence of a word.

4.2 Copy Editor

When a document has been entered or changed using the input editor (or changed using the proof editor, described below), it may be sent to the copy editor to produce a printed version. Creation of a command file for typesetting is the primary function of the copy editor, but it also can apply global checks that are inappropriate for incremental application by the input editor.

The document may contain explicit formatting marks, and is also governed by implicit rules where format is calculated from the text.

Files created by the input editor rely on implicit rules whenever possible, but a "foreign" document may contain low-level controls or no controls at all. The copy editor should convert foreign documents into a form that might have come from the input editor, but many queries will result from a conversion. It is important to automatically convert often-occurring, simple features; but a query is adequate for complex ones. For foreign documents there will be no hierarchical structures associated with the file, but the textual-section hierarchy can be automatically created. Thus the copy editor has the side effect of putting foreign documents in a form suitable for the input editor. The writer may choose the input editor as more suitable than the proof editor for an initial pass over a converted document.

Experimentation with implicit format rules will be the main research topic in the copy editor. The goal is to completely control the typeset form of the document with rules, although some explicit marks will probably always be needed. When explicit marks have been inserted, the copy editor may query when they do not agree with the rule-based implicit controls. Too many such conflicts will suggest that the rules should be changed.

However many queries the copy editor may file, it will produce a typeset document, so the final result can always be obtained by ignoring all queries. This is the proper use of an imperfect rule-driven program: its output is expected to be examined by a person.

4.3 Proof Editor

A writer using the proof editor works from a final typeset document annotated with the copy editor's queries. When something is to be done about a query, the position can be automatically located by the proof editor, say using a query number, or in a mode where the queries are located in order. When the writer notices an error that the copy editor has not caught, locating its position in the file requires better ideas than most conventional editors use. It would be an improvement to make use of the page and paragraph structure of the printed document, and to maintain these through as many drafts as possible.

When the screen display is centered on the position where a local change is needed, the proof editor should go as far as possible toward WYSIWYG, and on dumb terminals a clutter of explicit marks to show fonts, etc., will not be distracting in this final phase.

The proof editor will share with the input editor certain rule-based mechanisms. For example, it will not be possible to insert misspelled words nor destroy the beginning or end of a bracketed construction. The changes permitted will be limited to cases not needing the more extensive checks of the input editor. Since the proof editor is makes only minor, local changes, its corrective marks carry more weight than explicit controls used by the input editor.

5. Summary
A scheme has been described for a document-writing system that goes beyond existing text-processing tools in two ways. (1) Its editor is driven by hierarchical structures describing the document, so that it supports methods that have been successful in program development. (2) Typesetting format controls are implicit, based on rules rather than commands in the text file. These innovations are probably not an unmixed blessing, but it will require experimentation to discover their strengths and limitations. The program-development environment is a rich source of ideas and analogies for the implementation of this scheme.

References
[1] T. Allen, R. Nix, and A. Perlis (1981). PEN: a hierarchical document editor, in [SIGOA81], 74-81.

[2] V. Basili & A. Turner (1975). Iterative enhancement: a practical technique for software development, *IEEE Trans. Software Eng.* **SE-1**, 4, 390-396.

[3] V. Donzeau-Gouge, G. Kahn, B. Lang, & B. Mélèse (1984). Document structure and modulatity in mentor, *SIGPLAN Notices* **19**, 5, 141-148.

[4] R. Hamlet (1977). Testing programs with the aid of a compiler, *IEEE Trans. Software Eng.* **SE-3** (July, 1977), 279-290.

[5] J. Ossanna (1983). TROFF User's Manual, in *UNIX Programmer's Manual*, v. 2, New York, Holt, Reinhart & Winston, 196-229.

[6] SIGOA (1981). *Proceedings* of the ACM SIGPLAN SIGOA Symposium on Text Manipulation, *SIGPLAN Notices* **16** (June, 1981).

[7] W. Tichy (1982). Design, implementation, and evaluation of a revision control system, in *Proc. 6th Int. Conf. on Software Eng.*, Tokyo, 58-67.

[8] R. Trigg (1983). A network-based approach to text handling for the online scientific community, TR-1346, Dept. of Computer Science, Univ. of Maryland.

[9] J. Walker (1981). The document editor: a support environment for preparing technical documents, in [SIGOA81], 44-50.

[10] N. Wirth (1976). *Algorithms + Data Structures = Programs*, Englewood Cliffs, NJ: Prentice-Hall.

Semantic Guided Editing : A Case Study On Genetic Manipulations

M. NANARD[*], J. NANARD[*], J. SALLANTIN[*],
J. HAIECH[**]
* CRIM, 860 rue de St Priest, 34100 Montpellier,
** CRBM, Route de Mende, 34100 Montpellier, France

ABSTRACT
This paper describes the BIOSTATION, a generalized document preparation system, developed to guide an interactive editing of biological sequences by taking into account their semantics. This paper also focusses on the use of a document preparation system as the mediator for a larger application.

1. Introduction

The BIOSTATION is a generalized document preparation system, developed for the CRBM[**] and in use since May 85, able to guide an interactive editing of biological sequences by taking into account their semantics. This semantic is extracted at editing time from the document itself by an integrated expert system, and is used to express the structuration. This paper also focusses on the use of a document preparation system as the mediator for a larger application.

Genetic sequences are observed in this approach as generalized documents. This choice allows to associate convenient, and so more legible, visual representations to the abstract aspects of biological sequences semantic.

At first, we explain how semantic information on the sequences is obtained and used to guide editing. The biostation architecture is presented in a second section.

1.1. Problem position

The genetic information which allows organic cells to synthesize proteins is kept in *genes*. These genes are linear strings built with four types of molecules (Adenin, Thymin, Guanin, Cytosin) called nucleotids. The non biologist readers can refer to [Hélène 84]. The studied length of such strings can be up to 30000 atoms.

A gene can be analysed by the biologists to explicit its formula as a word on (A, T, G, C), and operations can be done on the gene (in vitro or in vivo) to modify it by insertions or deletions of some parts, at precise positions. This activity is called Genetic Manipulation.

The study of the genes sequences provides a very large amount of informations collected in international biological data bases. Genetic sequences formulas, informations on some characteristics of the structure and on the proteins properties can be found here. An example of such a base is EMBL [Gouy 84]. These data can be considered as a set of couples (global formulas versus global properties), but the relations between elementary properties and the structure of the formula are not explicited there.

An important activity in biological science is now to decipher the semantics of biological sequences, in order to be able to create new ones with specific semantics. This problem is similar to the analysis of an enciphered language about which samples of couples (ciphered text, global meaning) are available. This semantic analysis have yet lead to synthesize new proteins having some explicitely wished properties, e.g. : hormons synthesis for medical use (insulin), mutagenesis for agriculture needs (square section tomatoes for easier packaging), new proteins for industrial production (enzyms efficient at low temperature for washing powder)... and so on.

So, the biologist has to study in a formal way the semantic of the biological sequences before to build them. The complexity of this problem requires powerfull tools such as data bases, expert systems, learning systems, and graphical display, available on large computers. But these tools are ill-matched together, and their ergonomy is very poor when compared to the present state of the art in office automation [Gutknecht 83, Williams 84]. This lack of ergonomy forces the biologist to deal more with specific computer science problems than with his own job. So, an effort was to be done to unify access and treatment. It has lead to the development of the BIOSTATION [Nanard 85-2], the purpose of which was to provide an unified and user-friendly man-machine communication tool between the biologist and the computer application he needed.

1.2. Characteristics of the "BIOSTATION"

The biostation kernel is a generalized document preparation system used as the *mediator* [Coutaz 85] of the artificial intelligence applications needed to deal with the semantics of the sequences. This has lead to build an interactive editor in which semantics is used to guide editing. The man machine communication is object oriented. The object selection is done by pointing directly on the formatted document on the screen.

The user always operates on a visual graphical representation of the entities and has never to deal with their internal description. This formatting is typically multi-aspect : the representation of a given entity is not unique but depends upon the working context in which it is displayed. Furthermore, the user is allowed to define his own presentation rules. The biostation uses a multi-aspect, dynamically parametrable formatter.

The command language is object-oriented and mouse driven. It has no written expression. Any command is given by selecting an operand on the screen and an operator by poping up menus.

This interface is not limited to the editor, but is able to pilot all the applications attached to the biostation. It must be noticed that no application in the biostation has direct access to the screen, nor to the keyboard : its results are always displayed through the biostation formatter, and its data come from the generalized editor. Thus one can consider that the generalized document preparation system is used here as a mediator for all the biostation applications. The biostation is mainly a tool for planning biological experiments. Therefore, the document preparation system has not as its main purpose to produce papers, but to elaborate the formatted representations used for man-machine communication.

2. Principle Of Semantic Guided Editing

2.1. Editing Biological Sequences As Texts.

A gene is a word of the monoid generated by the four nucleotids *A, T, G, C*. A protein synthesized by this gene is a word of the monoid generated by twenty aminoacids. Each amino-acid of the protein has been induced by a triplet of consecutive nucleotids of the gene. The biologist may use either the nucleotid string or the associated amino-acid string according to the problems he is working on. In any case, the abstract object is a linear text that can be edited by standard tools. Editing per se has no interest here ; the important point is to guide the biologist in creating significative new sequences, by providing him structural and semantic informations on the consequences of any elementary editing action.

2.2. Displaying A Sequence As A Formatted Document

Why does the biostation uses a formatter to display sequences? The purpose of formatting is first to improve legibility. A user wants to be as efficient as possible. So he needs the objects he is working on to be very legible. A good way to improve legibility is to display the objects with the natural aspect they have in the mental working scheme of the user, and to organise them in an efficient geometrical manner on the screen. So, in the biostation, as it appears in figure 1, icons and graphical enhancements are used to represent sequences in what seems to be the most natural way for the biologist.

Another purpose of formatting is to focus the interest of the reader on important points by emphasizing them with graphical conventions, and to express the structure of the document through its geometrical aspect. In the biostation, colours, icons, and geometrical relations are used to express structure and semantics along the sequence, as it will be shown later.

So, formatting is a very important activity in the biostation as it improves the immediate legibility of the sequence and, by the way, the efficiency of the man-machine communication.

But, unlike most document preparation systems, the primary purpose of the biostation formatter is not to produce paper but rather to display the formatted aspect of a sequence as the normal man-machine communication method of the biostation.

 BIOSTATION, version 2.1 (11/85)

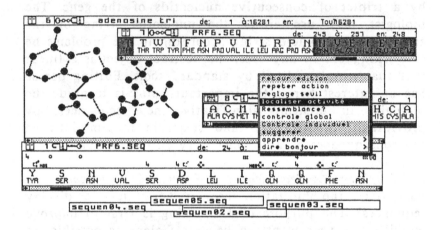

Figure 1 : a copy of the biostation screen

The biostation requires a multi-aspect formatting system because the points to be emphasized depend on the context of the work. For example, a sequence can be displayed either at its poorest level as the string of its components (sequence at the top of figure 1) or at a highly elaborate level as the 3D geometrical structure of the molecule, computed from informations provided in the data base. Furthermore, during guided editing, the sequence is displayed in most cases with attributes. Attributes are pieces of information which can be valued on each sequence element, and the value of which may affect the sequence semantics. Among all the possible attributes of a sequence element, the biologist may choose some of them, considered as significant and define their representation with colored icons. The sequences may then appear decorated with attributes colored according to their value or their part in the sequence semantics, as it can be seen on the figure 1.

2.3. Analysis of sequence semantics

Artificial intelligence methods, especially expert systems can be used to analyse the object properties in some domain. They operate with rule bases generally built by human experts. In the case of biological sequence analysis, it could be thought that the rule base would be obtained by a comparative study of some selected sequences. But this study is so complex that only a few human experts have been able, by their own, to discern structural specificities among the sequences. So, a systematic analysis is needed for an automatic building of the rule base characterizing a given problem. A particular kind of artificial intelligence methods called *learning* is used for this purpose.

In this section, after reviewing the principle of the learning methods, we will use an example to explain the strategy used to treat the semantics of the sequence. The example is a real one : *calcium binding by proteins*. Its expression is : "is there any active site in a given protein able to bind a calcium atom and if not, how can this protein be modified to induce this activity in it? ".

2.3.1. The "Learning" Principle

Learning theory has been developed for artificial intelligence applications. For example see [Sallantin 83]. We simply give here a brief and informal definition of the essential terms and concepts.

Let E be a set of sequences and (E1,E2,E3) a partition of E,

Let P be a property verified by X_i of E, such that

$\forall$ $X_i \in$ E1, X_i is known to verify P
$\forall$ $X_i \in$ E2, X_i is known not to verify P
$\forall$ $X_i \in$ E3, nothing is known on X_i about P.

Learning systems are able to elaborate a set of rules characterizing the structure of the sequences of E which verify P.

An important point on these methods is that, if E is consistent versus P, when the cardinality of E1 and E2 exceeds a specific threshold, the rule set is at its steady state. This is the origin of the learning aspect of this method.

Generalizing methods allow to forecast if any sequence of E verify or not P, by using the learned rules.

Argumentation methods express which learned rules has been used to forecast the property P for a given sequence, and so explain the actual structure responsible of the property.

On the biostation, an access to biological sequence data bases is provided and allows to extract the sample learning sets containing for example the sequences able to bind calcium. It must be noticed that this selection gives these sets of sequences only as texts but does not provide explicit information about their structural characteristics.

2.3.2. Sequence Semantic Description Using Attributes

The choice of the attributes associated to the components of a sequence is free. The biostation allows the user to define the attributes that provide the primitive semantic items adequate for his problem and consistent with his conceptual view of it. Any level of expression can be choosen for the attributes. They can be at the same level as the terminals of the sequence, e.g. "nucleotid A and G which are terminal for a gene have a chemical formula containing a pentagonal cycle". They can also condense a longer part of the sequence to express a more global information, e.g. "this part of the sequence has a geometrical shape organized according to the helix-alpha structure". They can also express a local result concerning a part of the sequence, resulting from a previous analysis on the biostation, e.g. "here is an active site for calcium binding".

As the man-machine interface of the biostation is graphics oriented, defining a new attribute is done by the user by specifying which components of the sequence have this attribute and by creating the visual representation expressing the presence or the absence of this attribute. On the previous example, an attribute of nucleotids A and G is drawn as a pentagon and the same attribute is drawn as an hexagon for C and T. In the calcium binding problem, a set of 8 attributes is used to characterize each amino-acid (cf figure 2). The formatter is able to display the sequence decorated with the attributes choosen for a specific problem (sequence at the foot of figure 1).

Yes	meaning of the attribute	No
−4	lateral chain with less than 4 main atoms (i.e others than Hydrogen)	4
+4	lateral chain with more than 4 main atoms	4
ccc	linear lateral carbon chain / ramified	cᴱ
c⁻	light lateral chain / bulky	c•
C=0	C=O link present	C̄=̄0̄
NOS	Nitrogen, or Oxygen, or Sulphur present	N̄ŌS̄
±	Electrical load on lateral chain (e.g. O-H⁻)	O
ᴴ-ᴴ	lateral chain with less than 3 C-H	ᴴ-ᴴ

figure 2 : icons and meaning of Calcium binding attributes

Rules provided by the learning system are expressed with the user defined attributes. They are logical expressions specifying the co-occurrence or mutual exclusion of some attributes in some precise positions within the sequence. An important feature of the biostation formatter is to visualize on the sequence the structural and semantic relations expressed by the rules activated during the expert system argumentation. This visual technique is very efficient for improving the legibility of the *argumentation* as it will be shown in the next paragraph.

2.3.3. Semantic guided editing
Once the attributes have been defined and the learned rule base is available, the biologist can search an active site in a given sequence or edit the sequence under semantic constraints to induce the active sites. The main purpose of the biostation is not to deliver him an automatically computed solution but to guide him in creating significative new sequences, by providing him structural and semantic informations on the consequence of any elementary editing action.

The general A.I. mechanisms provided by the biostation and used for this purpose are :

- *deduction* : the A.I. system deduces from the rule base wether the object matches the studied property or not.

- *argumentation* : the A.I. system explains its answer. It can especially explain why some property is verified or not.

- *induction* : the A.I. system can use the rule base for suggesting a new solution.

The semantic guided mechanism is as follows : until the wished property has been induced in the sequence, the biologist loops on the three following actions :

- deduction
- argumentation
- edition using the results of argumentation.

For a good efficiency of this process, the A.I. treatment response has to be immediately understood by the biologist so that he can at once interact by editing his sequence. The interest of the biostation is precisely to provide an efficient visual dialog to improve the understanding of A.I. responses.

For example, the biologist can choose the action *localiser activité* (active site searching) among all the actions of the menu displayed on figure 1. *Localiser activité* means that a semantic search is done by the A.I. system from the current position to find the sites which may bind calcium, i.e. the sequence parts with a structure as consistent as possible with the specification given by the rules. The next so selected site is displayed by the formatter as the A.I. response (figure 3). This sequence is decorated by its valued attributes. Only the attributes which have been significantly invoked by the activated rules are present and are painted with colors (but of course not colored on the present document) to show wether their actual states are compatible or not with the one requested by the rules.

This display provides informations to the biologist at two levels :

- *at the global level*

On the one hand, the density of attributes displayed on some position shows the density of constraints on this position. For example, see the pointed positions on figure 3. On the other hand, the colors immediately show to the biologist wether the sequence structure is rather good or rather bad according as there is more green attributes or more red attributes.

- at the detailed level

If an attribute is painted with a red color, the biologist first concludes that this attribute is inconsistent with the wished property. Furthermore, the attribute state is directly described with the icon used to represent it : for example, on the right pointed position on figure 3, there is a red attribute, its icon indicates that there is an aminoacid with a branching chain when there must be one with a linear chain.

This first *argumentation* given by the expert system is only at a *global* level. It indicates wether an attribute has a value consistent with the current context but does not express at this level the contextual constraints on this attribute.

The fact that this attribute is suspected at a global level does not mean that it has to be changed but only that there is a contextual conflict on it. This is a problem similar to the detection of an error by a parser : very often, the error is not on the symbol which exhibits off the error but on some other symbol contextually related to it.

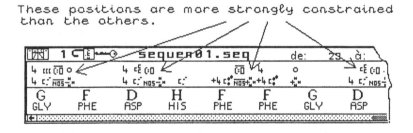

Figure 3 : An example of argumentation.

To be guided in his edition, the user can then ask for a *local argumentation* (*"Contrôle individuel"* on the menu) on a specific attribute. The system expresses the rules that constrain this attribute and the formatter displays this answer with the usual convention. The other related attributes causing the conflict then appear with a red colour on the screen, and the attributes which agree with the suspected attribute appear with a green colour. The user may study recursively the impact of attribute conflicts, and the biostation can also express graphically a quantitative expression of the contextual constraint on every attribute.

These tools provide to the biologist all informations necessary to elaborate his own editing decision. A suggestion module can suggest good editing decisions, but it is very . important to notice that the final editing decision is always taken by the biologist and not by the system.

The multi-window screen of the biostation allows the user to keep sight on a few *argumentations* to study more efficiently the consequence of a possible editing choice.

When all the conflicts has been edited out, an active site is considered as induced in the sequence, and the biologist now has to prepare his experiments. The global *argumentation* on this site then matches for all the attributes and expresses the effective global structure of the site. The biostation main purpose is to guide new sequences building without needing the previous existence of a theory on the studied aspect. *Argumentation* is only used as a working tool within this approach, and has not as purpose to deliver a scientific theory of the studied problem. In an artificial intelligence formulation, this approach is called a *winning strategy* by opposition to an *explicative strategy*.

3. Biostation Description
3.1. Hardware and implementation
The biostation is a moderate cost specialized workstation built on an IBM AT, with an AXEL high resolution colour graphic card (640x400x8) and a mouse. A CANON ink-jet colour printer is the standard output device. An EPSON LQ1500 monochrome printer is also supported by the station for good quality printing. As a high quality printer is needed for 'camera ready' documents, the Hewlett Packard LASERJET[+] is also supported by the

biostation. Through a network, the biostation can access to the IBM 3081 of the Centre National Universitaire Sud de Calcul, on which learning programs and biological data bases are available. All other functions such as editing, formatting, interpreting the command language, interfacing to remote applications, and artifical intelligence treatments such as *generalization* and *argumentation* are run locally on the AT.

The man-machine interface of the biostation is a generalized document preparation system. It has been designed with the benefit of the experience of the GTX system [Nanard 84] implementation, and some of the GTX modules have been caried over to the biostation. The AT system is written in Pascal, and the A.I. learning programs running on the CNUSC are written in APL.

3.2. External aspect of the biostation
Common man-machine communication concepts provide to the biostation a unified and consistent user interface.

3.2.1. Windows
The biostation offers a multi-window environment, able to deal with up to 16 simultaneous documents. This is an important feature for semantic sequence analysis, since the user needs to visually compare variants of a sequence or variants of an *argumentation*. All windows are of the same type, so an inter-window data exchange mechanism is available at the editor level.

3.2.2. Formatter
The document preparation system is responsible for all the displays in the biostation and can be considered as the mediator for all applications. Their results are always expressed as virtual documents to be displayed by the formatter on the bit map screen. The formatter maintains internal tables used for object selection and for fast redisplay operations. Screen updating is done in real time, even while editing.

3.2.3. Icons
Icons are dynamically associated to the applications, and

can be modified at any time with a font editor. Using the inter-window data exchange mechanism, the user can take advantage of existing icons to build new ones.

3.2.4. Colours
The biostation uses colour in a systematic way to present information : colour is not used for an aesthetic purpose, but as a means to increase man-machine communication efficiency. An unifying convention associates a colour to a concept which is significant within to the mental working scheme of the user. A consistent use of this convention induces reflexes in the user's behaviour. This principle leads to choose monochrome icons, so they can be painted with the right colour depending on their actual meaning. For instance, the same attribute icon can be painted either green if the *argumentation* agrees with its value, or red if it does not. It becomes yellow when used elsewhere. These constraints, expressed at the formatting rule level, are valid for any application.

The use of colour to attract the user attention to an important but isolated detail is more efficient than the use of any written message, and induces a more direct perception.

A colour display can also implicitly carry qualitative and quantitative informations : at a glance one can guess from an *argumentation* display how far the current state is from the solution.

3.2.5. Object oriented command language
The command language has no written representation. It is always expressed by direct selections on the screen of objects and operators. Icon menus are dynamically created at the adequate position of the screen whenever they are needed.

An object oriented approach is very user-friendly because commands are always given in their natural context. As an example, a local *argumentation*, which is specific to an attribute at a specific place of the sequence, cannot be invoked in an invalid context, since its invocation is precisely done by pointing on the wished attribute in the decorated sequence : it can only occur when a global or local *argumentation* has prepared this context by painting its own results.

3.2.6. *Working environment*

The learning phase shown in the first section of this paper is a preliminary for the semantics driven editing phase. But learning can be done once for all for a given problem, and the user need not invoke the learning process as long as he is editing on the same problem. Furthermore, a large set of learned rule bases relative to different problems can be kept on the biostation winchester disk, allowing immediate semantics driven editing according to these bases. This creates a working environment in which semantics can take a large place since many aspect can be studied together on a sequence.

3.2.7. *Paper document preparation*

This presentation of the biostation has focused on the semantics driven edition of sequences. But the biostation is at first a document preparation system, and can be used as such, for preparing traditional paper documents containing text, graphics, and, of course, sequences images. It is used by the biologist to print his experiment plans, transparencies for conference, reports and scientific papers. The formatter accepts as input a virtual document using a markup language similar to TROFF's. The graphical editor SCHEMATIX is available for preparing pictures to be included in the document. The inter-window data exchange mechanism allows to include in a paper any images from the biostation screen, such as sequences and their *argumentation.* Output can be obtained on the CANON JP1080 inkjet colour printer, mainly for tranparencies, but better quality is obtained on the LQ1500 EPSON or LASERJET[+] printers.

3.3. *The biostation architecture*

The document preparation system, around which the biostation is built, is used as a *mediator.* The different applications access data and express their results at the virtual document description level, and receive commands from the command language interpreter. A communication module adapts data to the external specifications of remote programs, such as the learning program. So the user of the biostation does not need to distinguish between local and remote applications of the biostation. This system architecture is illustrated in the following figure 4.

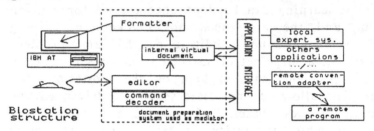

Figure 4 : The Biostation architecture.

4. Conclusion

The biostation is the result of pluridisciplinary joint research between the office automation team and the artificial intelligence team of the CRIM[*] and the macromolecular biology team of the CRBM[**]. It has been developed under the strong constraints of producing within a short delay a truly usable and efficient tool. This system, in use since May 85, has already shown to the biologists the interest of guided editing, and this method has been helpfull for the study of proteins [Haiech 85].

Our experience with this development suggests to us three thoughts :

- The first one concerns the use of formatters

Formatting was traditionally the last stage of document preparation and was invoked after document description was achieved. Some systems providing a better interactivity have shown the interest of interactively using a document preparation system since the conception stage of the document to its final production [Gutknecht 83, Nanard 85-1]. The real time access to the formatted document is fundamental in this approach. The meaning of "preparation" is slightly shifting from the final production to an activity including a larger part of draft handling. The use of Andra during the translation of a book is an example of such an interactive use [André 84]. Our experiments show that a document preparation system can also be used for other purposes than paper producing. Formatting is then used to associate pleasant and legible representations to abstract data, and allows user-friendly access to the applications. A document preparation system seems to be a more general computer tool than in the traditional paper oriented approach.

- The second one concerns the use of a mediator.

The purpose of a mediator is to provide the independance between a program and its external aspect. Building a general purpose mediator is a very hard problem. But partial solutions can be achivied when the mediator only covers a restricted area. In the biostation approach, the interface between the expert system and the external world is done through the virtual document. The document manipulation system is used for general man machine communication.

- The third point concerns semantic driven editing.

The biostation is also an experiment in integrating an expert system into a document preparation system to deal with text semantics and implicit structure. The general problem of semantic driven editing in a textual environment is of course far more complex than the specific problem of biological sequence editing, mainly due to the need of natural language analysis. But without diving down to the details of semantics, it is already possible and helpful to use expert and learning systems to display complex structural relations between larger entities. These deduced structures can be used either to pilot formatting [Virbel 84] or as in the biostation, to guide editing.

References

[1] André, J. (1984). *High quality book production using a text editor*, Protext I, Dublin.

[2] Coutaz, J. (1985). *Towards friendly systems, design concepts for interactive interfaces*, Southeast Regional ACM conference proceedings, Atlanta, p 56-61.

[3] Gouy, M. and al (1984). *ACNUC nucleic acid sequences database*, Nucleic Acid research N 12 p 121-128.

[4] Gutknecht, J., Winiger, W. (1984). *ANDRA : the document preparation system of the personnal workstation LILITH,* Software - Practice and experience 14, 1, 73-100.

[5] Haiech, J. (1985). *Computer search of calcium binding sites in a gene data bank : use of learning techniques to build an expert system,* Biochimie, vol 67 N 5.

[6] Hélène, C. (1984). *Les structures de l'ADN* La Recherche N 155, special issue on genetics.

[7] Nanard, J. & M. (1984). *Manipulation interactive de documents,* TSI Vol 3 N 6.

[8] Nanard, M. & J., Falgueirettes, J. (1985)-1. *Computer aided interactive preparation of document layout,* IASTED, Grindelwald.

[9] Nanard, M. & J. (1985)-2. *A user friendly biological workstation,* Biochimie, Vol 67 N 5.

[10] Sallantin, J (1983). *Algorithm for learning logical formulas,* I.J.C.A.I. Karlsruhe.

[11] Virbel, J. (1984). *Formal representation of textual structure for an intelligent text editing system,* Natural language understanding and logic programming, North Holland.

[12] Williams (1984). *The Apple Macintosh computer,* Byte.

The present document has been edited, formatted and printed using the Biostation with a HP LASERJET[+]. The figure 1 is a copy of the full screen. The figure 2 is a map formatted by the Biostation formatter. The figure 3 is a copy of an active window of the Biostation, adapted by the picture editor "Shematix" of the Biostation. The figure 4 has been composed with "Shematix". As the Times 14 points font needed for the title was not, at once, available with the printer, an approximative Times font has been drawn by the authors with the font editor of the Biostation.

Acknowledgements
We thanks Mr Giacomelli and Mr Mougin of the Hewlett Packard France, who lends to us a Hewlett Packard LASERJET[+] for interfacing to the Biostation.

Trends and Standards in Document Representation

Vania Joloboff

Bull Research Center. BP 68 - 38402 Saint Martin d'Hères Cedex. France

ABSTRACT

This paper starts by tracing the architecture of document preparation systems. Two basic types of document representations appear : at the page level or at logical level. The paper then focuses on logical level representations and tries to survey three existing formalisms : SGML, Interscript and ODA.

1. Introduction

Document preparation systems might be now the most commonly used computer systems, ranging from stand-alone text processing individual machines to highly sophisticated systems running on mainframe computers. All of those systems internally use a more or less formal system for representing documents. Document representation formalisms are very different according to their goals. Some of them define the interface with the printing device, they are oriented towards a precise geometric description of the contents of each page in a document. Others are used internally in systems as a memory representation. Yet others have to be learned by users ; they are symbolic languages used to control document processing.

The trouble is that there are today nearly as many representation formalisms as document preparation systems. This makes it nearly impossible, first to interchange documents among heterogeneous systems, second to have standard programming interfaces for developping systems. Standardization organizations and large companies are now trying to establish standards in the field in order to stop proliferation of formalisms and facilitate document interchange.

This paper focuses in the last sections on three document representation formalisms often called 'revisable formats', namely SGML [SGML], ODA [ODA], and Interscript [Ayers & al.], [Joloboff & al.]. In order to better understand what is a revisable format, the paper starts with a look at the evolution of the architecture of document preparation systems.

2. Architecture of document preparation systems.

Document preparation systems have appeared as soon as computer printing devices were able to output typewriter-like quality documents. Although the evolution of printing technology have been the major one, several factors have influenced the architecture of document preparation systems: low cost computing power, distributed systems, and the simple maturation of ideas in the field. The evolution of printing technology has lead to the digital representation of documents ready to be printed, called final form representation. The evolution of software techniques has principally lead to representations capturing the logical structure, the structure that is perceived by the author when the document is revised, i.e. constructed or modified.

2.1. Final form representation

On early document preparation systems, printing devices were basically typewriter-like terminals directly connected in character mode to the unique processing computer. Those devices were driven by sequences of control characters inserted in the data stream they received in order to produce layout rendition (underlining, overstriking). A formatting system basically had to translate the formatting commands into printer control sequences.

As printers from different vendors had different control sequences, transparency for the formatting system was needed to be able to print the same document on different sites with different printers. It was achieved by creating device independent formats. *Final form representation* had appeared, that is, the final digital representation of a document before it is printed. The main property of a final representation is that the number of pages in a document has then been computed. The way each object (character string or graphics) should appear on the page is totally determined.

As it becomes possible to introduce a processor into the printing device, yet keeping prices reasonably low (cheap chip), final form representations tend to become more and more complex. A final form representation is not any more a sequence of characters but an organized structure. A formal method is used to describe the page layout. For non impact printers, formalisms are needed that allow for the representation of images and graphics.

Virtually any image is reproducable on non impact printers: characters in any alphabet, graphics and images as well. There do not exist any more a specific set of imaging functions available from the hardware. Then the limit to the expressive power of the page creator is set by the *software interface*.

This fundamental change brought by technology has implied a fundamental change in the design of final form representation. Non-impact printing has introduced a new generation of final form representation formalisms, highly structured, trying to offer a maximum expressiveness. They aim at universality, that is, they allow for the description (in theory) of any page for any printer. They divide into static formats and dynamic ones, more recent. In a static format the page layout is described as a static data structure. The standard CCITT T73 [T73] is a typical example of such formats. In dynamic formats, also referred to as procedural page description languages, a page description actually describes *how to compute* the layout.

Brian Reid's paper [Reid86] in that very conference talks more extensively on procedural page description languages, such as PostScript[PostScript]. The point we want to emphasize now is that the architecture (figure 1) of document preparation systems has now a clean interface with printing devices. It generates a final form representation of documents in terms of a structured page description formalism.

2.2. Revisable form representation

A document has to undergo many additions or modifications before it is ready to be printed. Working on a page based representation when editing a document would be tedious and cumbersome both for users and the editing system. An unformatted representation of documents is necessary. This representation typically is the output of the editing system and the input of the formatting system. Figure 1 shows the three basic components of a document preparation system: editing, formatting and printing. Revisable form and final form are the two representations interfacing these components.

Figure 1. Typical architecture of a document preparation system.

The first document preparation systems have naturally imitated the method used in the publishing industry for typesetting: additional information is interspersed among the document contents to produce a data stream directly processed by the typesetting device. On those early systems the revisable form representation simply consists of a text file containing control sequences, directly keyed in by the user from a standard terminal.

Control sequences consists of a series of *markup signs*. That was the beginning of so called *procedural markup languages*, since those markup signs were interpreted as instructions controlling subsequent processing in the formatting system.

Procedural markup has well known inconvenients:

- the logical structure of a document is not much evidenced once the document is marked up. For example, if chapter titles have been marked with a centering command, it does not appear clearly that what follows a centering command is a title. If someone later wants to flush all titles right, changing all centering commands into flush commands will probably not give the expected result.

- the style of the resulting documents, i.e. the aspect of the document layout, is determined by the user who placed the markup signs. A good layout style, if some style at all, requires from the user some typographic knowledge. The lack of this knowlege is responsible for all of the ugly documents produced on procedural markup systems... Also, it makes it difficult to output the same document in a different style.

Disavantages of procedural markup have been avoided with a new method, known as *declarative markup*. The standpoint in declarative markup is that the user should describe the logical structure of a document, what is to be processed rather than how the document content is to be processed. A user enters mark up signs indicating logical properties of data, for example *paragraph* or *heading*, expressing its logical structure, which sounds more familiar, and does not imply a particular processing. The responsibility of making consistent styles, or applying specific functions is left to the system. GML [Goldfarb] and Scribe[Reid83] are two examples of declarative markup systems ; the reader is referred to [Furuta & al.] for an extensive survey of such formatting systems.

The SGML formalism is essentially the definition of an international standard by ISO for covering these systems. Yet a SGML entity may refer to non-character data, as shown in the next section, it has been designed in the spirit of all markup systems. As the standard says (page 3) "The millions of existing text entry devices must be supported. SGML documents can easily be keyboarded and understood by humans."

A user does not need a specific editor to build a markep up document. As far as there are only characters, any editor will do on any standard terminal. The revisable form representation of a document in a markup system, be it declarative or procedural, is (or should be) fully known from users, they have to key it in...

More recent approaches have a different viewpoint. They assume the revisable form representation is not directly accessed by users, but solely by the editing system. Thus a specific editor is needed, which generates that representation. It is intended such editors will not expose users to the revisable representation; that they will actually hide to the user the internal representation of documents, constructing themselves this representation from the user input.

These editors are expected to provide a more convivial user interface. Most of the editors from this new generation do not run on standard terminals, for example Grif, presented in this conference [Quint & Vatton]. They rather use bitmap display terminals, a window system and a pointing device.

The new type of document representation used in this approach may then be designed to be quite complex, nearly unmanageable by human beings, but very suitable to be handled by computers. Graphics and images may be directly inserted in documents more easily than for markup formats. Graphics may rely on existing standard graphics representation, images may be stored trough specific data compression techniques, while the user only sees on the screen a real layout.

Interscript and ODA both belong to this new genereration of formalisms. They assume more computing power from the editing system, they lose the possibility to be directly entered from a standard terminal, but promise many more possibilities.

3. Generalized Markup Language

SGML stands for Standard Generalized Markup Language. It is essentially a declarative markup language, which has inherited mainly from its ancestor GML. However it includes a lot of new interesting features.

A first difference with its predecessors is that markup is defined rigorously. It is possible from the SGML standard definition to build a general syntactic parser that will not arise ambiguities. According to this rigorous syntax, SGML documents may be processed very much like programs by a compiler. A document may be parsed to build an abstract syntactic tree together with its attributes.

Semantics of that tree may be evaluated by semantic functions according to the attributes values. Thus, SGML can be used for other tasks than formatting ones. Semantics of markup tags and attributes might be used for machine translation, automatic indexing or any other process needing parsing of documents.

A markup sign in SGML is named a tag. Any element which needs to be tagged starts with a start-tag and ends with an end-tag. Any tag is delimited by the characters '<' and '>'. A tag is defined by an identifier, which appears first in the start-tag. An end-tag repeats the same identifier preceded by '/'. Note that all of these mark characters are redefinable for each document. End tags may also be omitted under conditions specified in the standard. For example, a paragraph will appear as :

 This is a short paragraph.

A drawback of usual declarative markup systems is that one is forced to use the catalog of markup tags which is offered by the system. Since markup tags express the logical structure of documents, it means one cannot define the logical structure in other terms than the general tags set up once for all by the system.

A property of SGML is that tags are themselves described trough a formal language: the SGML meta-language, which may be used within SGML documents to dynamically define new symbols. Syntax to introduce a meta-language construct simply follows '<' by '!'.

The SGML meta language allows for the definition of complex constructs, named *elements*. An element declaration defines of a class of objects, i.e. an element type. Subsequent objects in the document may be tagged with the element name. Elements may have a hierarchical structure, and each element in the hierarchy may have its own attributes. Element types may be used either to facilitate the interactive creation of documents, to control the validity of a document structure, or to associate a layout style to a particular document type.

For example, one might define a document type for a conference paper as follows:

```
<!ELEMENT
 1   paper              (title abstract sections)
                language   CHARS
 2   title              (#CDATA)
 3   abstract           (p)
 4   body               (p*)
 >
```

This document type declaration specifies that a paper has a title, an abstract, and a body. The title consists of characters, the abstract is one paragraph and the body one or more paragraphs. A paper has a language attribute to indicate in which language it is written. More complex combinations can be designed to define document types that have some commonality.

The facility to define new elements brings troubles when laying out those elements, because the formating system then does not know how to format such constructs. SGML provide two ways for handling that situation. The first one is naturally to add to the SGML system a procedure to take care of the new tags. This requires a good knowledge of the system and prohibits further interchange of documents with such tags to systems which do not have this procedure. The second one is to use a LINK tag. A LINK tag says to the system that a construct should be handled as another one, presumably known from the system, with possible attributes modifications. For example, if one says <!LINK abstract paragaph indent=5>, it means an abstract has to be formatted like a paragraph, however using a different indentation value.

It is often required in a document to be able to refer to other parts of the document. Some binding mechanism is needed in the formalism to attach a value to some identifier, which resembles to progamming language variables. Binding is achieved in SGML trhough *entity declaration* and *entity references*. An entity (a value, a character string or any valid SGML constituent) may be bound to a name by the notation <!ENTITY name entity value>. From now on, that entity may later be referenced by its name either to set an attribute value, or to be included into the running text. Entities also provide means to handle non character data. An external entity is declared <!ENTITY name SYSTEM system information>. Then it is known that this entity is not in the document stream. The processing system will find in the system information how to access that content.

If the document is to be interchanged among different computers with different operating systems, this system information is specific to each system. SGML provides an IGNORE/INCLUDE mechanism for that purpose. Information relative to some particular system, let say osx, has to be encoded within the magic declaration <![osx;[<?commands for osx system>]]>. Then a user only needs to turn a switch at the beginning of the document to the local system for the document to be processed correctly.

4. Interscript

We mentioned previously Interscript is a representation formalism from a new generation. Interscript, which was originally designed at Xerox PARC, starts from the idea that a document representation should be suited to be processed by computers, not by the humans who manipulate documents.

Such things as traversing trees, evaluating expressions, searching values of variables within contexts are among what computers can easily do. Thus, a fundamental notion in Interscript is to rely on a formal language to describe document constructs, not only a document logical structure, but all formal constructs that could be necessary into a document representation. These abstract constructs may be data structures such as paragraphs, fonts, geometric shapes, but may also represent computations, like setting a context or evaluating expressions within some context.

The Intescript approach is very much like the approach used in software engineering: general programming languages are used by people to build abstract constructs and procedures to solve their particular problem. A document representation problem should be solved using the a document representation language. The Interscript base language is simple (around 25 grammar rules) and powerful. Its semantics are well defined but its syntax rapidly leads to document that cannot be managed by humans.

A document encoded in the Interscript base language is called a script. A script is very much like a program. The processing paradigm (figure 2) is that a script should be first internalized by a system. Internalizing a script implies *execution of computations*, which are dictated only by Intercript base language semantics, and result in the construction of another representation available for the client process.

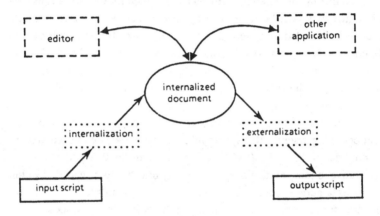

Figure 2. Interscript processing model.

This simply means that one translates a standard disk representation into a non standard memory representation, while achieving computations.

Computations are necessary in the internalizing process because the base language includes a binding mechanism and the evaluation of expressions within hierarchical contexts. For example, evaluating the expression :

$$rightmargin = leftmargin + linelength$$

needs to obtain the values bound to the variable names.

We will not in this paper enters into the details of the internalizing process, which looks like the evaluation of any interpreted programming language, to focus on the central concepts of *node* and *tag*.

A script is a hierarchy of nodes. Nodes have contents and tags. The authors have compared an Interscript node to a bottle of wine. The contents of the bottle is qualified by several tags on the bottle: a price tag, a product number tag. Interscript tags similarly qualifies the node contents. To some extent an Interscript tag is similar to an sgml tag, it introduces an element, it has attributes, it denotes structural properties of the contents.

The difference is that, first a Interscript node may have simultaneous tags, second attributes of a tag may be bound to an expression which must be evaluated. For example, a figure caption could be affixed with both a CAPTION and a PARAGRAPH tag. The paragraph tag says that the caption text has to be laid out as a parapragph, the caption tag restricts the placement of that paragraph relatively to the figure picture. The leftmargin attribute of the paragraph might be set to be equal to the margin of some object X. Then the node hierarchy is searched for that X.

Interscript syntax denotes nodes between curly braces. Tags are character strings followed by a dollar sign. A typical node is :

> { PARAGRAPH$ PARAGRAPH.leftmargin = 10
>   {CHARS$ <paragraph text content> }}

4.1. The pouring process

Markup languages do not provide good support for describing layout. They start from idea that a user should hardly be able to specify layout, in order to enforce style discipline. It is true that users of a document preparation system are usually not interested in setting line and page breaks, selecting fonts, positioning titles, etc. However, they are often concerned with placement of logos, page numbers, whether there are one or more columns ; what we might call macroscopic layout.

Interscript provides for that purpose a comprehensive mechanism we shall name *descriptive layout*. Descriptive layout does not prohibits the use of styles, it would rather enforce their use too, however it allows for the specification of high level layout. Tags have been defined which symbolically represent the layout process. By placing those tags at appropriate places and specifying attributes values, a user may indicate to a formatting process how layout should be achieved.

All of those specifications appear as parameters of the Interscript *pouring process*. The Interscript metaphor for this process is that the document content, is *poured* into some *liquid layout*, resulting in a *solid layout*. Liquid layout basically serves as a template which guides the pouring process in its actions. The pouring process is naturally described by means of constructs expressed in the base language. The fundamental pattern for invoking a pouring process is:

> { POUR$
>   POUR.template = {TEMPLATE$ -- template -- }
>   contents to be poured }

A template basically is a hierarchy of boxes. A box defines a rectangular area on which constraints apply to locate it relatively to other boxes. Assume a user wants a page layout as shown on figure 3. That page has a header at the top and a logo down the header. The content should be laid out in a right area on the page, leaving some place for margin comments that should be placed on the left.

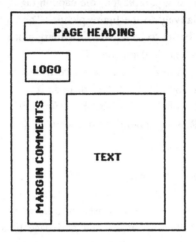

Figure 3. A page layout.

The template for that page will be a hierarchy whose root node is a page node. This page contains four boxes respectively specifying the position of the heading, logo, margin comments and text. The position constraints are those indicated by the user.

When the content is poured in the page, the pouring process must not pour any content into the heading or the logo box, neither does it pour text content into the margin comment box. This correct placement of data is ensured by the MOLD mechanism.

When a box is to receive data, it shows a MOLD tag accompanied by a label. The pouring process does not try to pour content into boxes that do not have a mold tag, it directly places them within the page box. If a box is a mold, then it looks in the node contents for some node with a matching label. All content portions with matching label are to be poured into that box.

It may be the case that there is too much content to be poured to fit on a single page. A template may specify that it is a sequential template, an iterative or an alternative one. In a sequential template, the pouring process will consider all boxes in the hierarchy sequentially. If a template is full, or no more matching content exists, it considers the next mold. An iterative template will repeat itself until all matching content has been poured.

The argument in favour of that unique representation seems to be that most editing systems have to manage both structures. The standard says (part 2 - page 75)

> "In a text processing system with separate editing and formatting subsystems, the specific layout is created after any changes to the specific logical structure and content have been made. In a word processor type editor, small editing changes may be incorporated directly into existing specific layout structure after every command, without recreating the entire specific layout structure."

This issue is discussed in the conclusion. This section only tries to present the ODA formalism. Figure 5 shows the main constituents of a document. It has six parts, a document profile, a document style, a generic and a specific logical structure, a generic and a specific layout structure.

An alternative template specifies different possibilities for pouring the content, the layout process is responsible for choosing one. One possibility is to try all of them, and pick up the best by its own criteria. Another possibility is to have additive tags indicating when or how to select an alternative. For example, one might indicate a template to be used on screens, another one for paper.

Templates may also be combined. Figure 4 shows an typical example, a paper like this one. The first page has a particular layout showing the title, authors, an abstract of the paper ; down of the abstract starts the paper. All subsequent pages are in the same format, showing only a page heading and text. The template for that document is a sequential one. It contains the first page as a single box (a page is a particular box), next an iterative page template.

Many others possibilities are offered by this descriptive layout process. We only described in this paper its general properties.

5. Office Document Architecture

Office Document Architecture is a standard elaborated within ISO to introduce a standard in the data structures used for the digital representation of documents. The most particular property of ODA is that it does not fit in the traditional architecture schema: ODA defines simultaneously the logical structure and the layout structure of a document, i.e. it is both a logical and a page description format.

A document may actually contain only one of the structure. This is indicated when transmitting in the document profile. The document profile also contain data related to the whole document: creation date, last alteration date, originators, status, etc.

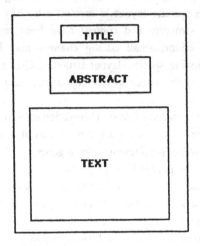

FIRST PAGE

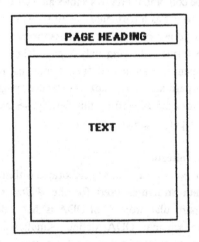

OTHER PAGE

Figure 4. Two different page layout in a single template.

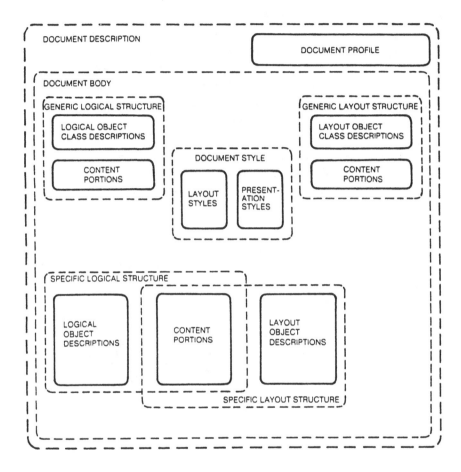

Figure 5. ODA document components.

Generic and specific are to be interpreted respectively as class and instance. For example a generic structure named *conference paper* will describe the general structure and properties of a conference paper, as shown in the SGML section. A particular instance of a conference paper will be described by its specific structure. Attributes defined in the generic will be valued in the specific structure, possibly to a default value specified in the generic part. The specific structure should be consistent with the generic one, and will probaly inherit properties from the generic structure. Specific logical and layout structure are trees whose leaf nodes are named basic objects and other nodes composite objects. Any node may carry attributes.

The specific logical structure expresses the structure of the document in, e.g. paragraphs, chapters, titles, etc. The specific layout structure is a tree of page sets (a set of pages identified as a single entity), pages, frames and blocks. Blocks and frames are rectangular areas located within frames and pages.

Blocks and basic logical objects both refer to the document content. This content is divided in content portions. A content portion is governed by a content architecture, which basically defines the content type (characters, images, graphics) and its encoding mechanism.

The logical and layout structure are clearly not independent, they refer to the same document content and they may have reciprocal pointers.

Figure 6 (reproduced from the standard) shows the coexistence of the two structures implies particular constraints. A paragraph which spans over two pages has to be split into two content portions.

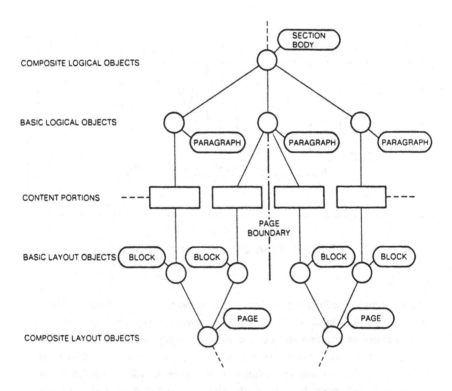

Figure 6. Simultaneous layout and logical structure.

Styles simply are a named set of attributes, which can be referenced from other components in the document. They divide in layout style and presentation style. A presentation style is attached to a basic object and depends upon the nature of that objects. For characters, it would indicate font information, for images it would probably indicate colors or half-toning. Layout style defines global style information. It can be referenced only from logical objects.

The standard is somewhat fuzzy about generic structures. There is no clause devoted to the description of generic structures, while there is one for each specific structure. It says that object class description are used by the editing process to construct a specific logical structure but it does not say much about such descriptions. Part 3 of the standard, which describes the layout process, indicates how the generic layout structure should be used, hence give a clearer idea.

The generic layout structure contains common content portions, for example logos or headings that should be used in many places in the document. It also serves as a guide for the layout process.

6. Conclusion

We have focused in this paper on three representation formalisms considered as revisable form representations, namely SGML, ODA and Interscript. On these three formalisms, SGML and ODA have reached the status of ISO draft proposal, which means they will become definitive standards with very little modifications.

SGML results from experience accumulated since more than ten years by current practice in the field of markup languages. The standard has a precise definition, which makes it possible to rigorously parse a document. Document markup tags may induce hierarchical structures expressing the logical content of a document. A simple binding system among entities has been introduced, which allows for cross referencing among entities.

Knowing that SGML has been running on many machines, that high quality text books have been produced through an SGML system, A vendor commercializing a markup document system would probably better take SGML rather than inventing a new formalism.

ODA did not follow the same standardization process as SGML. ODA is an attempt by an ISO working group, consisting mostly of text processing system vendors representatives, to define a standard before there are hundred of representation formalisms around the world that would not be compatible. Hence there is no current practice of ODA and it is only expected that most of new systems will use ODA. However there are a few objections to actually using ODA.

The choice of the two coexisting layout and logical structures. might lead to implementation problems. The content portions which have to be split to satisfy layout constraints will have to be recollected when the layout is modified.

Now that most printing device vendors have upgraded their machines to have a procedural page description language, the design of the layout structure in terms of frames and blocks looks old fashioned and contradictory with the fact that ODA claims to be a standard for future systems.

One might fear too with ODA that vendors will actually offer "ODA subsets". Particularly it is the case SGML can be considered as such a subset. The standard explicitly states, probabaly for reasons of compatibility among ISO standards, that an SGML document may be transmitted within an ODA document (part5-page 4):

> "Any subdocument within a (ODA) document may be represented either by descriptors and text units or by an SGML entity set. An SGML entity set is a self contained unit of SGML information, which is denoted but the term document in the SGML standard."

A vendor may actually sell an SGML system as an ODA subset system. If each vendor offers a subset of ODA, it might be the case that all of those systems will be actually incompatible, which is not desirable for an interchange standard. This argument is naturally true for all standards, but ODA design makes it easier to have closed subsets.

For example, it is possible to design an ODA editing system that would not take into consideration all of the layout part and restrict to the logical structures and styles. This editing system will output only documents with logical structures and styles. These documents may be interchanged using the ODA format.

It is possible too, in terms of delimiting an ODA subset, to design a simple word processing machine that would use no logical structure at all to produce office documents with only a layout structure. But both of those ODA systems will not be able to interchange a single document.

Morover, it seems from ODA complexity that a complete ODA system can hardly be implemented on a small word processing workstation. Implementors of these relatively small workstations, who are willing to manage documents with both logical and layout structure, will probably have to define a subset in order to maintain satisfying performance.

Though SGML has been designed so that human beings may enter markup tags into a document, it might well be used as an internal representation for an editor that would not appear to the user as a markup system. Then the structuring possibilities offered by SGML may be used by the implementors to represent complex internal structures, producing equivalent facilities to those of ODA. Documents produced by such an editor could hardly be revised by humans from a standard terminal, but they could still be output with the high quality of an SGML formatting system. Thus a vendor who is willing to implement a document preparation system has to choose among two international standards.

Interscript is not an international standard and it seems it will not become. The reason might be that Interscript design is too much a departure from their existing formalisms to be accepted by most vendors, who are mostly interested in standards. Remember that bitmap displays were developed at Xerox PARC in 1975. In 1985, still very few vendors offer text processing systems with a bitmap display and a pointing device. Interscript was also born at Xerox PARC in 1983 [Ayers & al], as a result of several years of experience with powerful text processing systems running on bitmap displays...

Yet Interscript will not be a standard in the eighties, it has introduced two important ideas, the notions of base language associated with an internalization process, and descriptive layout, which should be retained by people who are participating to the design of a new generation of document preparation systems.

Interscript proves that a base language can be defined which encompasses all abstractions that can be found in the document preparation world. It can describe as well a document logical structure, properties and structure of various kind of entities (font, paragraph, etc), and functional symbolisms like the pouring operation.

A base language considerably simplifies the software development of systems once it is implemented, but all over it gives cleanness to the systems and clarity in concepts. The Interscript base language is certainly not perfect. It can be improved and it might be actually too powerful for its goals.

Similarly, the idea of a layout process formally described and specified by abstract constructs, can be expressed in other terms than the particular Interscript pouring process. But both concepts have opened a direction for prresent research in the field.

References

[1] Adobe Systems Incorporated (1984). PostScript language manual. 1870 Embarcadero Road, Palo Alto California.

[2] Ayers, R.M., Horning, J.T., Lampson B.W, Mitchell J.G. (1984). Interscript : A Proposal for a Standard for the Interchange of Editable Documents. Xerox Palo Alto Research Center. 3333 Coyote Hill Road,

Palo Alto, California.

[3] CCITT (1984). Recommendation T73. Document interchange protocol for the telematics services.

[4] Furuta, R., Scotfiled, J., Shaw, A. (1982). Document Formatting Systems: Survey, Concepts, and Issues. ACM Computing Surveys, 14, 3, pp 417-472.

[5] Goldfarb, C.,(1978). Document Composition Facility : Generalized Markup Language (GML) User's Guide. Technical report SH20-9160-0. IBM General Products Division. ACM Computing Surveys, 14, 3, pp 417-472.

[6] International Standard Organization/ TC 97/ SC 18 (1985). Information Processing. Text and Office Systems - Document Structures. Draft Proposal 8613

[7] International Standard Organization/ TC 97/ SC 18 (1985). Information Processing. Text Preparation and Interchange. Processing and Markup Laguages. Draft Proposal 8879

[8] Joloboff, V., Pierce, R., Schleich, T. (1985). Document Interchange Standard "Interscript" International Standard Organization/ TC 97/ SC 18. Information Processing. Document N439R

[9] Reid, B.K. (1983). Scribe: Histoire et evaluation. Actes des journees sur la manipulation de documents, INRIA/IRISA, Rennes, France.

[10] Reid, B.K. (1986). Procedural Page Description Languages Proceedings of the conference on text processing and document manipultation, Notthingham, England.

[11] Quint, V., Vatton, I. (1986). GRIF: An interactive system for structured document manipulation. Proceedings of the conference on text processing and document manipultation, Notthingham, England.

TEXTMASTER - DOCUMENT FILING AND RETRIEVAL USING ODA

Michael H. Kay

International Computers Limited: Office Business Centre

ABSTRACT

This paper discusses a document retrieval system designed as an integrated part of ICL's networked office product line. The system is designed to use the ISO ODA standard for document interchange and to support a user interface that can be tailored to the needs of particular users. The CAFS-ISP search engine, a special purpose hardware device, is used to locate the document required.

1. Introduction

This paper describes a project within ICL's Office Business Centre that is designing a new document filing and retrieval system. The system is designed to integrate with ICL's networked office product line and to make maximum use of international standards for Open Systems Interconnection. The project is known internally as Textmaster, and an initial subset of the total system is being delivered to selected customers during 1986 under the name ICLFILE.

The system is designed to allow end-users to find the documents they are interested in by means of simple enquiries. They may then view these documents either directly on the screen, or by requesting a printed copy, or by having the document mailed to them electronically. Throughout this process both the typographical layout and the editability of the document are fully preserved. Thus if the user requests a printed copy this can be produced in high quality on a laser printer if required, while if he wishes to edit the document all the necessary layout directives will be preserved. If the document is viewed on the screen it can be presented in a format as close to the printed layout as the screen characteristics will allow: the popular 'what-you-see-is-what-you-get' feature of modern word processors.

The system may be used for personal filing and retrieval, for example of word processor and electronic mail documents. In practice it is even more useful for document collections that have a wider audience: company procedures and announcements, departmental records, and so on. The advantages of using Textmaster for such applications are that it reduces the proliferation of paper copies; it makes it easier to issue updates; and it means that the user of the information rather than the originator decides what he needs and when.

To meet these requirements the system must offer full-text retrieval (the ability to use any word appearing in the document text as a keyword) and it must be suitable for ordinary office use. Existing products such as STATUS [AERE1982] and STAIRS have achieved considerable success among research workers (including scientific, legal, and commercial applications), but they are not widely used among managers and other office workers in handling everyday office paperwork.

There are a number of reasons for this. We felt that the most important were:

a)   The existing systems are not easy enough to use. The style of their user interfaces seems to have advanced little since the days of teletypes and punched cards. The users of modern personal computers and word processors expect better than this.

b)   Most office documents are prepared on word processors, but existing text retrieval systems generally offer word processing interfaces only as an afterthought. In most cases the system only holds the document as a string of characters from a limited character set, with no control information needed for editing or quality printing.

c)   The technique used to support free-text retrieval in existing systems — file inversion — is expensive in processing time. In an attempt to reduce the costs, new documents are usually collected together in batches and added to the database at intervals, perhaps weekly. Removing documents is often even more expensive than adding them. This is not a serious problem with permanent high-value information, but it makes the systems quite unsuitable for rapidly changing office files.

d)   The user interface of most systems cannot easily be tailored to the particular requirements of the subject matter and the type of user. Our experience with the ICL Committee Minutes System [ICL1985] (a free text retrieval system designed for local authorities) suggests that by focussing on the specific requirements of a particular application it is possible to create a user interface that is far superior to that of any generalised system.

e)   Office documents are less formal than academic papers, and as a result retrieval based on content alone will not always be very successful. Often the attributes of the document — date, author, document type — will be as important as the textual content in narrowing the search. This will be especially true if the person filing the document (and wishing to retrieve it later) controls these attributes but does not control the document content.

f) Most text retrieval systems are free-standing: they do not allow the user to switch readily from text searching to other tasks, and they do not allow information to be extracted easily from the text retrieval system into other systems. This is acceptable for software installed in an academic library, but not for a system offered to an office worker.

In order to solve these problems the Textmaster software has three main differences from existing text retrieval systems. These are:

a) The CAFS-ISP search engine [Haworth1985] is used to search for documents. This is a special hardware device enabling very rapid searching of textual information or data files. Using CAFS-ISP enables the costs of inversion to be avoided or deferred, which means that it becomes economic to maintain a much more volatile document collection.

b) The software is designed from the start to deal with word-processed documents. All the information in the document is retained, including typographical details and editing information. This means that it is possible to request high-quality printed copies of the documents, and to send the document back to a word-processor for further editing. In addition to the document text, any external attributes of the document (date prepared, title, name of author and so on) are captured automatically from the details entered at the word processor; these may be supplemented by additional attributes supplied when the document is filed.

c) The software is constructed in the form of a server containing the document retrieval functionality, communicating via a message-passing protocol with a user interface component. The user interface component is designed to be locally tailorable. Local tailoring may adapt the interface to the type of user, or to the capabilities of the terminal he is using; or it may be designed to restrict or enhance the functionality offered to the user, or to integrate it with functions available from other packages.

This paper concentrates on two aspects, the user interface architecture, and the link with word processing and the rest of the office world. Brief details of the way the CAFS-ISP hardware is exploited are given in section 8; for more information, see [Kay1985].

2. Document Structure and ODA

Documents have structure: they have headings, footnotes, titles, named sections, numbered paragraphs, and so on. The more the retrieval software knows about the structure, the more helpful it can be in allowing the enquirer to specify exactly what he wants to see. If the document is divided into separate fields, the enquirer can say which field he is interested in; and different matching rules can be used for special fields such as dates and numbers.

The Office Document Architecture (ODA) [ECMA1985] developed by the European Computer Manufacturers' Association, and adopted by ISO, is designed as an interchange format for word-processed documents. Unlike many of the mark-up languages used in electronic publishing, it is not intended to be used directly by a human user, but is rather a common transmission format between office systems components such as word processors, filing servers, and print servers. While many of the functions in ODA are similar to those in mark-up languages, the encoding is more appropriate to software-to-software communication.

ODA allows two types of structure to be imposed on the text: a logical structure, and a layout structure. The logical structure defines the partitioning of the document into objects such as chapters, sections and paragraphs; while the layout structure defines objects such as pages, columns, and margins. The two structures are interrelated; for example a particular logical field may always appear in the same place on the front sheet of the document.

The ODA standard defines the logical structure simply as a hierarchy of components. Each component belongs to a particular component class (e.g. chapter heading, footnote), and the attributes of a component class indicate among other things the way in which components of that class should be formatted - these are called layout directives. For example, the layout directives for a chapter heading might indicate that it is to be centre-justified and printed in a particular font and character size. The logical structure, coupled with the layout directives, is needed by any process that attempts to edit the text: for example, such a process will be able to keep a chapter heading centred if extra words are added to the heading.

In Textmaster, we are attempting to use the logical structure for an additional purpose — to enable enquiries on the contents of documents to focus on specific parts of the text.

The structural model used by Textmaster is therefore closely based on that of ODA. (The current implementation uses an interchange format known as

Normalised Document Format, or NDF, which implements an early draft of the ODA standard).

Although ODA gives the potential to define a great deal of structure, it does not make it mandatory; a document may still appear as a chunk of amorphous text. No doubt documents from certain sources, such as optical character readers, will indeed take this form. In consequence of this Textmaster allows three methods of document structuring (which may be combined in various ways):

a) The structure of the document may be internally defined using the features of ODA. This allows Textmaster to recognise the logical components (such as sections and fields) of the document automatically.

This route is ideal when it is possible to create ODA documents with sufficient structure. For example it might typically be used if all the documents are prepared using a standard form at a word processor that generates ODA directly.

b) The structure of the document may be absent from the ODA representation, but implied by markers edited into the document content in the traditional way. This allows structured documents to be prepared on equipment that offers no support for ODA structure.

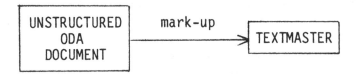

This route is necessary where the user wishes to record the full structure of the documents but has little control over how they are prepared. An alternative is to use conversion software that generates ODA structure from one of the standard mark-up languages such as SGML.

c)   The document is regarded as being unstructured text. Logical components of the document are not distinguished. However, for filing and retrieval purposes, a number of document attributes can be defined such as author, title, keywords, and reference number; these do not form part of the document content, but are held as an auxiliary document or file-card. The values of the attributes on the file-card default to the values recorded in the ODA document profile if available.

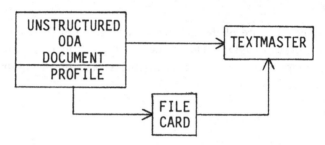

This case is more suitable for casual documents: memos, informal minutes, electronic mail. In this case the structure will tend to vary from one document to another and the organisation imposes very little control over the way they are written and typed. Traditionally the person filing the documents is responsible for creating order out of this chaos, but has no authority to alter the document text: the use of the file-card reflects this.

3. Document Classes

The ODA standard allows each component of a document (both logical components and layout components) to be of a defined class. For example several sections, or several pages, may have similar attributes, and these need only be specified once. In addition the document itself belongs to a document class, characterised by its structure: an example of a document class might be a tax return or a product description.

This concept of document class is extremely important when considering retrieval from large collections of documents. In ODA each document is self-contained: the class definitions are included in each individual document. For retrieval, however, we need to know what structural rules apply across all documents in the same class, and for this reason we allow document classes to be centrally defined in the ICL Data Dictionary System [Bourne1979]. This also allows additional properties of each component class to be defined: for example the list of stop-words (non-searchable terms) for a field, the names and synonyms of the fields to be used in enquiries, and so on.

The DDS Data Dictionary is used because it is a public place, where the definitions are available to any other software product that cares to use them. It already forms the centre of ICL's fourth generation application system, Quickbuild, and acts as the place where an organisation can keep all its 'information about information'. Using the Data Dictionary to record document collections as well as conventional databases is a new departure, which gives the potential for integrated data/text enquiry systems in the future.

The basic definition of a document class may be set up in the Data Dictionary by a Textmaster program that takes a specimen ODA document and analyses its structure. The current NDF implementation contains a lot of information about the layout structure, but little detail of the logical structure; the rest must be added by hand.

The elements that may be defined in the data dictionary are document classes, sections (composite logical object definitions in ODA), fields (basic logical object definitions in ODA), and blocks. The block element may be used to define any of the ODA layout objects: page-sets, pages, frames, and blocks. Sections and blocks are recursive: a section may contain subordinate sections, and a block subordinate blocks, to any depth. An additional element, the form-description, is introduced to allow a document class to have several permitted layout structures.

The structure is illustrated by Figure 1.

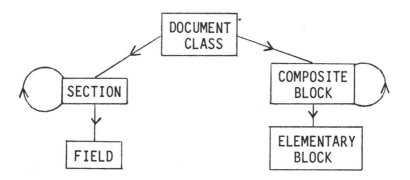

Fig. 1: Logical structure and layout structure

The structure may be very liberal, or it may impose constraints on the existence, position, and contents of each field. When documents are added to the database they will be validated against these constraints and rejected if necessary.

A field is a set of terms. For a text field the terms are words; fields may also be defined to contain numbers, dates, times, or arbitrary strings. The definition of a field class in the data dictionary includes rules for recognising fields of this class in the document (if this is not implicit from the ODA structure), for splitting it up into individual terms, and for 'indexing' the terms. There may also be validation rules for a field class, for example a range of valid values for a date field.

4. Document layout

Within the ODA standard, a document may be represented in three forms: image form, processible form, and formatted processible form.

In image form the document contains layout definitions and layout objects only. This makes the document suitable for printing, but not for further editing. It corresponds to 'final form text' in IBM's proprietary document architecture, DCA [IBM1983].

In processible form the document contains logical definitions, logical objects, and layout definitions. This means it contains the definitions of what page headers look like, for example, but the text is not actually formatted into pages. The document can be converted from processible form into image form by applying formatting algorithms.

In formatted processible form the document contains both the logical structure and the layout structure. Strictly speaking, the layout structure is redundant, as it can be generated from the logical structure and the layout directives.

In Textmaster the document will be stored either in processible form or in formatted processible form. The choice depends on a trade-off between space costs and processing costs, which have yet to be evaluated. Either way, the full logical structure is retained for subsequent editing, and the layout structure is either retained or can be generated when the document is displayed or printed. This means that documents can be displayed or printed in response to an enquiry with their original pagination and typography, limited only by the capabilities of the enquiry terminal or printer.

ODA currently allows documents to be a mixture of character-based text and photographic image; other types such as line graphics are being added. Textmaster only offers retrieval based on the content of text portions, but in principle pictures and diagrams in the document could be displayed when the hardware allows it.

The character repertoire used in text content portions is ISO-6937 [ISO1982], which caters for the needs of all European languages using a latin alphabet, and is being extended to handle other alphabets such as Greek and Cyrillic, as well as character sets required for technical and scientific applications. Typographical features such as character size and font are controlled by directives separate from the character string itself; these directives may be specific to individual components of the document, or they may relate generically to classes of component (for example, display all chapter headings in bold face).

5. Retrieval Capability

The retrieval capability of Textmaster corresponds broadly with that offered by established products such as STATUS and STAIRS. It includes the ability to search for any word, with stem searching, range searching, and fuzzy matching, and the ability to combine search terms using the Boolean operators **and, or,** and **not**. The search term may be sought in any named field class or in a field in the file-card; if no field is specified it may appear in any text field of the document.

A limited collocation facility is provided by the operators **with** and **without**. A **with** B means that A and B must both be present, and in the same field; A **without** B means that A must appear in a field in which B does not appear.

The main strength of the Textmaster search capability relative to other systems is in fuzzy matching. This exploits the searching power of the CAFS-ISP hardware. Three omnibus (or wild-card) characters are provided:

* Matches one unknown character appearing at that position
? Matches an unknown character, or a null string, at that position
! Matches any string of characters (including the null string) at that position.

These characters can be used anywhere in a search term and in any combination. Thus, for example, STE*?EN! will match STEVEN, STEPHEN, STEPHENS, and STEVENSON.

In contrast, some of the more sophisticated features of other systems, such as proximity searching and thesaurus handling, are excluded from Textmaster, at least for the time being. We feel that these facilities will not usually be needed by the casual office worker.

In general all term matching ignores case and accents: thus "COUPE" will match "Coupé". Similarly date and numeric fields are matched by their values rather than their representatations: 1.0 will match 1.00, and 1/5/83 will match 01-05-1983. The principle is that the normalised value of a search term is compared with the normalised value of the term as it appears in the document. The normalisation rules depend on the properties of the field class, defined in the data dictionary.

Standard normalisation procedures are supplied for text fields, dates, times, and numeric fields; but the installation may use locally-written procedures to normalise fields such as personal names or County names. This could be used, for example, to ensure that a search for "Shropshire" finds a document referring to "Salop".

6. Access Control

Not all users are entitled to see all documents. In order to regulate who may see what, some kind of access control mechanism is needed. The effect required is that a user who is not entitled to see a document remains unaware of its existence: there will be no evidence of it in the results of a search.

In selecting an access control model, our aims were to reflect normal office practice, to keep it simple (for the users and for the implementation), and to make it efficient at run-time.

The model we chose is borrowed from ICL's VME operating system. It is a two-dimensional model, with a horizontal partitioning by seniority, and a vertical partitioning by department.

Each user has a seniority level between 0 and 15, and each document has a 'required seniority'. A user may only see a document if his seniority is greater than or equal to the required seniority. In addition each document belongs to a department (departments are numbered 0 to 255), and users may see only those documents belonging to departments they have access to. All users have access to department 0, but they may also have access to other departments.

A user is only allowed to see a document if both the department rule and the seniority rule are satisfied. To illustrate this, consider a user who is given seniority 10 and access to departments 0, 3, and 4. The documents he may see are indicated by the shaded areas in Figure 2.

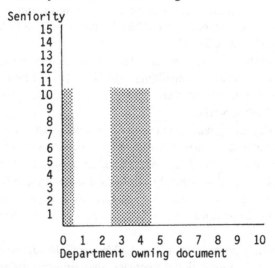

Fig.2: Documents available to a user with seniority 10 and access to departments 0, 3 and 4

Users are registered centrally by an administrator; at present we do not allow him to delegate this authority.

The access control rules are implemented using the selection functions of the CAFS-ISP hardware. As well as the user's search terms, additional terms are added by Textmaster to restrict the search to the seniorities and departments the user has access to.

There are no access constraints affecting parts of a document. If a user may see a document, he may see all of it. This reflects normal office practice with paper documents. Given that documents are displayed in their original layout, suppressing part of a document would only be possible by blanking it out, which would give the game away.

7. User interface

From the beginning we have recognised that there is no ideal user interface that will suit all users. This arises for a number of reasons:

a) Different users speak different native languages

b) The user interface should ideally exploit all the capability of the terminal equipment in use, which may vary from a simple dial-in portable terminal to a fully bit-mapped screen using a mouse, icons and windows

c) Different users have differing levels of computer skills, typing ability, knowledge of the subject matter, and research skills

d) One user will want compatibility with the word-processor, another with the corporate database enquiry language, another with his favourite application.

e) Any user interface imposes compromises − in particular the compromise between keeping things simple and offering extra capabilities. It is better to make these compromises locally, by tailoring, than to impose them on all users of a general-purpose package.

f) There are considerable benefits in tailoring the user interface closely to the class of document to be handled. A user interface designed specifically for retrieval of committee minutes or personnel records, say, will always be superior to one designed for documents in general.

For these reasons we have adopted an architecture in which Textmaster is driven by an internal protocol quite independent of a specific user interface.

The architecture is illustrated in Figure 3.

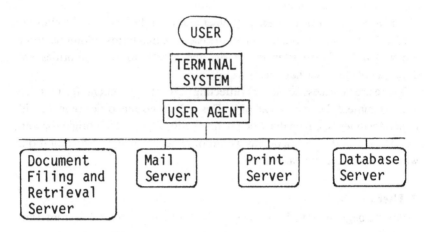

Fig. 3: Server Architecture

The terminal system consists of the terminal hardware itself, with whatever features it offers for exploiting the hardware: this might be something as simple as a forms-handling package, or an advanced environment offering pop-down menus, windows and so on.

The user agent software contains components that understand the protocols used to drive the various servers, and present to the user a coherent view of the functions available. In practice it is also likely to deliver some services to the user directly: these might include word processing and personal computing.

Note that this architecture has many possible realisations in terms of actual network configuration. The obvious realisation is to put the user agent software on an intelligent terminal and the other functions on distributed minicomputers or mainframes; but in some cases it may be cheaper to locate the user agent on the mainframe as well. The protocols driving the servers may go across a network or operate within a single machine. The main strength of the architecture is that each component may have multiple realisations for different circumstances: there may be different mail servers, for example, on different machines in the network, and there may be different user agents supporting different kinds of user.

Within ICL's Networked Office product line, the first product to fully adopt this architecture is the electronic mail system, ICLMAIL. The effect is that the ICLMAIL service can be used from a wide variety of terminals, personal computers, and word processors connected to message transfer agents (post rooms) which are themselves implemented on a variety of machines from micros to mainframes. In this case the protocols between user agent and server are international standards in the CCITT X.400 [CCITT1984] series.

By implementing Textmaster as a server using the same architecture for document filing and retrieval we will be able to gain the same benefits: the ability to use the system from a wide variety of terminals tailored to different kinds of user. The use of ODA as the interchange format for documents allows Textmaster to use the other servers such as mail and printing. And the all-important function of displaying documents can be implemented as part of the user agent software, allowing an identical user image for viewing documents whether they have just been prepared on the word-processor, received via electronic mail, or retrieved from the filing system.

8. Search techniques

This section discusses briefly the way in which the Textmaster software uses the CAFS-ISP search hardware. More detailed information is given in [Kay1985].

CAFS-ISP is a hardware device inserted into the disc controller, whose function is to filter data as it comes off the discs, returning only what is relevant to the host computer. As a result, it can search data many times faster than a program running in the host could achieve; and at the same time it frees the processing resources of the host computer for more productive work.

The ODA document format is not searchable by CAFS-ISP directly. Instead, Textmaster extracts all the search terms from the ODA document, normalises them, and puts them in a separate file used for searching. When the volume of text becomes so large that even CAFS-ISP cannot scan it in a reasonable time, indexing techniques are used to improve access times. In a single search Textmaster may retrieve some documents that have been indexed and others that have not: the difference is not apparent to the user.

The normalisation rules convert "Coupé" to "COUPE", for example, or 31/3/86 to 19860331. This normalised form is used only for searching; the original ODA text is used whenever the document is displayed or printed. Similarly, search terms entered as part of an enquiry are normalised before the search commences.

When the user issues a search request, Textmaster examines it to see how much of it can be delegated to CAFS-ISP. The search criteria passed to CAFS-ISP will always include the document class, the department, and the seniority, to restrict the search to the relevant set of documents. In addition they will include term values requested by the user. If there are more search terms than CAFS-ISP can handle (it has a limit of 16), Textmaster will perform several scans and combine the results by software.

The search expression passed to CAFS-ISP includes only **or** operators. All matches against the individual terms are returned to Textmaster, which combines the reference lists for each term using the operators actually requested in the user's search expression. Although CAFS-ISP is capable of handling **and** and **not** operators, this feature is not used because it works only if documents are limited to a maximum of about ten pages.

Search terms including omnibus characters are handled using CAFS-ISP as far as possible. In fact the Textmaster facilities for fuzzy matching are more powerful than those provided by CAFS-ISP, so additional filtering is done by software. For example if the user's search term is 'BR!SKY' (all words beginning with 'BR' and ending with 'SKY'), CAFS-ISP will find all words starting with 'BR', and the Textmaster software will check which of these end in 'SKY'. In the extreme case this results in a pure software scan, except of course that CAFS-ISP is still filtering on document class, field class, department, and seniority.

9. Conclusions

Textmaster represents an attempt to apply text retrieval technology in the office. To achieve this we needed to provide good support for word-processed documents; to make the software much easier to use than its predecessors; to allow flexible updating of the document collection; and to allow the software to be adapted to local needs and to be integrated with other services available at the same terminal.

This is achieved by use of a server architecture in which the handling of the user interface is separated from the filing and retrieval functionality; by the use of ODA as a format for interchanging documents between servers and the word processor; and by the use of the CAFS-ISP search hardware to simplify update and speed retrieval.

References

[1] AERE Harwell, Computer Science and Systems Division (1982). *STATUS User Manual*, ST-UM80.3-1.

[2] Bourne, T.J. (1979). *The Data Dictionary System in Analysis and Design*. ICL Tech J, **1**, 3, pp 292-298.

[3] CCITT (1984). *Message Handling Systems: System Model Service Elements*. Recommendation X.400.

[4] ECMA (1985). *Office Document Architecture*. ECMA-101.

[5] Haworth, G. McC. (1985) *The CAFS System Today and Tomorrow*. ICL Tech J, **4**, 4, pp 365-392.

[6] IBM (1983). *Office Information Architectures: Concepts*. GC23-0765-0.

[7] ICL (1985). *Committee Minutes System Administrator's Manual*. R50051/02.

[8] ISO (1982). *Coded Character Sets for Text Communication*. ISO-6937.

[9] Kay, M.H. (1985). *Textmaster - a document-retrieval system using CAFS-ISP*. ICL Tech J, **4**, 4, pp 455-467.

Acknowledgments

I am indebted to numerous colleagues at ICL who contributed to the design of the Textmaster system and of the architecture used to integrate it with the rest of the networked product line.

This paper is adapted from a paper published in the ICL Technical Journal [Kay1985]. I am grateful to the editor for permission to republish the common material.

This paper was prepared on an ICL DRS 8801 word processor, and prepared for typesetting using the COMPOSE software running on that equipment. It was then transmitted to a Visutek Scantext typesetter. The diagrams were produced on an Apple Macintosh and pasted in.

Combining Interactive Document Editing with Batch Document Formatting

D. D. COWAN and G. DE V. SMIT

Computer Science Department, University of Waterloo, Canada

ABSTRACT

The paper presents the design of a document preparation system that allows users to make use of existing batch formatters and yet provides an interactive user interface with what-you-see-is-almost-what-you-get feedback.

1. Introduction

Increasing numbers of people are using computers for the preparation of documents. Many of these new computer users are not "computer types"; they have a problem (to produce a neatly formatted document), they know the computer can help them, and they want the result with a minimum of (perceived) fuss and bother. The terms in which they present the problem to the computer should be "theirs" – easy for them to use and understand and based on previous document experience.

Many powerful document preparation tools exist that are capable of producing high quality output. However, they are often awkward (some would say difficult) to use, especially for the novice or casual user, and a substantial amount of training is usually necessary before they can be used intelligently.

This paper presents the design of a document preparation system that allows users to make use of existing formatters and yet makes document entry relatively easy. The following topics are discussed:

- the requirements and overall design for such a system, and

- some of the issues to be resolved in constructing the system.

First, some terminology is clarified.

2. Terms and Concepts

We use Shaw's model for documents [Shaw80, Furuta82, Kimura84]. A document is viewed as a hierarchy of objects, where each object is an instance of a class that defines the possible components and other attributes of its instances. Typical (low level) classes are document components such as sections, paragraphs, headings, footnotes, figures, and tables. Documents themselves are instances of document classes such as business letters, papers for a particular journal, or theses for a given university.

Objects may be composed of other objects. The composition may be a combination of full and partially ordered sequences and unordered sets of objects. For example, a technical paper may consist of a sequence of objects: a header, body, appendix and bibliography. Each of these objects are in turn composed of other objects: the body may consist of a sequence of sections, each a sequence of subsections. A given subsection may again be a sequence of paragraphs and figures. Though the figures might be ordered in relation to each other (fig.1 first, then fig.2), they might not be ordered with respect to the paragraphs. The bibliography may be a set of reference items, the order of which will be determined by the class to which the document belongs: in one instance they may be ordered alphabetically and in another, in order of reference.

Objects are either abstract or concrete. Abstract objects are the logical entities comprising a document (such as those listed earlier), while concrete objects are the external representations of abstract objects and are (usually) two-dimensional formatted images.

2.1. Document Descriptions

In order to describe a document fully, three components have to be specified: content, syntax, and semantics.

The **content** of the document is the text of the document – the string of characters that forms the visible part of the document. Ideally this should also include any drawings, figures or other graphical material.

The **syntax** or structure of a document defines the relationships between the various objects in the document. The structure may be a tree, a linearly ordered list, or a set of unordered objects, or any combination of these or other structures.

We define the **semantics** or meaning of a document to be a description of the visual form or layout into which the content would be formatted.

2.2. Description Languages

Languages used to describe documents can generally be divided into two categories: procedural and declarative.

In a **procedural language** the description contains the procedure for actually formatting the document. In such a language the form of the document is generally not defined through the form of various objects, but is 'hard coded' into the description. When giving a procedural description, the user is usually in direct control of the final appearance of the document. Pure procedural descriptions are to document formatting as assembler languages are to programming: very powerful, but usually low-level. Some procedural description languages like SCRIPT [IBM85, Waterloo85b] and TROFF [Ossana76] allow the definition of macros that can give the language the appearance of a declarative one, but since the low-level instructions are still available for use (and are often used), it is difficult to regard such a language as a declarative one.

In a **declarative language** (e.g. Scribe [Reid80] or GML [IBM84, Waterloo85a, McKee84]) only the logical components of the document (the items that are called objects in our model) are specified in the document description. The objects are formatted uniformly during the formatting process according to the form specified in the class description (also referred to as a style sheet or layout file).

This approach has the advantage that the format of a document can be easily changed by merely specifying a different layout style. Documents are also fairly portable since they can be reformatted easily for viewing on different devices. Note however, that the user has less immediate control over the layout of the document, since only pre-defined objects and no layout parameters can be specified in the document itself. This problem may be partly overcome in two ways:

- Object instantiations may be parameterized. When an object is instantiated, certain (mostly layout-related) parameters, called attributes, may either be assigned new values, or retain the default values assigned to them in the class description. For example, a list may have an attribute specifying whether or not it is a compact list, where a compact list is one that has less white space between its items than a non-compact list.

- Users could be allowed to define new classes and subclasses of objects. Creating such class definitions can be compared to defining new data structures or creating new subroutines in a program.

2.3.   Batch-oriented and Interactive Systems

Document processors usually come in variations of two distinct forms: batch-oriented and interactive.

Batch-oriented document processors are also referred to as pure formatters since they do not have an editing function directly associated with them. A file containing the document description is prepared with a general text editor and passed to the document processor for formatting and displaying/printing. If the user has made any mistake in the description, it will only be detected by the formatter during formatting, or by the user after formatting has been completed.

In interactive document processors, the editing and formatting tasks are combined to various degrees. They may be fully integrated in a what-you-see-is-what-you-get approach as in MacWrite [Johnson84], or just partially integrated in that the formatting process is only invoked intermittently during the editing process, either automatically or on demand by the user as in WordStar [MicroPro81]. Most interactive formatters use a procedural description language, probably because of its similarity to the operation of a typewriter.

3.   Requirements

One set of requirements for a system that should appeal to the document processing needs of the computer user identified in the introduction, is the following:

- Ease of document creation,

- Immediate, readable feedback on the structure of the document,

- Flexibility in choosing the type of output device, and

- Flexibility in choosing the final appearance or layout of the document.

Each of these requirements is discussed in more detail in the next sections.

3.1.   Ease of Document Creation

Many sophisticated and powerful batch-oriented document formatters exist today, such as TEX [Knuth84], Scribe, TROFF, GML-based formatters and SCRIPT. These formatters are often not straight-forward and easy to use, especially for the novice or casual user, since the formatting language is often complicated. Reading such a document description is not easy either; the commands and/or declarations to the formatter tend to interfere with reading the content, and the content in turn interferes with reading the commands/declarations.

The editors used to prepare document descriptions for batch-oriented formatters are usually general purpose editors and are not designed for the specific task of editing text documents.

An interactive processor using a procedural document description language can provide a simple, intuitive, typewriter-like interface. The procedural approach can at the same time make the description language extremely powerful; by including only a small number of programming constructs it should be possible to "program" any desirable effect. Furthermore, the user gives a direct description of exactly how the formatting should be done, which makes things easier for the formatter. However, a user unfamiliar with programming concepts may have trouble in producing a quality document, and understanding some of the more advanced features of the language.

3.2. Immediate Feedback

Batch-oriented document processors can be very powerful and can devote substantial effort into producing high quality output. They can use global information to "optimize" the appearance of the final document [Knuth81]. Their major drawback comes from this batch-orientation; the time lapse between entering a document description and seeing the result of that description is often too long. The user might want to experiment with various formats and layouts, but the delay in turnaround inhibits this and reduces productivity [Meyrowitz82].

Similarly, the elapsed time between making a mistake and discovering it is much longer in a batch-oriented system than in an interactive one. An interactive document processor can immediately point out errors, or even prevent them from occurring. Furthermore, on-line, context sensitive help can be provided that can guide the inexperienced user to use the processor effectively.

3.3. Flexibility in Choosing the Output Device

Some output devices are more expensive to use than others. It is not surprising therefore, that the choice of output device will differ depending on the intended use of the document.

A major advantage of current batch-oriented document processors is that they usually support a large variety of output devices. One can therefore use the same processor and document description to produce documents for a number of diverse output devices.

3.4. Flexibility in Choosing Layout

Most journals and publication houses and many companies have their own layout standards. Hence the need to be able to change the format of a document often arises.

The declarative approach to document specification caters exactly for this need and greatly reduces the amount of necessary formatting detail that the user has to supply. It provides more structure and portability to the document, usually with fewer commands. However, the user has less direct control over the final appearance of the document.

4. A Framework For A Document Preparation System

In order to meet the requirements mentioned in the previous section, a system with the following characteristics seems desirable:

- Minimal learning is necessary to produce a well-formatted document.

- What the user sees on the screen must be close in appearance to the final output.

- Good on-line help must be available

- The system must provide access to current and future powerful and sophisticated (batch-oriented) formatters.

- The layouts defined for these formatters should as far as possible still be available to the users.

- The same system must be available on as large a variety of machines and display devices as possible.

- The documents that are created must be portable over a variety of output devices.

The framework for such a document preparation system is described in the next few paragraphs, with more detail presented in subsequent sections. A diagram representing the system is shown in Figure 1.

The user creates a document using an editor imbedded in the system. Four pieces of information are needed: the class of the document, its content, syntax and semantics. The document class and content is determined by the user, while the syntax and semantics are determined by the document class. For example, the document class could be: business letter, technical paper, personnel form or legal document. General document classes have been given here as examples, obviously there could be many types within each class.

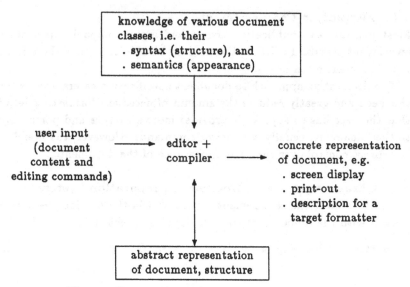

Figure 1: Framework for a document preparation system.

The document syntax and semantics are predefined in a file or data base of class descriptions. The data base may contain several semantic definitions (or layouts) for the same document class. This document class data base may be created by the user, but preferably by a "document designer".

While the document is being entered, the editor uses the information in the document class data base to assist the user in creating a "correct" document. The editor creates an abstract, internal representation of the document containing both the content and syntax of the document.

The abstract document can now be compiled into a concrete one by selecting a semantic definition from the document class description and generating the appropriate output. Two concrete representations are normally required: a screen display which approximates the final appearance of the document, and a description of the document in the input language of some target formatting system.

The individual parts of the system are described in more detail in subsequent sections.

4.1. The Document Class Data Base

The document class data base contains the definitions of various classes of documents. Since a class description is basically a document template, a document description without the content part, the class data base consists of two parts: a syntactic and a semantic part.

4.1.1. The Syntactic Part

This part of the data base contains a description of the syntax or structure of a document that belongs to a given class. The structural description includes definitions of the classes (types) of objects in the document class, their composition and ordering, and how objects may be combined to form documents of the given class. For example, in a "business letter" class there could be such object classes as sender's address, receiver's address, salutation, body and close. The body might be composed of other classes such as paragraphs and lists. One of the (ordering) syntax rules might state that the salutation must be preceded by the receiver's address and succeeded by the body.

Included in the syntactic part of an object class definition, even though it is not purely syntactic information, is a list of all attributes associated with that class of object, the possible values that each attribute may have, and the default value of each attribute. For example, the class "figure" might have an attribute "frame", with possible values box, rule, or none, indicating which kind of frame, if any, should be drawn around a figure.

4.1.2. The Semantic Part

This part of the data base contains layout information for each object in the class data base. It assigns "meaning" to the objects in a document class by specifying the form or layout in which each object would be presented to the user. This part may also be referred to as the presentation data base.

More than one layout may exist for the same document class. There may therefore be a one-to-many relationship between object structure definitions and object layouts.

The information contained in the presentation data base is used at least twice: to determine how an object will be displayed on the screen, and to generate a target document description.

4.2. The Editor

The editor is an easy-to-use, interactive, formatter-independent document editor that allows the user to create documents in a consistent way, regardless of which formatting system is eventually used. The user specifies the document class and the editor obtains the class description from the class data base. The user then proceeds to give a declarative description of the document.

Apart from the usual editing functions of copying, moving and deleting selected portions of text, a create function is provided through which the user creates specific document objects (such as headings, paragraphs, and list items). The attributes of each object are obtained from the structural part of the document class description, while the presentation data base determines how each object is displayed.

The editor is syntax-driven. It allows the user to create only legal objects (ones defined in the current document class) in their legal positions (determined by the syntax rules). For example, while entering the receiver's address in the business letter mentioned earlier, the user is not supplied with any other create function than that of creating the salutation. This implies a dynamic, state-driven user-interface: the functions/commands/menus available to the user change as the state of the document or edit-session changes. Specifying a new document class can cause a complete new menu-tree to be constructed.

4.3. The Compiler

The compiler generates formatter-dependent document descriptions. Using the abstract document object produced by the front-end, together with a semantic description obtained from the class data base, it generates a document description in the target formatter's description language. The compiler might also have to generate the appropriate layout files if the target formatter is a declarative ne.

Note that the display hardware is regarded as a target formatter and the display instructions as its document description language. The output produced for the display gives a visual feedback of the objects that are in the document. What the user sees on the screen may not necessarily be the exact form of the final output, since the display unit might not have the capability to display the object in its true form. However, the visual feedback enables the user to recognise each object clearly and determine that the display is approximately what is required, yet the user is not distracted by formatting commands as in document descriptions for batch-oriented formatters.

5. Issues

There are a number of issues to be resolved before the system outlined in the previous section can be constructed. These issues are discussed next.

1. While the syntax-oriented approach of the editor ensures that only "correct" documents are created, care should be taken that it does not become too restrictive, for example, the user might want to create the body of a letter before having to be concerned with the

receiver's address. Partially correct documents should therefore be allowed.

2. The editor has to be flexible during the editing of an existing document. Usually when a something is modified, it is taken apart and then reconstructed. Similarly, while a document is being edited (modified), it is possible that one or more of the syntax rules will be violated in order to perform the edit effectively. The editor must allow the user freedom to violate the rules while still encouraging the correction of such a violation as soon as possible.

3. The creation and editing of class descriptions both need more research. In most existing object-oriented systems (e.g. Scribe, LaTeX [Lamport86], JANUS [Chamberlin82] and GML) new class descriptions are defined by writing procedures in some programming or low level formatting language. This process should be made much easier, possibly by building some kind of expert system that will allow the document designer to "program by example".

4. It is not always clear how much semantic information should be included in the document class definitions. If enough semantic information is included, the compiler should be able to generate a. document description for any target formatter without making assumptions as to the availability of external layout or macro definition files. Since it has a complete description of every object (including the parameters that will determine its layout), the compiler can generate the appropriate tag and/or macro definitions for declarative target formatters, or sequences of formatting commands for procedural ones.

   However, most declarative target formatters already have layout files for the various styles that are being used. To be able to use these layouts, they have to be "translated" and included in the semantic part of the class data base. It might be much better if the semantic part of the class data base only specifies the semantic class to which an object belongs. The additional semantic information necessary to format the object is then obtained by the target formatter from the external layout file.

6. A Particular Design

One design to handle the issues raised in the previous section is presented in this section. In this design a decision was made in favour of a true declarative approach with a strict separation of form and content. The

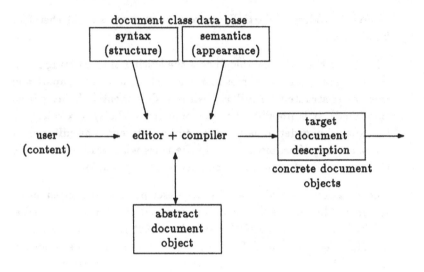

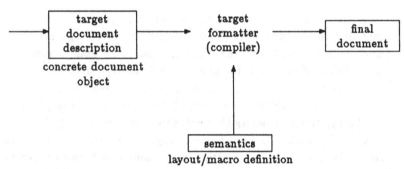

Figure 2: The expanded framework.

binding of an object to its layout form is postponed as long as possible. This allows for the most flexibility in targeting the document; it is easy to change the target formatter, output device, and/or layout style without changing the document description. At the same time existing layout files can be used with little difficulty.

This design also allows a certain kind of incomplete document: while objects may not be transposed, they may however, be missing. For example, if the objects A, B, C and D must all be present in the document and follow each other in that order, the system will accept "subset incomplete" documents such as ABC, ACD, and BD. However, the documents ACBD and DA would not be accepted.

The framework of Figure 1 is expanded in Figure 2. The expanded description is given in the following paragraphs.

6.1. The Document Class Data Base

6.1.1. The Syntactic Part

The syntax of each object in the class data base is defined by a regular expression. The symbols used in each regular expression are the names of (user-defined) objects. An object may be defined as either a terminal or non-terminal symbol. A deterministic finite automaton (DFA) is constructed for each object class and these automata are used to drive the syntax-directed editing.

6.1.2. The Semantic Part

An "unparsing scheme" similar to that used in [Medina-Mora82] is associated with each regular expression in the class data base. The exact nature of these unparsing schemes are still under investigation, but at this stage it is envisaged that a sequence of unparsing instructions would be associated with each transition in the corresponding DFA. Whether this would prove to be powerful enough, remains to be seen.

6.2. The Editor

The user interface of the editor is a menu-based system combined to some degree with mnemonics and function keys, since at least some investigations [Aderet84, Hodgson85] have indicated that this approach is the most effective.

Structure editing is separated from text editing while the relation between text and structure is still maintained and clearly indicated. The screen is divided into two parallel areas: one area indicates the structure of the document using labels that are indented to indicate nesting levels, while the other area contains the corresponding (formatted) text. When the cursor is moved through the structural part, the corresponding text parts are marked. On the textual side the cursor behaves in the normal way.

The syntax-directed editor is constructed using two DFA's for each regular expression in the class description. The first is the usual minimal state DFA [Hopcroft79] and is used in checking for legal and complete documents. The second DFA is constructed in the same way, except that every symbol in the regular expression is regarded as an optional one. This second DFA provides a mechanism to handle subset incomplete documents. The second DFA is also used for constructing the create menus.

6.3. The Compiler

The compiler becomes an interpreter. It interprets the appropriate unparsing schemes given in the semantic part of each object class description and produces the required output. The only complication in the interpreter is that it must be able to work incrementally for at least one of the unparsing schemes, namely the one associated with the terminal display.

7. Conclusions

We have described the design of a document preparation system suitable for use by the casual or novice user as well as the expert. The design has tried to make the entry and production of documents relatively easy while still providing all the flexibility and power of the powerful batch-oriented document processors. In this way it is hoped experts will only be needed in certain areas such as creation of layout descriptions

There are a number of issues which need to be resolved before such a system can be constructed, including

1. design of an editor, and

2. methods of defining, constructing and inputting the document class data base.

Research is continuing in both these areas, especially in ways of defining the class data base. Current investigation indicates that regular expressions provide sufficient power to describe the structure of most documents, while unparsing schemes similar to those used by [Medina-Mora82] could be used to define the necessary semantics.

Acknowledgements: The authors are indebted to Eric Mackie, John Wilson and Carl Durance for stimulating discussions on this and related material.

References

[1] Aderet, A. and Hoffman, P. (1984). Mnemonic strategies in word process-ing systems, *Proc. Second ACM SIGOA Conf. Office Info. Systems, SIGOA Newsletter* 5, 1-2 (June), 188-198.

[2] Chamberlin, D. D., Bertrand, O. P., Goodfellow, J. C., King, J. C., Slutz, D. R., Todd, S. J. P. and Wade, B. W. (1982). JANUS: An interactive document formatter based on declarative tags, *IBM Syst. J.* 21, 3, 250-271.

[3] Furuta, R., Scofield, J. and Shaw, A. (1982). Document formatting sys-tems, *Computing Surveys* 14, 3 (Sept.), 417-472.

[4] Hodgson, G. M. and Ruth, S. R. (1985). The use of menus in the design of on-line systems: a retrospective view, *ACM SIGCHI Bulletin* 17, 1 (July), 16-22.

[5] Hopcroft, J. E. and Ullman, J. D. (1979). *Introduction to Automata Theory, Languages, and Computation*, Reading, Massachusetts: Addison-Wesley.

[6] IBM (1984). *Document Composition Facility: General Markup Language Starter Set User's Guide* (Third Edition). Document No. SH20-9186-2, IBM, White Plains, New York.

[7] IBM (1985). *Document Composition Facility: SCRIPT/VS Language Reference* (Release 2). Document No. SH35-0070-2, IBM, White Plains, New York.

[8] Johnson, L. (1984). *MacWrite*, Apple Product No. M1502, Apple Computer Inc., Cupertino, California.

[9] Kimura, G. D. and Shaw, A. C. (1984). The structure of abstract document objects, *Proc. Second ACM SIGOA Conf. Office Info. Systems*, *SIGOA Newsletter* 5, 1-2 (June), 161-169.

[10] Knuth, D. E. and Plass, F. P. (1981). Breaking paragraphs into lines, *Softw. Prac. Exper.* 11, 11, (Nov.), 1119-1184.

[11] Knuth, D. E. (1984). *The TEXbook*, Reading, Massachusetts: Addison-Wesley.

[12] Lamport, L. (1986). LATEX: *A Document Preparation System*, Reading, Massachusetts: Addison-Wesley.

[13] McKee, D. S. and Welch, J. W. (1984). *WATCOM GML Tutorial and Reference Manual*, Watcom Systems Inc., Waterloo, Ontario.

[14] Medina-Mora, R. (1982). Syntax-directed editing: Towards integrated programming environments, Ph.D Thesis, Dept. of Computer Science, Carnegie-Mellon University, Pittsburgh, Pennsylvania.

[15] Meyrowitz, N. and van Dam, A. (1982). Interactive editing systems: Part II, *Computing Surveys* 14, 3 (Sept.), 353-415.

[16] *MicroPro WordStar User's Guide* (1981). MicroPro International Corp., San Rafael, California.

[17] Ossana, J. F. (1976). NROFF/TROFF user's manual, Computer Science Tech. Rep. 54, Bell Laboratories, Murray Hill, New Jersey.

[18] Reid, B. K. (1980). Scribe: a document specification language and its compiler, Report CMU-CS-81-100, Dept. of Computer Science, Carnegie-Mellon University, Pittsburgh, Pennsylvania.

[19] Shaw, A. C. (1980). A model for document preparation systems, Tech. Rep. 80-04-02, Dept. of Computer Science, Univ. of Washington, Seattle, Washington.

[20] *Waterloo SCRIPT GML User's Guide* (1985). Department of Computing Services, University of Waterloo, Ontario.

[21] *Waterloo SCRIPT Reference Manual* (1985). Department of Computing Services, University of Waterloo, Ontario.

Formatting Structured Documents:
Batch versus Interactive?

Giovanni Coray, Rolf Ingold, Christine Vanoirbeek
Swiss Federal Institute of Technology at Lausanne

ABSTRACT
The use of a multi-task system seems to open up new perspectives in document preparation. This paper presents such an approach, bringing together the wide possibilities of old markup techniques with the convenience of recently appeared interactive systems. It requires a very clear separation between a document's content and its formatting specification. Furthermore the latter can be favourably expressed with a descriptive formalism based on the document's logical structure.

Introduction

The subject matter of this paper stems from ideas developed in the context of a research contribution made in Lausanne on a document preparation project. The initial goal to produce technical reports has been broadened to solve more general document preparation problems (flexibility, modularity).

As interactive editing systems that include sophisticated typographical features become more fashionable, one might expect traditional formatting techniques to give way. The fact that this is not really the case is due to the advantages and shortcomings inherent in either approach: fast viewing and nice man-machine interface on the WYSIWYG systems, highest typographical quality and greater portability of documents through a variety of text processing software on the markup based textfile formatters.

Attempting to combine the good sides of both above mentioned approaches entails several requirements. First, the formatting process needs a flexible parametrisation that provides descriptive formatting specification, clearly separated from the document's content. This approach should offer more flexibility and guarantee portability of a document to several systems with different printing devices. Second, a multi-tasking environment should permit to blend user-comfort with the high typographic quality realized by sophisticated formatting functions.

The aim of this paper is not to describe all the problems that occur in text processing techniques in general. It takes into account features related to document producing, i.e. preparation for printing on paper. It presents neither storage managment and access methods to data-base nor utilities like spelling or syntax-checker.

The first chapter presents current approaches in text processing techniques and situates our new point of view, and its special requirements. Chapter two describes an architecture of a new document processing system which should conform to these requirements. A formalism based on the logical structure of a document to describe its formatting, is presented in chapter 3. Finally chapter 4 gives a short overview of the user's possibilities.

1. The formatting process

This chapter summarizes the state of the art in present day text processing developments, and contrasts our approach with other existing avenues.

1.1. State of the art

Present day text processing systems for document production can coarsely be classified into two families: interactive versus batch systems. We shall first characterize both families.

1.1.1. Batch-mode text processing

Historically, for obvious technological reasons such as the availability of alphanumeric terminals and the prohibitive size of existing formatting software, most text processing tools were used in batch mode. The text to be processed was held on printable files, containing both characters as actual text, and commands as layout conventions. Compilation of the whole file was the standard means to produce a readable document, when correctly printed (figure 1).

The merit of these large and somewhat clumsy systems is to provide the user with a wide range of formatting, layout and macro primitives. The specific needs of any document composition application can thus be met by adapting or combining the functions from a body of existing software.

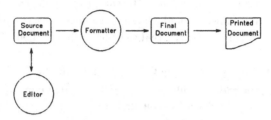

Figure 1: Architecture of batch formatter

Several drawbacks that would particularly weigh on the user's comfort and efficiency are inherent in this approach. The user is forced to pollute his text with quantities of commands, often spelled in illegible and rigid syntax; turn-around time for testing the commands is often too long for an efficient interaction during document "debugging", which as a whole appears as a fastidious and time consuming process.

A few systems palliate these drawbacks by simulating the printed document on a graphic screen [Chamberlin81], or by preprocessing the file for checkout purposes.

1.1.2. Interactive text processing

Recent technology, using graphic or bitmap screens, fast microprocessors, and less expensive laser printers, has given raise to an entirely new software. Individual workstations with fast graphic ouptut now are responsive to windows and mouse driven dialog.

Through the screen, the user has a realistic perception of his document as if it were printed (the ideal is coined WYSIWYG: What You See Is What You Get). This interaction is obtained through an integrated software that combines both editing and formatting (figure 2).

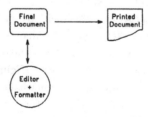

Figure 2: Architecture of interactive formatter

Although such systems are convincing by their user-friendly assets, such as fast response time, pointing devices to document sections (mouse or stick), a.o.m., they suffer from a lack of flexibility on the functional level. They may provide a fair number of formatting commands, but at the cost of less elaborate structuring capabilities that would make them fit for more sophisticated applications. As it comes to extensions of their functionality these systems, by their very interactiveness, tend to shift the burden onto the user!

1.2. Objectives for a novel approach

The above considerations have led us to attempt a well integrated approach, that would combine the advantages of the old offline formatting technique, with the new practise of workstation type interaction. Let us detail the suggested objectives that such a combined approach ought to meet (figure 3).

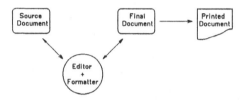

Figure 3: Integrated approach

1.2.1. Integration and extension: modularity

Besides the actual text, which constitutes the heart of the document, we usually find other entities such as logotypes, mathematical formulae, pretty- printed examples of Pascal programs or figures. In general, such graphical entities are produced by ad-hoc software [Lesk78]. From the formatting point of view they constitute inserts, either of binary data or of structured objects [VanDam82], within the final document.

Our preference goes to a system where such extraneous entities can be dealt with, not by tricks and patches, but according to the same general rules of an integrated concept. Any extension to the minimal set of formatting primitives ought to interface properly and explicitely with the others.

1.2.2. Parameterization

The last section gives room for vast generality. However, this precious potentiality should not burden the user with immoderate complexity, unless directly required for his own application. We advocate a solution that allows the system to be tailored according to given user applications.

For instance, business correspondence sets requirements which are different, -almost complementary- to those expected in the process of producing scientific papers. One promising avenue is the a priori specification of the document's structure, which is then to serve as a guide for the editing and formatting process. We have chosen this type of parameterization of the process: by a document description. An adequate formalism for the structural description of a document will be presented in chapter 3.

1.2.3. Portability

Transferring a document from one textprocessing system to another remains a largely unsolved problem. Welcome standardisation efforts have been undertaken recently [Goldfarb81]. The actual trend is to use a descriptive rather than procedural specification, i.e. to abstract from any formatting action or implementation while presenting the document's structure.

Following this convincing philosophy we enforce a strict separation between the content of a document (i.e. the actual text and information to delimit its logical constituents) and its description (how this content is to be mapped onto typographical and layout conventions, for printing)

2. Architecture

This chapter presents a special architecture for a document production software which should satisfy closely the requirements set in chapter 1. After a brief presentation of the later used vocabulary one section analyses the formatting process, whereas another one sketches the system environment required.

2.1. Document structure and stepwise formatting

Different points of view may prevail when documents are produced. As a consequence, at least two types of structure can be associated with each document for formatting purposes:
- the logical structure, which corresponds to the natural decomposition of the matter as seen by the author;
- the typographical structure, which embodies all external aspects of the printed document, in particular its page and line breaks, its

layout, fonts a.s.o.

In our approach, at every time, we consider a document in several different forms, of which we retain the following two extreme aspects:

- the source document: it contains information given by the author, i.e. the textual data and its particular logical structure;
- the final document: it corresponds to the printed view of the document; it embodies all the typographical structure.

In this workframe, formatting can be defined as processing from source document to final document, stepping through one or more intermediate forms as indicated below.

2.2 Splitting of the formatting process

The conventional way of formatting in batch systems consists of running the whole source document to generate automatically the final document. This technique requires at first sight a response time proportional to the document length. This solution is therefore inadequate in an interactive context and all the more penalizing as the involved algorithms are sophisticated.

With the aim of increasing user convenience, it means conferring an interactive characteristic to the system, we split the formatting process of a whole document into several more elementary processes. The advantage of such a decomposition is to quickly provide the user with a partially and only locally formatted document that he can interact with.

On one hand, formatting can be split chronologically into several steps. For instance, line breaking of paragraphs can be done previously to page layout. On the other hand, documents including objects of same nature can be formatted independently from one another; among others this is the case for page breaking of the different chapters in a book.

Although this general scheme is quite appropriate, some particular situations are difficult to handle. This is the case when several apparently independant steps must satisfy interlaced constraints; a typical rule in good typography requires that words do not get split at a page break. Here some arbitration may be necessary, possibly by human interaction.

The interactive editing and the look-out of the different formatting steps naturally lead to the use of a multi-windows system where each one displays a piece of a partially formatted document. Its presence, size and position on the graphic screen are driven by the user.

As an example, let us consider the following situation: a first window is associated with the source document such as it appears before any formatting operation; a second one shows a local portion of broken paragraphs; at last, a third one displays the aspect of the final document including page breaking and numbering.

Manipulation of document objects in the way described above is advantageously done in a multi-tasking environment of which a model is given in the next section.

2.3. Multi-tasking environment

Thus we consider on one hand an editing process to dialogue with the end-user and, on the other hand a number of formatting processes. All these processes are implemented as concurrent tasks under the control of a scheduler. The user is thus relieved from the obligation to direct explicitly all formatting steps.

The scheduler performs the processor's allocation according to a time-sharing scheme using fixed time slices. Furthermore it provides the necessary primitives to handle competition (mutual exclusion) and cooperation (synchronisation) of the coexisting tasks.

The data is shared by the processes in order to avoid redundant copies of the information. It is therefore necessary to provide mutual exclusion primitives for the access to the data by different processes.

Although the formatting algorithms can conveniently be expressed independently of each other, the order of their execution must obey strong constraints. For instance the process of formatting a chapter cannot be started unless all the paragraphs that occur within that chapter have previously been broken into lines. A synchronisation mechanism between the various processes is needed.

Last but not least an essential feature of our system is the dynamic nature of the formatting processes. Typically when a paragraph is modified due to an editing command, while its formatting is under way, the process associated with it must be killed, and subsequently replaced by a new process started on the modified data.

The system environment for a multistep formatting procedure must evidently support time-sharing and dynamic parallel processes.

3. The formal description of a document type

This chapter exhibits a formalism to describe first the logical structure of a source document and second the way it must be formatted.

3.1. Structure driven formatting of a document

According to our model, a document to be composed for typesetting should have two parts: the textual content and a style description valid for that type of document. Document samples that are destined for the same publication, such as papers that fall under the same heading in a periodical, will vary in content, but their style will be identical. Conversely, the same text may be subject to several styles of composition. This happens quite naturally when a textbook is first printed on a lowcost printer, while later versions are prepared for high quality typesetting. An even more drastic case is that of transparent foils, prepared for projection, whose content is taken from a densely printed manual. The forced layout for foils suits the needs of readable projection in contrast to prints of the same material.

The advocated approach also favors the crystallization of preferred styles, typically in the form of a library of document style descriptions. For the user, such a system can naturally be tailored to his specific applications and constitutes a discreet compromise between either a too sophisticated general purpose system or a limited specialized tool.

What rules must a text obey in order to fit a given formatting style? Conversely, just what typographical variations are permissible on a given source document? The articulation is determined by the logical structure of the type of document. Let us call document description the definition of a document type in terms of its logical structure, along with the specification of the associated typographical attributes. The next section illustrates an adequate formalism for both parts of a document description.

3.2. A formalism for document descriptions

Our formalism is inspired by declarative rather than procedural methods; this should enhance the independance between logical structure description of the source document and the specification of the actual processing needed to produce the desired printout. We therefore split the document description in two tables, one for the structure and the other for the typographical attributes.

```
Paper          = Header Abstract MainText References .
Header         = Title Authors Affiliation .
Title          = Char * .
Authors        = Char * .
Affiliation    = Char * .
Abstract       = AbstractTitle Paragraph * .
AbstractTitle  = String .
MainText       = Chapter * .
Chapter        = MainHeading Entity * Section * .
MainHeading    = String Char * .
Section        = Heading Entity * Section * .
Heading        = String Char * .
Entity         = Paragraph | TableEntity | FigureEntity .
Paragraph      = Char * .
TableEntity    = Table Caption .
FigureEntity   = Figure Caption .
Caption        = String Char * .
References     = Reference * .
Reference      = ( * not specified * ) .
```

Figure 4: A formal grammar

The present paper is taken as an example to illustrate both parts of the formalism (figures 4, 5, 6).

3.2.1. The formal grammar as a structure description

A document is quite naturally broken into constituent parts, that occur either in a sequence or possibly as alternatives. The entire document, as well as each of its constituent elements will be called objects. An object undergoes a similar analysis and may well be decomposed itself into smaller objects. Some objects are primitive, i.e. not further amenable to decomposition; these include single characters or entities like logotypes and inserted figures.

Paper : FontFamily = ? (*Times*),
MainTextFontShape = ? (*Roman*),
MainTextFontSize = ? (*10*),
MainTextLineSpacing = ? (*13*),
MainHeadingFontShape = ? (*Bold*),
HeadingFontShape = ? (*Italic*),
CaptionFontShape = ? (*Roman*),
CaptionFontSize = ? (*8*),
CaptionLineSpacing = ? (*10*),
TextAreaWidth = ? (*312*),
TextAreaHeight = ? (*528*),
AbsoluteTopMargin = ? (*100*),
LeftMargin = ? (*100*),
RightMargin = LeftMargin + TextAreaWidth,
Language = *English*,
PAGINATE (AbsoluteTopMargin, TextAreaHeight);

Header : LeftMargin = ? (LeftMargin + *36*),
FormattingMode = *LeftAdjusted*,
MaxVertSpace = ? (*182 - 26*);

Title : FontShape = ? (*Italic*),
FontSize = ? (*14*),
LineSpacing = ? (*17*),
TopSpace = ? (*4* * LineSpacing),
BREAK (LeftMargin, RightMargin, FormattingMode,
LineSpacing);

Authors : FontShape = ? (*Roman*),
FontSize = ? (*10*),
LineSpacing = ? (*13*),
TopSpace = ? (*2* * LineSpacing),
BREAK (LeftMargin, RightMargin, FormattingMode,
LineSpacing);

Affiliation : FontShape = ? (*Italic*),
FontSize = ? (*8*),
LineSpacing = ? (*10*),
TopSpace = ? (MainTextLineSpacing - LineSpacing),
BREAK (LeftMargin, RightMargin, FormattingMode,
LineSpacing);

Abstract : LeftMargin = ? (LeftMargin + *36*),
FontShape = ? (*Roman*),
FontSize = ? (*8*),
LineSpacing = ? (*10*),
FormattingMode = *Justified*;

AbstractTitle : FixedWordValue =
CASE Language OF
English: 'ABSTRACT',
French: 'RESUME',
German: 'ZUSAMMENFASSUNG',
ELSE ? ('');

MainText : FontShape = MainTextFontShape,
FontSize = MainTextFontSize,
LineSpacing = MainTextLineSpacing,
FormattingMode = *Justified*;

Figure 5: An attribute table (first part)

Chapter   :   ChapterNumber = COUNTIN (Paper),

MainHeading   :   FontShape = MainHeadingFontShape,
                    BuiltString = ChapterNumber & '.',
                    BREAK (LeftMargin, RightMargin, FormattingMode,
                    LineSpacing);

Section   :   SectionNumber = COUNTIN (Chapter),

Heading   :   FontShape = HeadingFontShape,
                    BuiltString = ChapterNumber & '.' & SectionNumber & '.',
                    BREAK (LeftMargin, RightMargin, FormattingMode,
                    LineSpacing);

Paragraph   :   ParagraphNumber = COUNTIN (Section),
                    Indentation =
                        IF ParagraphNumber = 0 THEN 0,
                        ELSE *em*(FontSize),
                    JUSTIFY (LeftMargin, RightMargin, Indentation,
                    FormattingMode, LineSpacing, Language);

TableEntity   :   FixedWord =
                        CASE Language OF
                        English: 'Table',
                        French: 'Table',
                        German: 'Tabelle',
                        ELSE ? (''),
                    BuiltString = FixedWord & COUNTIN (Paper),
                    AlignmentMode = *Centered*;

FigureEntity   :   FixedWord =
                        CASE Language OF
                        English: 'Figure',
                        French: 'Figure',
                        German: 'Bild',
                        ELSE ? (''),
                    BuiltString = FixedWord & COUNTIN (Paper),
                    AlignmentMode = *Centered*;

Caption   :   FontShape = CaptionFontShape,
                    FontSize = CaptionFontSize,
                    LineSpacing = CaptionLineSpacing,
                    FormatingMode = *Centered*;
                    BREAK (LeftMargin, RightMargin, FormatingMode,
                    LineSpacing);

String   :   CHARS (BuiltString);

Table   :   SETENTITY (AlignmentMode);

Figure   :   SETENTITY (AlignmentMode);

Char   :   CHARGEN (FontFamily, FontSize, FontShape);

Figure 6: An attribute table (second part)

All other objects are obtained by one of the three following
operations: sequential composition, alternative choice among objects
("|") and repetition ("*") of any number of some type of objects.
Figure 4 shows a formal description of the type of document this
paper conforms to; it is given in terms of the primitive objects

character, figure and table.

The notation used is derived from that of formal language grammars. As a consequence, some objects may be defined recursively and thus contain parts which are of the same generic type as the main objects themselves. In the example of figure 4 a section encompasses (sub-)sections in precisely this self-embedding fashion. The formal grammar that specifies a type of document is called its structure description

3.2.2. The attribute table as a complement for the formal grammar

To complete the description of a document by indicating how it should be processed, we need an additional table. An entry in the table is provided for each object that occurs in the grammar; it contains a set of attributes which are characteristic of the formatting processing for that particular kind of object. The set of attributes is not the same for every object; for instance, characters are attributed font parameters, whereas paragraphs need other data such as margins and justification mode.

In order to avoid tedious and error prone repetitions of similar attributes, an inheritance mechanism passes attributes down the hierarchy of objects. Thus FontFamily , an attribute for Paper, in the example of figure 5, is set to the actual value Times at the top level but is available to all objects throughout the description of the type Paper.

Since inheritance can be a bind, a masking mechanism is provided in compensation. Any inherited attribute may "temporarily", i.e. for the scope of a lower level object, be redefined with a different and better suited value. All hierarchically subordinate objects will inherit from that superimposed value, according to scope rules inspired by common practice in bloc-structured programming languages. For an example, consider LeftMargin as defined at the top level of Paper; its value (100, or alternately, AbsoluteLeftMargin) is redefined locally in the constituent object Header, with an indentation of 36 pica. Values of attributes are given in the notation of arithmetic expressions or symbolic constants. When preceded by a question mark the given value is considered as a default definition; the user has then the option of defining the value as he wants it to be, either within the source document, or in a separate file or even throuh an interactive dialog.

Most attributes serve as parameters for the formatting routines. Typically paragraphs are justified within given left and right margins and according to a specified formatting mode; these attributes are all inherited from the higher levels.

4. Using the system

This chapter describes how the system is used by several categories of users. The final users are in charge of the document acquisition and its preparation for printing according to a pre-established style. The skilled users have to define the document's style including the variety of its typographical appearances.

4.1. Document production by a final user

The final user of the system, as described in chapter 2, is placed in front of a multi-window screen, showing different views of the processed document; each window is tied to a formatting step.

Figure 7 illustrates the beginning sections of the present paper in the course of processing. One window is used to echo the source version of the document and another one to reflect its final aspect.

Relevant actions that may be performed on each window, from source to final document, will be specified.

4.1.1. Document editing

Necessary operations for source document manipulation include both usual editing functions and marking operations for the delimitation of typical objects in the document. To support the former it is enough to echo any typed-in keys from the keyboard and to provide a suitable basic set of primitives such as selection, cursor moves, search in plain text, and so on. To achieve the latter requires on-line recognition of markup commands, which may be given either by function keys, explicit in-line tags, or interactive mouse driven menu selection. Consistency checking must take into account the logical structure as defined by the prevailing document description.

For reasons of efficiency, it appears desirable to minimize the processing time of the high priority editing task, in order to avoid competition with other formatting processes. With this perspective, we advocate the use of a a rather simple editor, operating with a single non-proportional font.

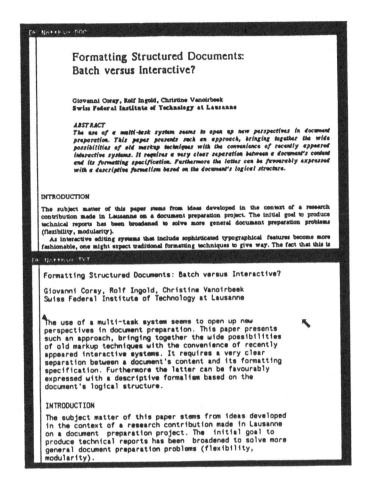

Figure 7: Different views of same document

4.1.2. Document formatting

The final user is allowed to tune the formatting result by modifying the values of some typographical attributes, provided these have been set as user-definable in the document description! This can be done interactively through the window associated with the completely formatted document.

4.2. Document description by a skilled user

The specification of a document description with the formalism explained in chapter 3, is a matter for an experienced person in typography as well as in computer science formalisms. Afterwards a distinction is made between the specification of a logical structure and the definition of formatting attributes.

The logical structure description part delimits a class of documents. The source version of a document is generally compatible with only one document description. Also any modification of this description brings into question the compatibility of the source documents marked according to it. Consequently it can be relevant to aim at a completeness of formatting possibilities when conceiving a new document description. Particulary it seems judicious to provide a trivial structure construction, which gives the final user a free hand to control himself any unplanned document items.

As for the attributes table, it can be modified without altering the consistency of source documents tied to it. The most important constraint is the adequate use of formatting procedures available in library.

4.3. Formatter extensions

The system, conceived in a modular way, should allow to extend the formatting features to satisfy new requirements. The planned mean to do this consists of joining to the formatting library new procedures consacrated to new applications. This programming job is the responsibility of a computer scientist and requires clearly defined interfaces with existing packages.

Conclusion

The aimed at generality of document preparation processes can only be achieved by wide parameterization and by a modular design.

The suggested approach, originally meant to combine advantages of both batch and interactive systems, has brought to the fore two issues: the need to separate the document's content from it's presentation style, and the advantage to split the formatting process into several steps.

This decomposition is favourably achieved in a system environment, that supports time–sharing of dynamic processes.

Also, in order to suit specific user needs and to enhance

portability, we advocate the use of a declarative formalism for document type description.

While presenting a particular document description, the paper touches upon a few typographical problems (paragraph justification, page breaking, automatic numbering ...) and presents a general model to solve them. Other situations, such has foot-note handling, integration of tables and diagrams, can be settled by suitable extensions within the same framework. Among remaining open problems, the resolution of internal references, coherent with page and section numbering, introduces an additional inter-dependance among formatting processes, yet to be analysed.

A more fondamental problem raises with the enrichment of a given logical structure to accomodate more complex document processing while preserving the compatibility with existing documents.

This paper, essentially devoted to fundamental problems, hardly mentions user- dialog facilities. Convinced by the implementability of these novel concepts, we are considering an investigation oriented towards user-interfaces, as well for document production as for document description.

References

[1] J. Andre. Bibliographie Analytique sur les "manipulations de textes", in TSI, vol. 1, no 5, p. 445-455.

[2] P. Bratley, G. Coray, G. Tiphane. COMPO: un langage de description de textes, in Actes des Journées sur la Manipulation de Documents, Rennes, 4-6 mai 1983, p. 47-68.

[3] Donald D. Chamberlin, James C. King, Donald R. Schultz, Stephen J.P. Todd, Bradford W. Wade. JANUS: An Interactive System for Document Composition, in Proceedings of the ACM SIGPLAN SIGOA Symposium on Text Manipulation, Portland, Oregon (USA), June 8-10, 1981, ACM SIGPLAN Notices, vol. 6, no 6, June 1981, p. 82-91.

[4] C.F. Goldfarb. Generalized Approach to Document Markup, in Proceedings of the ACM SIGPLAN SIGOA Symposium on Text Manipulation, Portland, Oregon (USA), June 8-10, 1981, ACM SIGPLAN Notices, vol. 6, no 6, June 1981, p. 121-122

[5] B.W. Kernighan, L.L. Cherry. A System for Typesetting Mathematics, Communications of the ACM, vol. 18, p. 151-157, March 1975.

[6] Donald E. Knuth. TEX and Metafont: new directions in

typesetting. Digital Press, 1979.

[7] M.E. Lesk. TBL - A Program to Format Tables, in UNIX Programmer's manual, 7th edition, vol. 2, Bell Lab., Murray Hill, New Jersey, August 1978.

[8] J. Nievergelt, G. Coray, J.D. Nicoud, A.C. Shaw. Document preparation Systems, North Holland, 1982.

[9] J.F. Ossana. NROFF/TROFF User's Manual, in UNIX Programmer's manual, 7th edition, vol. 2, Bell Lab., Murray Hill, New Jersey, August 1978.

[10] B.K. Reid. The Scribe Document Specification Language and its Compiler, in Abstract of the Presented Papers, Internatinal Conference on Research and Trends in Document Preparation Systems, February 1981, p. 59–62.

[11] J. Seybold. Xerox's Star, The Seybold Report 10, 16, April 1981.

[12] A. Van Dam, J.D. Foley. Fundamentals of Interactive Computer Graphics, 1982.

Acknowledgments

This work has been partly supported by the CERS (Commission d'Encouragement à la Recherche Scientifique), grants 1220 and 1427 n.A.

Advanced Catalogue Production at Unipart

Berin Gowan
Managing Director, Abbey Information Systems Ltd, UK

ABSTRACT
An advanced catalogue production system is described which has three elements: creating and structuring a database; assembling or transforming data; and publication. The major points examined are the design of the system so that compilers of information can access and update from various starting points, the use of dictionaries for multiple language publications, the use of publication parameters to allow different devices. Also emphasized is the use of publishing tools which enable subject and marketing experts to maintain direct control over the publication process.

Introduction

This paper deals with a recently completed project to develop a publishing system which provides users with responsive methods for the collection of information, and flexible ways for producing different publications.

It concerns a major supplier of replacement car parts which uses a range of publications to enable dealers and individuals to identify parts to fit cars. While it is obviously a specialised application, it represents an important market sector and also demonstrates a number of issues concerning the structuring of data and passing control directly to the users.

Context

Unipart is the largest supplier in Europe of replacement car parts and accessories for all makes of cars. It has been a leader in the development of systems for the distribution of product information, and has been using computerised publication systems for a number of years. As an indication of scale, it provides 12,000 parts for 3,500 vehicles and produces 135 major publications.

The system described provides a technical information service on parts, suppliers, and vehicle applications, as well as generating parts catalogues and supplementary publications for the trade.

With a change planned in computer systems, came an opportunity for examining the publication systems and meeting demands for publication formats which could not previously be provided.

The tasks
Unipart has three major tasks: compiling information; assembly; and publication. There is a large compilation operation where subject experts assemble the information about the parts required for individual models and variations, and also about suppliers of these parts. The product specialists are responsible for storing and maintaining the records for their own products and subsequently for producing the appropriate publications. Access is continuous throughout the day.

The second requirement is for the marketing department to decide on the publications required; their format and their content. The third requirement is for a means of production of the distribution media - currently print, although alternatives will be looked at later.

The system produces four main publications; the application catalogue, which is the primary publication; and the supplementary publications of buyers guide, menu card and cross reference.

Design considerations
The basic principle is the publishing of information in a suitable form for the enquirer, and is applied as much to Unipart's own staff as to the dealer network and members of the public. The incentive is to exploit the valuable information resource that is being built up and maintained by the operational system.

The system is required to manage effectively the technical information that is used for publishing. Structuring this information for computer-based publishing is a major investment, but it is seen to have many additional uses within the organisation. The system was therefore designed as a central resource that serves publishing analysis, interactive information services and links to other systems. The major features of the design specification were:

    a fully structured database with safeguards against unauthorised access

    extensive online access

    dynamic compilation by users

    online specification of publications

online editing of compiled material

Layout flexibility to allow users to specify numbers of columns and to rotate a page to landscape to suit their publication

generation of representative proof print

generation of typesetter tapes including symbols for fully made-up pages.

Overall plan

Following on from these requirements is the need to establish a database which can be accessed by parts and publications to be transformed by selection, sorting, merging and translating into a form suitable for composition.

A structure has been adopted to allow immediate access from different starting points. For example, a user is able to display the vehicle applications for a part and to display the parts supplied for a nominated vehicle.

The basis of the publishing system is the creation of a draft catalogue by applying stored parameter sets to the technical data. In draft form the text may be edited and paginated then be formatted by a style specification. Page proofs are produced automatically on a laser printer, and tapes generated for typesetting on an APS5 phototypesetter.

Parts information

The information contains the relationship between a part number and the vehicle it fits. This includes the familiar model names and also the precise specification for a vehicle. It contains the manufacturer's own part number and the potential suppliers with their quoted part numbers.

The facilities available to the product specialist are presented in the form of a menu screen. Typically he can retrieve a part record and browse through the information available through a dictionary. Thus the technical information can be viewed by part number, supplier code, vehicle builder code and model.

Responsibility for the technical information resides with the marketing department. Using facilities for browsing, the technical specialists in the marketing department are able to review the information and make appropriate additions and amendments.

Data structures

As the same information can be viewed in different ways, the list of vehicles or suppliers for a specified part number can be in the conventional form, but the same information can be viewed as all the Unipart numbers for a given vehicle. It may also be seen as a list of supplier's numbers or vehicle manufacturer's numbers with the Unipart equivalents.

Within the database, information is structured in a logical sequence so that, for example, applications for a part number are displayed in vehicle sequence.

For consistency of information, and to enable automatic translation into foreign languages, the system uses a range of dictionaries. These contain suppliers names, product descriptions, and publication details such as footnotes. These dictionaries may also be browsed.

The technical information is grouped into database segments with a number of different relationships between them. These segments are further divided so that optional information is separated from mandatory information. The basic structure is displayed in diagram 1.

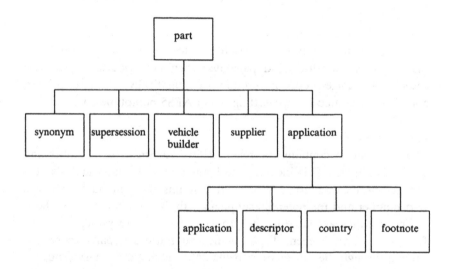

Diagram 1 Technical data database map

User interface
Great emphasis has been placed on providing users with tools which are easy to use and perform the sort of jobs which they require them to do. Thus, even for complex operations menus are used extensively, along with form-filling on screen. Where the information overflows one screen, forward and backwards browsing is available.

Thus it is possible for a technical expert to access the database through a menu to change a part number and also to check directly to see the effect on the cross-reference.

Publication

To achieve a good, readable publication, a complex transformation is performed to extract, regroup and format the detailed content. For each catalogue, the product content and vehicle content can be selected for a particular market area, such as the UK or Scandinavia. Different product ranges can be combined and dispayed with choice of Unipart number, cross-reference number, synonym or descriptive text for any column.

Similar transformations are provided for compiling Buyers Guides, Cross-references and Menu Cards from the same technical data.

The control of these transformations is provided by publication parameters stored on a further database. Separate parameters are required for the different publication types, but long lists of names, such as vehicles to be excluded from all Scandinavian publications, are entered only once and incorporated in each relevant parameter set.

Publication parameters

Publication parameters are maintained for all publications and identified by publication number. Multiple occurence items, such as models and countries, which may be used on more than one publication are stored as lists and identified by list number. The general parameters may be displayed, browsed, printed and amended.

Compilation and editing

For economy and speed of development, and where appropriate, extensive use has been made of existing packages, which have been incorporated into the system. Compuset has been used for page breaking, handling of headings, font changes, character sizes, vertical and horizontal alignments, and other layout considerations. Amendments to these definitions, known as style specifications, generate different page images from the same compiled material.

Compuset style specifications operate on flags or copymarks embedded in the text. These are generated automatically by another publishing tool, Format.

At best this transformation can provide a good approximation to the final copy, so facilities have been incorporated for browsing and revising the material. The effect of doing this is important: the computer is used to perform the operations which require bulk manipulation of data, but the user always has the opportunity to make revisions to content and appearance, so control is not taken away, but enhanced. Even in an area where such considerations in the past have not been considered paramount, it is important and practicable to do this.

Copy production
The first sight of a compiled publication is a soft proof on the wide plasma panel IBM 3290 screen which gives a 160 character display, so that a reasonable representation of the completed image can be seen. The compiled material is held on an editing database and can be revised as necessary, and also retained for display until it is replaced by a subsequent issue.

From this soft proof stage, a hard copy proof can be produced on a Xerox 9700 laser printer. This closely resembles the final photoset output. In conjunction with Compuset, the laser printer can create pages of publications very close in appearance to photosetting. For short-run publications this can be used to produce complete issues or for longer runs, a master for printing.

Fir high-quality publications with long runs, typesetter output is used. This uses the APS5 driver extension to Compuset and produces a drive tape for dispatch to the photosetter. The result is fully made-up pages with logos, symbols and special characters ready for printing.

Use of software packages
Three software packages were used: UFO, and Langton Electronic Publishing System's Format and Compuset.

UFO (User Files On-line) is a package for maintaining databases and displaying items on a screen. It is used for accesses to all databases items including the publication entries generated for editing.

Format takes a data processing file containing information to be published and inserts the copymarks required. They are inserted in the edited data before or after defined fields and at specified points in the publication structure. It allows the editing of defined fields and the insertion of text, such, as page titles into specified positions.

Compuset takes the files prepared by Format and converts them into a form to drive an output device. It requires a style specification which is a collection of statements that define the copymarks. This is used to create an intermediate file which is then interpreted through a device driver for output.

Alternative distribution media

So far, all the distribution is paper-based, but because of the way that the information has been handled the composition stages could be replaced by different software for other media such as optical disc. The operation would in essence be to establish another set of publication parameters governing the items selected and the format.

A pilot video disc project has also been undertaken which combines information taken from this database with a video programme. The material, instead of being sent to a typesetter is re-presented on a floppy disc and the user sees both video and computer data together.

Conclusion

We have tried to show the importance of two concepts:

1. providing users with easily usable tools running on a computer system so that they maintain control, with the computer department providing background support. This applies not only to entering the information and setting parameters for publication but also for personal intervention at the output stages.
2. structuring so that it can be accessed from a number of points of view and output in a variety of ways.

While lip service only is still often paid to providing publishing tools for direct user control, they are vitally important to providing the benefits of electronic publishing services.

1. the use of commonly available packages to do specific jobs. This saves time and money in development, and provides proven software (usually) and also support.
2. the use of an in-house team to develop expertise and maintain control.
3. the use of outside consultants for specialised skills for one-off problems such as designing a new system in consultation wit users.

Legibility of Digital Type-fonts and Comprehension in Reading

C. Y. Suen* and M. K. Komoda**

* *Comp. Sc. Dept., Concordia University, Montreal, Canada*
**Psych. Dept., Concordia University, Montreal, Canada*

ABSTRACT

Two experiments were conducted to investigate the effects of font-styles on legibility and on reading proficiency. The font-styles studied include Letter Gothic, Courier, and DECwriter font. Both upper and lower case letters were studied. The results revealed the significant effects of different font-styles, ambiguities between letters, and method of presentation. Directions for future research were suggested.

1. Introduction

Advances in computer technology have brought many new methods of conducting research in typesetting and typography. One area which benefits a lot from the use of modern computers is related to type-font design and evluation. With the aid of a computerized optical scanner, characters in different font styles can be read and converted into digital images. Once these images have been binarized [Suen 1986], they can be stored in matrices and reproduced easily by computers and matrix and laser printers. Hence it is not surprising to see that digital fonts have become more and more widely used in the computer environment. While these binary matrices can be stored and used later for printing, they form a new tool to study several subjects in typography such as legibility of font styles, reading speed/comprehension and font style, spacing of words and texts on the page, line lengths and character sizes. These topics have been of great interest to many psychologists and others (see e.g. Burt 1959, Tinker 1963, Hartley et al 1983). Using modern equipment, these topics can be studied much more rigorously and efficiently than before due to the fact that many parameters such as font styles, character shapes, exposure time, presentation speed, format and spacing, etc. can be controlled precisely by the computer. Our investigation is concentrated on the effects of font-styles on legibility and on reading proficiency.

Three font-styles were studied, viz.: (a) Letter Gothic, (b) Courier, and (c) DECwriter font. These type-fonts were chosen because of their common use and their special properties, i.e. the absence or presence of serifs in Letter Gothic and Courier respectively, and the matrix/letter quality of fonts between the DECfont and the other two. All three type-fonts were first digitized by an optical character reader to produce binary matrices within a frame of 21 dots wide and 42 dots high. This matrix size was chosen so that the characters can be displayed reasonably quickly while at the same time preserving the essential characteristics of the font style. Upper and lower case letters and special symbols of the 3 different digitized type-fonts are shown in Fig. 1. Using these three font-styles, Experiment 1 investigated the legibility of individual letters while Experiment 2 investigated the readability of texts.

2. Experiment 1

The legibility of individual characters was ascertained in Experiment 1 by using the visual backward masking paradigm (see Neisser, 1967, for a description of the paradigm). In the backward masking paradigm, a target letter is briefly flashed and then is followed by a masking stimulus after varying periods of time, the inter-stimulus interval or ISI. As Sperling (1963) has demonstrated, as the ISI between the target and mask is increased, the legibility of letters is increased due to the increased amount of time available for the processing of the letters before they are degraded by the mask. With respect to the present experiment, then, letters presented in inherently more legible fonts should lead to superior performance, especially at the shorter ISIs.

2.1 Method

Subjects. Three males and three females with normal (20/20) or corrected to normal vision participated in the experiment. The subjects were paid for their participation.

Apparatus and Stimuli. Apple II microcomputer was used to generate the stimuli, control the temporal presentation of the letters and mask on a high resolution screen, and acquire and store the responses made by subjects.

Procedure. Each subject was tested individually and completed 10 sessions, of approximately two hours, over a period of two weeks. In each session, subjects were presented with each of the three fonts (Letter Gothic, Courier and DECwriter) in combination with each of three ISIs (0, 16.7 and 33.3 ms). The presentation of fonts and ISIs were blocked within a session while the presentation of the 52 target letters (26 upper case and 26 lower case letters) were randomly presented within each block.

2.2 Results and Discussion

The mean percentages of correct responses as a function of font-style and ISI are presented in Table 1. The results shown in Table 1 were subject to a 3 x 3 (Font x ISI) analysis of variance for repeated measures. The analysis revealed a main effect of Font [$F(2,10) = 28.5$, $p<0.001$], a main effect of ISI [$F(2,10) = 70.0$, $p<0.001$] and a significant Font by ISI interaction [$F(4,20) = 4.7$, $p=0.007$]. As can be seen from Table 1, the main effect of Font arises from the overall poorer performance with the DECwriter font.

Font	ISI(ms)		
	0	16.7	33.3
Letter Gothic	.46(.18)	.87(.07)	.91(.04)
Courier	.39(.18)	.89(.05)	.91(.03)
DECfont	.28(.13)	.80(.08)	.88(.04)

Table 1: Mean proportion correct recognition of letters.
Note: standard deviations are presented in brackets.

Consistent with the findings of Sperling (1963), Table 1 also shows that the main effect of ISI arises from the improvement of performance with increases in ISI. However, the most interesting result is the interaction between font-style and ISI. The examination of Table 1 reveals that, at the ISI of zero, performance with the Letter Gothic font was the highest followed by that with the Courier font and that with the DECwriter font was poorest. In contrast, at the ISI of 33.3 ms, performance with all three fonts were very similar. These results, then, suggest that the sans serif font Letter Gothic is the most legible among the three fonts and that the DECfont is the least legible among the three.

Unlike most studies which concentrated on the legibility of either the lower case or upper case letters [see e.g. Mayzner 1975, Gilmore et al 1979, and van der Heijden 1984], the present experiment also studied case differences. In order to assess within font discriminations among the letters, confusion matrices were computed for each of the three fonts for the ISI of 16.7 ms; these results are presented in Table 2. The results presented in Table 2 reveal the following:

FONT # 3   ISI = 16   Case Differentiation

	A	B	C	D	E	F	G	H	I	J	K	L	M	N	O	P	Q	R	S	T	U	V	W	X	Y	Z	
A	0	0	0	0	0	0	0	0	0	0	0	1	0	0	0	0	0	0	0	0	0	0	0	0	0	0	2
B	1	0	0	0	0	0	0	0	0	0	1	0	0	0	0	0	0	0	0	0	0	0	0	0	0	0	4
C	0	0	0	1	0	0	1	0	0	0	0	0	0	0	0	0	0	0	0	0	0	0	0	0	0	0	4
D	1	0	0	0	1	0	0	1	1	0	0	0	0	0	1	0	0	0	0	0	0	1	0	0	0	0	11
E	0	0	1	0	0	1	0	0	0	0	0	0	0	0	0	0	0	0	0	0	0	0	0	0	0	0	3
F	0	0	0	0	1	0	0	0	0	0	0	0	0	0	0	0	0	0	0	0	0	0	0	1	0	0	5
G	0	0	1	0	0	0	0	0	0	0	0	0	0	0	0	0	0	2	0	0	0	0	0	0	0	0	3
H	0	0	0	0	0	0	0	0	0	0	0	0	0	0	0	0	0	1	0	0	0	0	0	0	0	0	6
I	0	0	1	0	0	0	0	0	0	0	0	2	0	0	0	0	0	0	0	1	0	0	0	0	0	0	5
J	0	0	0	0	0	0	0	1	0	0	0	0	0	0	0	0	0	0	0	0	0	0	0	0	0	0	6
K	1	0	0	0	0	0	0	0	0	0	0	1	0	0	0	0	0	0	0	0	0	0	0	0	0	0	14
L	0	1	0	0	0	0	0	0	0	0	0	0	0	0	0	0	0	0	0	0	0	0	0	0	0	0	3
M	0	0	0	0	0	0	0	0	0	0	0	0	0	2	0	0	0	0	0	0	0	0	0	0	0	0	6
N	0	0	0	1	0	0	0	0	0	0	0	0	1	0	0	0	0	0	0	0	0	0	0	0	0	0	3
O	0	0	0	5	0	0	0	0	0	0	0	0	0	0	0	0	0	2	0	0	0	0	0	0	0	0	10
P	0	0	0	0	0	0	0	0	0	0	0	0	0	0	0	0	0	1	0	0	0	0	0	0	0	0	9
Q	0	0	0	0	0	0	0	0	0	0	0	0	0	0	0	1	0	0	1	0	0	1	0	0	0	0	5
R	0	0	0	0	0	0	0	1	0	0	1	0	0	0	0	1	0	0	1	1	0	0	1	0	0	0	8
S	0	1	0	0	0	0	0	0	0	0	0	0	0	0	0	0	0	0	0	0	0	0	0	0	0	0	3
T	0	0	0	0	0	0	0	0	0	0	0	1	0	0	0	0	0	0	0	0	0	0	0	0	0	0	1
U	1	0	0	0	0	0	0	0	0	0	0	0	0	0	0	0	0	1	0	0	5	0	0	0	0	0	10
V	0	0	0	0	0	0	0	0	0	0	0	0	0	0	0	0	0	1	0	0	0	0	0	0	0	0	6
W	0	0	0	0	0	0	0	0	0	0	0	1	0	1	0	0	0	0	0	0	0	0	1	0	0	0	10
X	1	0	0	0	0	0	0	0	0	0	0	1	0	0	0	0	0	0	0	0	0	0	1	0	0	0	9
Y	0	0	0	0	0	0	0	0	0	0	0	0	0	0	0	0	0	0	0	0	0	0	1	0	0	0	1
Z	0	0	0	0	0	0	0	0	0	0	0	0	0	0	0	0	0	0	0	0	0	0	0	0	1	0	3
a	2	4	3	1	0	0	0	0	1	0	0	0	0	0	0	0	0	0	1	1	0	0	0	0	0	0	28
b	0	1	0	0	0	0	0	0	0	1	0	0	0	0	0	0	0	0	0	0	0	0	0	0	0	0	9
c	0	0	10	0	0	0	0	0	0	0	0	0	0	0	0	0	0	0	0	0	0	0	0	0	0	0	10
d	0	0	1	0	0	0	0	0	0	0	0	0	0	0	0	0	0	0	0	0	0	0	0	0	0	1	3
e	0	0	0	0	1	0	3	0	0	0	0	0	0	0	0	1	0	1	0	0	0	0	0	0	0	0	11
f	0	0	0	0	0	0	0	0	0	0	0	0	0	0	0	0	0	0	0	0	0	0	0	0	0	0	4
g	0	1	0	0	0	0	0	0	0	0	0	0	0	0	0	0	1	1	0	0	4	0	0	0	0	0	49
h	0	0	0	0	0	0	0	0	0	0	0	0	0	0	0	0	0	0	0	0	0	0	0	0	0	0	6
i	1	0	0	0	0	0	0	0	0	0	0	0	0	0	0	0	0	0	0	0	0	0	0	0	0	0	9
j	0	0	0	0	0	0	0	0	0	6	0	0	0	0	0	0	0	0	0	0	0	0	0	0	0	0	8
k	0	0	0	1	0	0	0	0	0	0	0	0	0	0	0	0	0	0	0	0	0	0	0	0	0	0	6
l	0	0	0	0	0	0	0	0	3	0	0	4	0	0	0	0	0	0	0	0	0	0	0	0	0	0	8
m	3	0	0	1	0	0	0	0	1	0	0	0	1	2	0	0	0	0	0	0	0	0	0	0	1	0	21
n	2	0	0	1	0	0	1	0	0	0	0	0	1	0	0	0	0	0	0	1	0	0	0	0	0	0	10
o	0	0	0	0	0	0	0	0	0	0	0	0	0	0	5	0	0	0	0	0	0	0	0	0	0	0	8
p	1	0	0	0	0	1	0	0	0	0	0	0	0	0	0	0	7	0	1	1	0	0	0	0	1	0	33
q	2	0	0	0	0	0	3	0	0	0	0	0	0	0	0	0	21	0	0	0	0	0	0	0	0	0	46
r	0	0	0	0	0	0	0	0	0	0	0	1	0	0	0	0	0	0	0	0	0	0	0	1	2	0	8
s	0	0	0	0	0	0	0	0	0	0	0	0	0	0	0	0	0	0	0	8	0	0	0	0	0	0	9
t	0	0	0	0	0	0	0	0	0	0	0	1	0	0	1	0	0	0	0	0	0	0	1	0	0	0	5
u	0	0	0	0	0	0	0	0	0	1	0	0	0	0	0	0	0	0	0	0	19	0	2	0	0	0	24
v	0	0	0	0	0	0	0	0	0	0	0	0	0	0	0	0	0	0	0	0	0	15	1	0	0	0	18
w	0	0	0	0	0	0	0	0	0	0	0	0	0	0	0	0	0	0	0	0	0	0	20	0	0	0	25
x	1	0	0	0	0	0	1	0	0	0	0	0	0	0	0	0	0	0	0	0	0	0	1	10	0	0	16
y	1	0	0	0	0	0	0	0	0	1	1	1	0	0	0	0	0	0	0	0	1	0	1	0	2	0	23
z	4	0	0	0	0	0	0	0	0	0	0	0	1	0	0	0	0	0	0	0	0	0	0	0	0	5	19
	22	8	17	11	3	2	9	3	6	9	4	13	3	6	10	9	28	3	17	3	22	24	26	12	7	6	

ble 2: Confusion matrix for DECfont, excerpt from
entire table of 6 pages.

Font 3

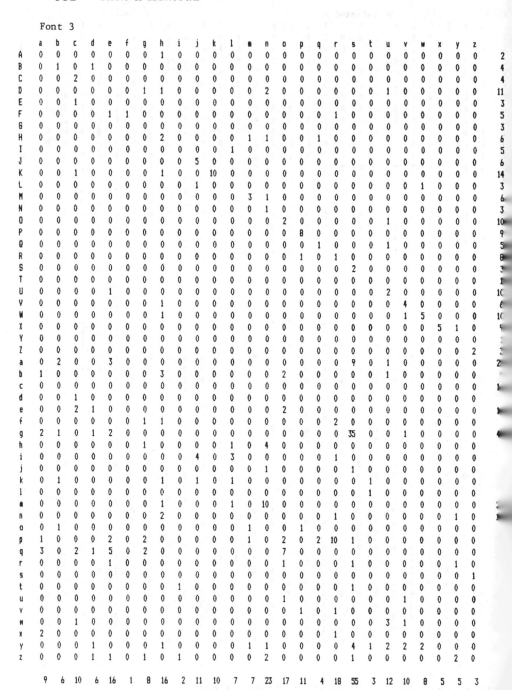

	a	b	c	d	e	f	g	h	i	j	k	l	■	n	o	p	q	r	s	t	u	v	w	x	y	z	
A	0	0	0	0	0	0	0	1	0	0	0	0	0	0	0	0	0	0	0	0	0	0	0	0	0	0	2
B	0	1	0	1	0	0	0	0	0	0	0	0	0	0	0	0	0	0	0	0	0	0	0	0	0	0	4
C	0	0	2	0	0	0	0	0	0	0	0	0	0	0	0	0	0	0	0	0	0	0	0	0	0	0	4
D	0	0	0	0	0	0	1	1	0	0	0	0	0	2	0	0	0	0	0	1	0	0	0	0	0	0	11
E	0	0	1	0	0	0	0	0	0	0	0	0	0	0	0	0	0	0	0	0	0	0	0	0	0	0	3
F	0	0	0	0	1	1	0	0	0	0	0	0	0	0	0	0	0	1	0	0	0	0	0	0	0	0	5
G	0	0	0	0	0	0	0	0	0	0	0	0	0	0	0	0	0	0	0	0	0	0	0	0	0	0	3
H	0	0	0	0	0	0	0	2	0	0	0	0	1	1	0	0	1	0	0	0	0	0	0	0	0	0	6
I	0	0	0	0	0	0	0	0	0	0	0	1	0	0	0	0	0	0	0	0	0	0	0	0	0	0	5
J	0	0	0	0	0	0	0	0	0	5	0	0	0	0	0	0	0	0	0	0	0	0	0	0	0	0	6
K	0	0	1	0	0	0	0	1	0	0	10	0	0	0	0	0	0	0	0	0	0	0	0	0	0	0	14
L	0	0	0	0	0	0	0	0	0	1	0	0	0	0	0	0	0	0	0	0	0	1	0	0	0	0	3
M	0	0	0	0	0	0	0	0	0	0	0	0	3	1	0	0	0	0	0	0	0	0	0	0	0	0	6
N	0	0	0	0	0	0	0	0	0	0	0	0	0	1	0	0	0	0	0	0	0	0	0	0	0	0	3
O	0	0	0	0	0	0	0	0	0	0	0	0	0	0	2	0	0	0	0	1	0	0	0	0	0	0	10
P	0	0	0	0	0	0	0	0	0	0	0	0	0	0	0	8	0	0	0	0	0	0	0	0	0	0	9
Q	0	0	0	0	0	0	0	0	0	0	0	0	0	0	0	0	1	0	0	0	1	0	0	0	0	0	5
R	0	0	0	0	0	0	0	0	0	0	0	0	0	0	0	0	0	1	0	1	0	0	0	0	0	0	8
S	0	0	0	0	0	0	0	0	0	0	0	0	0	0	0	0	0	0	2	0	0	0	0	0	0	0	3
T	0	0	0	0	0	0	0	0	0	0	0	0	0	0	0	0	0	0	0	0	0	0	0	0	0	0	1
U	0	0	0	0	1	0	0	0	0	0	0	0	0	0	0	0	0	0	0	0	2	0	0	0	0	0	10
V	0	0	0	0	0	0	0	0	1	0	0	0	0	0	0	0	0	0	0	0	0	4	0	0	0	0	6
W	0	0	0	0	0	0	0	1	0	0	0	0	0	0	0	0	0	0	0	0	0	1	5	0	0	0	10
X	0	0	0	0	0	0	0	0	0	0	0	0	0	0	0	0	0	0	0	0	0	0	0	5	1	0	5
Y	0	0	0	0	0	0	0	0	0	0	0	0	0	0	0	0	0	0	0	0	0	0	0	0	0	0	
Z	0	0	0	0	0	0	0	0	0	0	0	0	0	0	0	0	0	0	0	0	0	0	0	0	0	2	
a	0	2	0	0	3	0	0	0	0	0	0	0	0	0	0	0	0	0	9	0	1	0	0	0	0	0	2
b	1	0	0	0	0	0	0	0	3	0	0	0	0	0	0	2	0	0	0	0	0	1	0	0	0	0	
c	0	0	0	0	0	0	0	0	0	0	0	0	0	0	0	0	0	0	0	0	0	0	0	0	0	0	
d	0	0	1	0	0	0	0	0	0	0	0	0	0	0	0	0	0	0	0	0	0	0	0	0	0	0	
e	0	0	2	1	0	0	0	0	0	0	0	0	0	0	0	2	0	0	0	0	0	0	0	0	0	0	
f	0	0	0	0	0	0	1	1	0	0	0	0	0	0	0	0	0	0	2	0	0	0	0	0	0	0	
g	2	1	0	1	2	0	0	0	0	0	0	0	0	0	0	0	0	0	35	0	0	1	0	0	0	0	
h	0	0	0	0	0	0	1	0	0	0	0	1	0	4	0	0	0	0	0	0	0	0	0	0	0	0	
i	0	0	0	0	0	0	0	0	0	0	4	0	3	0	0	0	0	0	1	0	0	0	0	0	0	0	
j	0	0	0	0	0	0	0	0	0	0	0	0	0	1	0	0	0	0	1	0	0	0	0	0	0	0	
k	0	1	0	0	0	0	0	1	0	1	0	1	0	0	0	0	0	0	0	1	0	0	0	0	0	0	
l	0	0	0	0	0	0	0	0	0	0	0	0	0	0	0	0	0	0	1	0	0	0	0	0	0	0	
■	0	0	0	0	0	0	0	1	0	0	0	1	0	10	0	0	0	0	0	0	0	0	0	0	0	0	
n	0	0	0	0	0	0	0	2	0	0	0	0	0	0	0	0	0	0	1	0	0	0	0	0	1	0	
o	0	1	0	0	0	0	0	0	0	0	0	0	0	1	0	0	1	0	1	0	0	0	0	0	0	0	
p	1	0	0	0	2	0	2	0	0	0	0	0	1	0	2	0	2	10	1	0	0	0	0	0	0	0	
q	3	0	2	1	5	0	2	0	0	0	0	0	0	0	0	7	0	0	0	0	0	0	0	0	0	0	
r	0	0	0	0	1	0	0	0	0	0	0	0	0	0	1	0	0	0	1	0	0	0	0	0	1	0	
s	0	0	0	0	0	0	0	0	0	0	0	0	0	0	0	0	0	0	0	0	0	0	0	0	0	1	
t	0	0	0	0	0	0	0	0	0	1	0	0	0	0	0	0	0	0	1	0	0	0	0	0	0	0	
u	0	0	0	0	0	0	0	0	0	0	0	0	0	0	0	1	0	0	0	0	0	1	0	0	0	0	
v	0	0	0	0	0	0	0	0	0	0	0	0	0	0	0	0	0	1	0	1	0	0	0	0	0	0	
w	0	0	1	0	0	0	0	0	0	0	0	0	0	0	0	0	0	0	0	0	0	3	1	0	0	0	
x	2	0	0	0	0	0	0	0	0	0	0	0	0	0	0	0	0	1	0	0	0	0	0	0	0	0	
y	0	0	0	1	0	0	0	1	0	0	0	0	1	1	0	0	0	0	4	1	2	2	2	0	0	0	
z	0	0	0	1	1	0	1	0	1	0	0	0	0	2	0	0	0	0	1	0	0	0	0	0	2	0	
	9	6	10	6	16	1	8	16	2	11	10	7	7	23	17	11	4	18	55	3	12	10	8	5	5	3	

Table 2: Confusion matrix for DECfont, excerpt from
entire table of 6 pages.

	Letter Gothic	Courier	DECfont	Sum
c-C	21	9	10	30
C-c	2	21	2	25
k-K	3	3	0	6
K-k	7	3	10	20
o-O	26	0	5	31
O-o	2	27	2	31
p-P	3	3	7	13
P-p	10	11	8	29
s-S	20	11	8	39
S-s	0	3	2	5
u-U	13	1	19	33
U-u	1	11	2	14
v-V	19	7	15	41
V-v	2	20	4	26
w-W	25	5	20	50
W-w	7	10	5	22
x-X	13	11	10	34
X-x	6	8	5	19
z-Z	19	8	5	32
Z-z	0	7	2	9

Table 3:   Major erroneous responses due to case differences
for ISI=16.7 ms.

(a) Major lower and upper case confusions, e.g. c-C, j-J, k-K, o-O,
p-P, s-S, u-U, v-V, w-W, x-X, z-Z as shown in Table 3.
(b) Major letter confusions, e.g. l-I and U-V in Letter Gothic, and
a-s, g-s, m-n, p-r, q-Q, and O-D in DECfont as can be seen in
Table 2.
Further examination of the results points out the important aspect
that while there is a tendency for some lower case letters to be
more easily mistaken as their upper case counterparts, including c-C,
o-O, s-S, u-U, v-V, w-W, x-X, and z-Z in both Letter Gothic and
DECfont; however, this trend does not occur in Courier. To the

contrary, more upper case Courier letters were mistaken as lower case than the other way round including C-c, O-o, P-p, U-u, V-v, and W-w. These trends seem to have more to do with the design of the character shapes in their respective fonts.

Note that case confusions will affect the performance of optical readers in data and text processing [Suen 1986] which must be able to differentiate upper and lower case characters correctly. This effect is more accute in military applications and cryptography where lower case and upper case letter confusions could be catastrophic.

In the Letter Gothic font, the small v shape at the bottom part of U produced 8 errors as V, and the short horizontal bars on top and bottom of I resulted in 7 l-I confusions.

The large number of letter confusions between letters in the DECfont suggests its deficiency in resolution as a 5 x 7 matrix font. A considerable number of confusions were caused by the absence of descenders in the lower case letters.

Based on the above findings, one can correct the deficiencies by modifying the shapes of the characters and re-design the type-fonts to make them more legible, e.g. by making the characters with similar shapes more distinct and emphasizing their different features.

3. Experiment 2

The results of Experiment 1, then, indicate that differences in font-style can influence the legibility of individual letters. However, whether the results obtained in Experiment 1 can be generalized to reading is not clear. Investigators such as Rumelhart (1977) suggest that reading is accomplished through a set of interactive processes. In particular they suggest that a skilled reader utilizes his or her knowledge of the language (e.g., the orthographic, syntactic and semantic contsraints in a language) to facilitate the recognition of individual words and, thereby, increase reading proficiency. From this point of view, the more readers use their knowledge of the language the less the reliance on the purely visual characteristics of the texts being read. This implies that differences in font styles may not influence reading proficiency.

Accordingly, Experiment 2 assessed the effects of different font-styles on the readability of texts wherein subjects were required to read texts presented using the rapid sequential visual presentation (RSVP) procedure for comprehension. (See Potter et al, 1980, for a description of the RSVP procedure.) In the RSVP procedure, the words that comprise the text being read are presented singly in rapid sequential order. Using the RSVP procedure, the rationale for

Experiment 2 is that the more legible a font, the higher the comprehension of texts presented in that font should be for a given rate of presentation.

3.1 Method

Subjects. Nineteen females and 17 males with normal or corrected to normal vision who were paid for their participation served as subjects. Subjects' reading proficiency were assessed using a reading test by Educational Testing Service (Don Mills, Ontario). The mean reading rate of subjects to achieve at least 70% comprehension was 320 words per minute.

Apparatus and Stimuli. The apparatus used in Experiment 2 and the manner in which letters were displayed were similar to that used in Experiment 1. However, in Experiment 2, whole words rather than single letters were presented at a rate of 600 words per minute. All words, irrespective of length, were presented for the same duration and centered on the monitor screen.

The texts presented were 32 paragraphs taken from different articles published in READER'S DIGEST. Five paragraphs served as practice texts while the remaining 27 texts served as experimental texts. All paragraphs were approximately 160 words in length.

Procedure. The 27 experimental texts were divided into three groups of nine texts. Each group of texts was paired with each of the three fonts (e.g., Letter Gothic, Courier and DECwriter font) to produce nine combinations of text group and font-style. These nine combinations were used to produce nine different orders of presentation such that a) each order presented each font and each text group once and b) over orders, each font-text group combination appeared equally often in each position of the order of presentation (e.g., first, second or third). Each subject, assigned randomly to each order or presentation, read each text, albeit, in different font-styles.

3.2 Results and Discussion

The results of interest are the total number of questions correctly answered over the nine texts presented in each of the three fonts, results which are presented in Table 4. The results in Table 4 were analyzed using a one-way analysis of variance for repeated measures with Font being the only factor. As suggested in Table 4, the analysis revealed a significant effect of Font [$F(2,70)=11.3$, $p<0.001$]. As is apparent from Table 4, the highly significant result of the analysis arises from the poorer performance with the DECwriter font. As in the case of Experiment 1, the DECwriter font appears to be the least legible font.

Font	Mean	SD
Letter Gothic	31.1	4.34
Courier	31.0	4.44
DECfont	27.9	4.17

Table 4: Mean number of multiple-choice questions
answered correctly over nine texts.

On the one hand, the results of Experiment 2 appear to be consistent with those obtained in Experiment 1. That is, whether in terms of single letter identification or of the readability of texts, DECwriter font produces the lowest level of performance. Again, such results may not only be due to the dot-matrix format of the font but also may be due to the lack of ascender and desender elements within the font. On the other hand, the results of Experiment 1 and Experiment 2 are not entirely consistent. In Experiment 1, the Letter Gothic font was found to be more legible than the Courier font. However, in Experiment 2, very little, if any, differences was observed in the reading performance of texts presented in the two fonts. Thus, the reading skills and strategies brought to the reading situation can apparently attenuate the effects of the purely visual characteristics of the texts being read.

4. Conclusion
The results obtained in Experiments 1 and 2 suggest that when materials are presented in an unfamiliar font (i.e., the DECwriter font) both the legibility of individual characters and the readability of texts are diminished. Given these results and with the advent of dot-matrix printers, questions arise about the legibility and readability of texts printed with such printers. One avenue of future research is, then, an examination of the legibility and readability of materials printed with various dot-matrix printers, especially those with ascenders and descenders. Given the findings from the confusion matrices, another fruitful direction for research is to examine whether the systematic redesign of individual characters would yield a font in which individual letters would be more legible and texts written in such a font, more readable.

5. Acknowledgement
This work was supported research grants from the Natural Sciences and Engineering Research Council of Canada and the Department of Education of Quebec.

5. REFERENCES

[1]   Burt, C. (1959). *A Psychological Study of Typography*, Cambridge: Cambridge University Press.

[2]   Gilmore, G. C., Hersh, H., Caramazza, A. & Griffin, J. (1979). "Multidimensional letter similarity derived from recognition errors," *Perception & Psychophysics*, vol. 25(5), 425-431.

[3]   Hartley J. & Rooum, D. (1983). "Sir Cyril Burt and typography: a re-evaluation," *British Journal of Psychology*, vol. 74, 203-212.

[4]   Mayzner, M. S. (1975). "Studies of visual information processing in man," in *Information Processing and Cognition*, ed. R. L. Solso, pp. 31-54, Hillsdale, N. J.: Lawrence Erlbaum Associates, Publishers.

[5]   Neisser, U. (1967). *Cognitive Psychology*, Englewood Cliffs, N. J., Prentice-Hall.

[6]   Potter, M. C., Kroll, J. F. & Harris, C., (1980). "Comprehension and memory in rapid sequential reading," in *Attention & Performance VIII*, ed. R. Nickerson, Hillsdale, N. J.: Erlbaum.

[7]   Poulton, E. C. (1965). "Letter differentiation and rate of comprehension in reading," *J. Applied Psychology*, vol. 49(5), 358-362.

[8]   Rumelhart, D. E. (1977). "Toward an interactive model of reading," in *Attention & Performance VI*, ed. S. Dornic, Hillsdale, N. J.: Erlbaum.

[9]   Sperling, G. (1963). "A model for visual memory tasks", *Human Factors*, vol. 5, 19-31.

[10] Suen, C. Y. (1986). "Character recognition by computer and applications," in *Handbook of Pattern Recognition and Image Processing*, eds. T. Y. Young & K. S. Fu, Orlando: Academic Press.

[11] Suen, C. Y. & Shiau, C. (1980). "An iterative technique of selecting an optimal 5X7 matrix character set for display in computer output systems," *Proc. Soc. Infor. Display*, vol. 21(1), 9-15.

[12] van der Heijden, A. H. C., Malhas, M. S. M. & van den Roovaart, B. P. (1984). "An empirical interletter confusion matrix for continuous-line capitals," *Perception & Psychophysics*, vol. 35(1), 85-88.

[13] Tinker, M. A. (1963). *Legibility of Print*, Ames, Iowa: Iowa State University Press.

An Overview of the W Document Preparation System.

Peter R. King.
University of Manitoba; Winnipeg; Canada.
Centre de Recherche en Informatique de Nancy; France.

ABSTRACT

This paper describes both the use and the implementation of W, an interactive text formatter. In W, a document is interactively defined as a hierarchy of nested components. Such a hierarchy may be system- or user-defined. The hierarchy is used both by the W full-screen editor, and by the W formatting process, absolving the user from providing any layout commands as such. W manipulates text, such non-text items as mathematical formulae, and has provision for the inclusion of general graphical items.

1. Introduction

W is an interactive text-editor and document preparation facility being developed within the department of Computer Science at Manitoba. A working prototype of W, known as W-p, has been described elsewhere [King84]. W is a considerable development of that earlier system, but retains the same basic philosophy:

- W is an interactive, extensible, integrated editor and formatter;

- W adheres as closely as possible to the "what you see is what you get" (wysiwyg) philosophy;

- W encompasses a wide range of document items, incuding text, tables, mathematical formulae, and provision for general graphical items;

- W is portable and adaptable; that is, several versions of W are being produced to run on different architectures; although the user interface will differ in its detail, the underlying system will be common;

- W is user extensible in a variety of ways.

The remainder of this paper is organised as follows. Section 2 describes W from the user's viewpoint and gives some details of its implementation. For the most part, it is a review of material which is covered in greater depth in [King84]. Sections 3 and 4 deal with particular aspects of the use and implementation of W in further detail, covering for the most part features which have been developed or added in extending W-p to W. Section 5 indicates the current status of the project and our plans for its continued development, and section 6 concludes.

2. Overview of W

2.1. Hierarchical documents and Syntactic Editors.

In traditional formatting systems, both interactive and batch, format commands are low-level, relating closely to particular formatter actions. In a number of recent systems, such as Scribe [Ried80] and Mint [Hibbard84] it is the task of a 'document compiler' to interpret the hierarchical composition of the document as specified by the user so as to produce a suitable appearance. W belongs to this latter class of system. Mark-up in W consists in specifying a document as a hierarchy of nested components, by giving the textual contents of each component, indicating where the various components begin and end, and by stating to which class of component each belongs. In W, these components are termed 'format ranges' (abbreviated to 'FR') while the class is specified by a 'format command' ('FC'). The essential difference between W and the other two systems mentioned is that W is an interactive wysiwyg system, whereas Scribe and Mint operate in batch mode.

2.2. Syntactic Editors.

A number of program editors now exist [Teitelbaum81, Donzeau80] in which all editing operations respect the sytax (and in some instances, the static semantics) of the language in question, so that the text produced always comprises a partial, correct program. The W system is heavily based on this notion. Each class of document which the W system can produce is, conceptually, defined by a context-free grammar; mark-up is, in essence, indicating which regions of the document comprise which non-terminals. Further, the editor may make use of the displayed hierarchy, as will be explained in section 3.2.

2.3. Integrated Full-screen System.

W combines the functions of editing, mark-up, formatting, and printing into a single full-screen system. The editor permits the usual operations of insertion, replacement, deletion, cut and paste, and is thus unexceptional, except in respect of being usable in a syntactic fashion, as just mentioned.

Mark-up is performed by indicating the position of each format range by a combination of cursor movement and issuing the desired format command. In W, mark-up does *not*, in default mode, imply any formatting. Thus, inserting or modifying an FR, or modifying the text in an FR, will not in itself normally change the appearance or position of any of the document. Inserting a new FR causes appropriate icons to appear on the screen, whose purpose is to record the current format-range hierarchy. The icons may themselves be edited or be used by the editor as we describe below.

A simple command is available which will cause all or a part of the document to be reformatted on the screen. In fact, any format range (including the entire document - a default format range) may be so reformatted. When reformatting in this way, the icons marking the format ranges remain on the screen, as far as possible in their same positions relative to the text, and may therefore be employed by the editor for further mark-up.

What we have described here is the 'preferred' or default mode of use. We have selected explicit request of formatting for three major reasons:

- reformatting is slow;
- when marking-up and editing, the user is not normally concerned with the characteristics of the particular printing device, including font; ultimately to be used;
- a sequence of several markup instructions may be required to accomplish what the user regards as one logical change (such as splitting two paragraphs into three); the user will positively not want current work reformatted and moved about the screen.

In fact,

- W *does* provide a continuously reformatting mode, normally only used when inserting into existing text format ranges, such as paragraph;
- existing mark-up may itself be edited in a mode in which just the icons (with no text) appear on the screen.

2.4. Format Parameters.

Formatting in W, as in Scribe and Mint, is performed in terms of a set of internal, low-level 'format-parameters' (abbreviated to 'FP'), the quantities needed in order for the formatter to layout the document components in the correct manner. The data structure used by W to store the document is, conceptually, a tree whose nodes contain the text within the corresponding FR, plus the values of the FPs (which change at FR boundaries) and other dynamic information needed by the formatter. FPs are of four classes, depending on their mode of computation; we will give further details in section 4.3.

If the user requests a predefined W document class at the start (or any other stage) of the session, a sub-tree, corresponding to the pre-defined FR matching the user's request, will be attached to the current tree and the dynamic information updated. Alternatively, a tree may be created by 'parsing' a marked document from an earlier session; the parser uses a striaghtforward top-down parenthesis match algorithm.

2.5. User Extensibility.

W provides two ways in which the user may 'extend' the system and provide templates for his own document classes.

Firstly, W provides a mode in which the user, wishing to create a new class of document not already within the W system, may interactively menu-select the desired component FRs and indcate how they are to be placed on the page. Secondly, and more usually, any existing FR may be displayed in 'style-sheet' form. The user may then, again by menu selection, request changes to a subset of the FPs for that FR. The effect is again displayed in style-sheet form. When the user is satisfied, the 'new' FR may be treated as a replacement, for the current document, or may be designated as an entirely new FR. A particularly common use of this feature is to modify text which may appear in certain FRs in a predefined docoment.

2.6. Summary.

To summarise, a typical W session will comprise an arbitrary mixture in arbitrary order of the following activities:

- opening and reading in (including parsing) earlier W files;
- requesting a predefined document template for part or all of the document;
- editing, to create the text for the component FRs;
- mark-up, to insert or modify FRs;
- definition, to create new FRs *ab initio*, or by modification;
- reformatting all or part of the document on the screen;
- requesting the document in summary or 'model' form;
- printing the document;
- saving the document, or parts of it, for future sessions;
- requesting on-line help on any W feature.

3. W - the User's View.
In this section we describe in greater detail some aspects of the use of W.

3.1. The User's Environment.
We mentioned earlier that several 'compatible' versions of W are being developed to run on various architectures. These versions are being kept compatible both in the sense that as much of the code as possible is common, but also in the sense that the user can move easily between versions. Each version will provide the same instructions with the same effect; they will, however, be issued and their screen effect will be portrayed in different ways across the versions. With this in mind, we will describe user actions at a fairly conceptual level without precise details of exactly how they are performed.

3.2. Edit and Mark-up.
While it is true that the W user works with a single full-screen editor, a distinction is made between 'edit mode' and 'markup mode'. While in edit mode, operations are performed on text, not on the FR hierarchy. However, the editor is extensible, in that one may edit according to the icons marking the FRs. Thus one may easily perform actions such as locating the third paragraph, replacing the upper bound (of an integral) etc. provided that FRs for these commands exist. One may also ascend and descend, and move left and right in the hierarchy. Thus, as we mentioned earlier, W behaves much as a structured editor. There are, however, two important distinctions between W and the program editors mentioned above. In the first place, the W user is never *forced* to use the document structure for editing. Straightforward cursor (or mouse) movement to any position is always available. If, for example, one wished to change to lower bound of an integral from $'a+1'$ to $'a-1'$, this could be done quite independently of the structure. In the second place, W is a formatter, not a syntax checker. Thus W will not guarantee the *correctness of data* to any great extent. W will ensure that the document's syntax definition is respected, and will not permit the insertion of a 'chapter heading' within an 'equation', for example, but would *not* ensure that an 'expression' is mathematically correct.

In mark-up mode, one may edit the hierarchy itself, by positioning on the icons and issuing the appropriate edit commands. Icons may thus be moved, removed, replaced etc. Such operations, of course, have the effect of changing the composition of the document and will usually imply the need for consistency checks on the part of the system. To facilitate in such operations, the hierarchy may be displayed in a variety of ways. Normally the screen contains a window into the marked-up (and possibly partially reformatted document) complete with whatever icons are present. One has the option of displaying just the icons (with no text) or to display part or all of the document in *summary mode,* where the FRs together with a portion of the text in each are displayed.

3.3. Pre-defined Documents.
Earlier we mentioned that a number of predefined document classes, defined as context-free grammars, exist within the W system. Some additional points concerning these *templates* are:

- there will usually be be several variants of a particular template corresponding to the various terminal productions of the grammar defining the template. For each such, there exists one 'normal form' which is displayed when that particular document class is selected;
- the user may then add or delete FRs, provided the template still conforms to the grammar; in addition, with system help an alternative FR hierarchy may be requested;
- certain FRs may contain fixed text which the user may not edit, and text which the user is invited to edit. These would be useful for instance in, respectively, mathematical formulae and form letters;
- such a template may be displayed in 'model form', that is, with the FRs in their correct relative position. For many simple instances, such as form letters, completing the document simply amounts to typing the appropriate text in the required fields.

3.4. User-defined Documents.
A user defined document implies creation of a template containing an FR hierarchy with, possibly, some fixed text in certain of the FRs, together with a description of the appearance of the document. Such a document description is created by the user menu selecting the desired FRs in the appropriate order. Alternatives and options are permitted, and internally a context-free grammar is constructed. Normally, a user will create one single form of a document for his own personal use.

While our present system works well in permitting the user to menu select the required FRs, and to check the selection for consistency, it is still somewhat rudimentary in how the user is permitted to indicate the positioning of the component FRs. At present, the user may select a relative position between two successive FRs, and an absolute position tor a single FR. Further, the only relative positions currently provided are 'beside' and 'below', while only 'left', 'centre', and 'right' (for empty FRs), and exact positioning for FRs with fixed text, are the only absolute positions available in the present version. Even these are not easy to implement and require considerable consistency checking. This area is one where we plan considerable further work, both on the facilites to be provided and the maner of their use.

An existing template is user-modified by displaying it in model form (as described above) and performing a combination of editing commands on the FRs and on any text they contain. Additionally, some internal format parameters may be modified, such as the line disposition and spacing, the font, etc. These modifiable parameters are menu selected, consistency checks on the new parameter values are applied, and the effect of their change is displayed in model form.

3.5. Mathematical Text.

W can produce a wide range of mathematical formluae. Each class of formula corresponds to a document template which, when displayed indicates the component FRs, fixed text (or , more correctly, symbols) and the overall positioning, just as for any other FR. For example, a definite integral would be displayed with the '$\int$ ' and the 'd ' signs as fixed text and with FRs indicated for the expression and for the upper and lower bounds. These are three ranges for the user to complete.

As the reader will observe, there is some similarity between W and the Edimath system [Quint 84], but there are also significant differences. W imposes no order in which the FRs must be completed. Also, the user is free to select any position within the formula both by using mouse or cursor keys, disregarding the logical structure, as an alternative to using the structure of the formula. In the former case W will identify and highlight the FR which corresponds to the selected cursor position. Further, since W retains FR delimiters as icons on the screen, it is always clear in which component an insertion or other change is being made; thus the distinction made in Edimath between *insert before* and *insert after* is not required in W.

We have endeavoured to make the manipulation of mathematical text identical to any other FR, rather than be a special case. Two advantages have accrued from this. First, virtually no special atention has had to be paid to coping with mixed text and mathematics. Each FR occupies a 'box' on the screen (and on the printed page), and if text surrounds a formula, this would appear as a nested FR (the formula) inside the FR of which the text is part, and so on. Second, some features which at first sight appeared to be of use solely for coping with mathematics have proved to be of great use elsewhere. Alignment, for example, was an obvious need for mathematical equations. Alignment is represented as a non-inheriting parameter (as discussed in section 4.3); one may align on a position or a symbol in each component.

This notion proved to be a clean way in which to implement many other types of tabular and columnar FRs outside of mathematical formulae.

4. The Implementation of W.

There are several logically distinct components to the implementation of the W system. In this section we will deal with certain aspects in detail while making brief remarks about certain others.

4.1. Editor and Tree-handler.

There are three logical components to the editor. display, command input, and command interpretation. The first two, of course, are device and hence version dependent. The UNIX[1] version, for example, uses the *Curses* package [Arnold82], while the version being developed on the Macintosh uses the mouse and icon software available. We will not give further details of these here.

The command interpreter is common across all current versions. As mentioned earlier, the tree used to store the FR hierarchy also stores the document text in its leaves. A fully dynamic space allocation scheme is used. Perhaps the only feature of the editor worthy of special note is the ability to edit whatever is on the screen, which need not be contiguous lines in the document. One may, for example, display all first lines of chapters and then edit among these.

There is absolutely no restriction in W over the order in which FRs may be inserted or deleted and hence the tree will change quite drastically in shape during a W session. The tree is a father-son-brother tree, with special treatment for lists of similar FRs (such as a list of paragraphs, or a set of simultaneous equations) and while the tree handler uses standard recursive techniques, it is a fairly elaborate piece of code. The grim details, and a Pascal version appear in [King85].

4.2. Templates.

A template (or document class) is an FR consisting of a context-free grammar, whose non-terminals are other FRs. One particular terminal production from this grammar is the preferred or normal form of the template and is displayed when this particular document class is requested; other paths through the grammar resulting in alternative forms of the same document are available upon request. Upon display, the relative and absolute placement parameters are respected on the screen.

---

1 UNIX is a trademark of Bell Laboratories

A second internal form, in addition to the grammar, has proved useful for the representation of document templates. A *tree template* is a subtree corresponding (usually) to the normal form of the document class. The root of this tree is the FR corresponding to the particular document class. The subtree will contain a good deal of the statically computable FP values. A copy of this template is hooked onto the existing tree when this document class is requested. Similarly, *layout templates*, essentially a screen image of how an FR will appear when the layout parameters for the FR have been interpreted, avoid much dynamic formatting when displaying an FR. In fact, both tree and layout templates are stored internally as strings representing linearised forms of the actual tree and screen respectively. These forms are also suitable for storage across sessions. User definition of a document class will also result in the creation of such strings. These notations will not be described here. They are not at all oriented to the human reader (probably a design error, since debugging them has proved very difficult) and will be described in a forthcoming report [King 86].

4.3. The Formatter.

We recall that formatting must be explicitly requested and that any FR (including its component FRs) may be formatted. Our description here will be at the conceptual level. When reformatting, the system prompts the user for the name of a printing device, or of a page setup; W will do its best to represent the appearance of the formatted FR on that particular page or device. The format parameters, in terms of which formatting is performed, are of four classes:

- *inheriting;* that is, computed by using the FR hierarchy;
- *non-inheriting;*
- *computed;* that is calculated from other FP values in the FR tree;
- *output;* that is, computed during formatting the FR, and available for inheriting or computing by other FRs.

The FP vector calculation is performed as each left or right icon is encountered, that is, as the formatter enters and leaves FRs. (Leaving an FR corresponds to re-entering the outer one). The majority of FP values are immediately available as values in the corresponding node of the FR tree; others require computation, especially those of the third and fourth categories. These two classes of parameters are, in fact, almost exclusively concerned with page layout. Each FR when formatted will occupy what W terms a *box* on the page, and the placement of one FR will frequently depend on the size and position of a second and would therefore be *computed* from size parameters *output* from the second. The majority of non-placement parameters are computed statically, and stored in the tree node corresponding to that FR when the FR is inserted; they are hence immediately available for use during formatting. In this regard, the implementationn of W is guided by the fact that mark-up may be very efficiently implemented, whereas formatting is of its nature slow; hence overall performance will be superior if wherever possible computation is done at mark-up rather than when formatting.

5. Other Implementation Details and Future Plans.

5.1. Graphical Items.
W itself does not provide features for the creation of bit-mapped graphical objects. Such objects may, however, be incorporated into a W document, by supplying an appropriate set of relative and absolute placement parameters. The intention is that such an object would first be created by some other suitable package and then incorporated into the W document, and FR hierarchy, in this manner.

5.2.Printed Output.
One area where W in currently deficient is in the form of its output. The present system produces output for immediate printing on a single specified device. We plan in future to produce Postscript [Adobe84] as output. We are also considering outputting TEX [Knuth79] as in [Andre85]; one major reason for this is the availability of several TEX systems at Manitoba and the use of TEX there for the production of several journals from several departments, including several series from within the departmment of Computer Science. A system integrating 'raw TEX' with 'W TEX' would be a distinct advantage.

5.3. User Interface.
The present user interface is less than perfect in several important respects. Ideally, the user should need to know nothing about the format parameters in the W system; it is the intention that these be hidden from the user. However, in the present system the user does need some knowledge of the parameters and their effects when defining new templates or modifying existing templates for his personal needs. The FRs can be selected with no knowledge of their parameters, but not so, alas, their placement, if any degree of precision is desired. We have been experimenting with a number of alternative approaches; our ideal is to allow the user as much latitude as possible in placing FRs in a graphical manner as a *style sheet*, and to interpret the placement as a series of constraint equations which must be

solvable for consistency and which must have a unique solution for complete specification. Quite apart from this consideration, we have become increasingly convinced that much of the user interface will depend on experience gained from usage of the versions of W described in this paper; we will probably regard this version, therefore, as a second prototype.

6. Concluding Remarks.

W as described herein is being implemented in three versions under three systems: VMS on the VAX, UNIX on a medium resolution graphics workstation, and as a stand-alone on the Macintosh. The original work on the W-p prototype began when the author was at Bell-Northern Research in Ottawa, Canada, and was written in a UCSD-like Pascal superset. At Manitoba, W-p was ported into VAX Pascal and into SVS Pascal. After this the author had become thoroughly weary of the problems of incompatible Pascal supersets, and most of out current work is done in C.

Acknowledgements. The original work at BNR owed much to many helpful discussions with Bill Williams, who also,provided the code of the full-screen editor on which W-p was based. At Manitoba, Al Stephens has been responsible for the VAX port and is working on the Macintosh version, while Pat Niesink has been collaborating on the UNIX version. Additionally, many helpful suggestions have been received from the author's colleagues at CRIN, Nancy France during two visits there in 1985.

References

[1] Andre, J., Grundt, Y. & Quint, V. (1985). Towards an interactive math mode in TEX. *Publication no. 257, IRISA, Rennes France.* May 1985.

[2] Arnold, K.C.R.C. (1982). Screen updating and cursor movement optimization: a library package. In *4.2BSD UNIX User Manual.*

[3] Donzeau-Gouge,V., Huet, G., Kahn, G. & Lang, B. (1980). Programming environments based on structured editors: the MENTOR experience. *Research Report no. 26, INRIA, Rocquencourt, France.*

[4] Hibbard, P. (1984). *Mint Users Manual.* Department of Computer Science, Cannegie-Mellon University.

[5] King, P.R. (1984). W-p: A prototype text-processor and document formatter. In *PROTEXT I,* ED. J.J.H. MILLER, pp. 161-172. Dublin, Ireland: Boole Press.

[6] King, P.R. (1985). A tree-handler for a general structured editor. *Scientific Report.* Department of Computer Science, University of Manitoba, Canada.

[7] King, P.R. (1986). Linear notations for   trees and displays. *Scientific Report.* Department of Computer Science, University of Manitoba, Canada. In preparation.

[8] Knuth, D.E. (1979). *TEX and Metafont: New directions in typesetting.* Digital Press.

[9] Adobe Systems Inc. (1984). *Postscript language manual.* Palo Alto, California.

[10] Quint, V. (1984). Interactive editing of mathematics. In *PROTEXT I,* ed. J.J.H. Miller, pp 55-68. Dublin, Ireland: Boole Press.

[11] Reid, B.K. & Walker, J.H. (1980). *SCRIBE Reference Manual.* UNILOGIC Ltd.

[12] Teitelbaum, T. & Reps, T. (1981). The Cornell program synthesizer: a syntax-directed programming environment. *Comm. ACM,* **24,**9, pp 563-573.

Grif: An Interactive System for Structured Document Manipulation

Vincent Quint*, Irène Vatton**

*INRIA
**CNRS

ABSTRACT

Grif is an interactive system for editing and formatting complex documents. It manipulates structured documents containing objects of various types: tables, mathematical formulæ, programs, pictures, graphics, etc... It is a structure directed editor which guides the user in accordance with the structure of the document and of the objects being edited; the image displayed on the screen also being constructed from that structure. Flexibility is one of the most interesting characteristics of Grif. The user can define new document structures and new types of objects, as well as to specify the way in which the system displays these documents and objects.

1. Presentation

Existing document manipulation systems may be classified into various categories. There are batch formatters [Furuta] and interactive systems [Meyrowitz]. Some formatters such as Scribe [Reid] or Mint [Hibbard] consider the logical structure of the documents they manipulate. Some others, like TEX [Knuth] or Troff [Kernighan], are more concerned with layout, even if macros allow some structure to be introduced in the document.

Formatters have also evolved towards more friendly tools, that allow the user to see quickly on the screen the result of his work: TEX, for example, has several 'preview' systems. Janus [Chamberlin] is an original system that has been developed with the same approach. Although they allow the user to see the final form of the document on the screen, these systems cannot be considered as really interactive, as they do not allow the user to interact directly on the final form of the document. Other extensions to formatters have been proposed, by adding a truly interactive editor [André].

Interactive systems may also be classified as layout oriented or structure oriented, but structure oriented interactive systems are mainly used for a particular class of documents: programs. Mentor [Donzeau], the Cornell

Program Synthesizer [Teitelbaum], Gandalf [Medina] or Adèle [Estublier] have been primarily developed for programming environments.

Interactive or not, all systems accept text. Some of them accept other forms of information, like Troff with its specialised preprocessors for mathematics, tables, and graphics. TEX, Scribe and Mint accept mathematics and tables. Some interactive systems also manipulate mathematics [Quint], or graphics [Joloboff83], or both [Joloboff84] in a structured way.

Finally there are interactive systems designed with an agreeable user interface which allows text, tables and graphics to be manipulated. The first commercially available system of this kind was the Star [Harslem]. The same principles have been used in the Macintosh or in Interleaf WPS, but the structure taken into account in these systems is limited.

An interesting synthesis of all these systems has been realised with Andra [Gutknecht]. We propose to go further in that direction with Grif, by trying to put together the most interesting features of these various kinds of system. Grif uses the structure of the documents it manipulates; it accepts text as well as other forms of information; it is really interactive and flexible, allowing the user to define his own structures and layouts and it presents a modern user interface with mouse, windows, menus, variable size characters, etc...

2. Document Structure

2.1. The Logical Structure

Documents, and specially scientific and technical documents, frequently include objects of various types: mathematical formulæ, tables, photographs, programs, etc... Most of these objects are logically structured. As an example, a mathematical formula may be considered as a sequence of expressions such as fractions, integrals, or summations. A fraction contains a numerator and a denominator which are themselves expressions. An integral contains an integrand and two limits, which are also expressions. A summation or any other mathematical expression may be described in the same way.

We call that the *generic structure* of mathematical formulæ; any formula can be built following that structure which defines the class 'formula'. A *class* is a set of objects built with the same generic structure. Each object of a class has a *specific structure* which conforms to the generic structure of the class and decribes the logical organisation of that particular object.

As well as formulæ, tables may be considered from a logical point of view. Some tables are constituted by a heading and a sequence of lines; each line containing a title and a sequence of cells. This simple model defines a class 'table1'. Other tables may be considered as a sequence of columns, each one having a title and the same number of cells. This generic structure defines another class, 'table2'. It is also possible to define a more general generic structure which encompasses these two kinds of organisation and defines a unique class 'table'. In Grif, we allow the user to choose the level of generality for his generic structures.

Programs also may be structured in the same way, the generic structure being then directly derived from the grammar of the programming language. Pictures and photographs, as opposed to formulæ, tables and programs, are often considered with a very poor structure: an array of pixels.

In addition to these structures, a general structure organises the document for the objects included therein. For example, a report comprises a title, the author's name, an abstract, a sequence of chapters and a bibliography. Each chapter contains a title and a sequence of sections, and so on. This may be the generic structure for the class 'report'. Other classes of documents, like letters or contracts, have different generic structures.

While creating or editing a document, the author has this kind of structure in mind. If he uses a system that knows about that structure, he can express himself in his own terms and the system can help him in building a correct document, i.e. a document which conforms to the generic structure of its class.

The logical structure of the document helps the user, but also the system. Most functions of the system are based on the structure. Numbering is one of these functions. In a complex document, chapters, sections, footnotes, figures and bibliographic quotations may be automatically numbered by the system, just by using the structure. Moving across the document is another function based on the structure. The system may provide the user with commands, as for example "move to the next chapter", or "to the previous table".

As several generic structures are simultaneously needed for editing a complex document, the higher level structure is called the *document structure*, the others being called the *objects structure*. Grif does not make any difference between a class of documents and a class of objects. The same generic structure may be used for editing an isolated table (for example when preparing a slide) or a table within a document. The class 'paper' may be considered as a class of documents by the author of a paper submitted to a conference, or as a class of objects by the proceedings editor.

Structures manipulated by Grif are trees. The main structure is a tree representing the whole document, but most objects included in the document are sub-trees of that tree. Each node of the tree has a type (title, chapter, numerator...) and may have *attributes* which add semantics to the element. Examples of attributes are the language in which a part of the document is written, or the importance of a fragment of text (keyword or index). These attributes are useful for several different applications working on the document. An information retrieval system uses keywords, a formatter hyphenates words according to the language.

In addition to the main tree structure, there are *references* which represent non-hierarchical relationships between elements; this allows an element to be referenced from another independently of their relative positions in the tree. It is thus possible from any paragraph to refer to a chapter ("As seen in chapter X..."), a figure or a bibliographic quotation. The system may then substitute the number of the referenced element or its title or any other of its sub-elements for the reference.

2.2. Presentation Based on Structure

Using this kind of structure, the system can display or print the document with very little additional information from the author. The presentation of a document or object may be automatically generated from the structure. For example, a fraction is displayed with the numerator centered over the denominator, with a horizontal bar between the expressions; the title of a report is printed with large letters and centered in the page.

If the system knows about the structure of the objects it manipulates and if it has rules for presenting these structures, the user does not have to worry about presentation: when the title of a report is entered, the system can automatically change the character size and center the text.

Another advantage of this automatic presentation is that it leads to a homogeneous presentation for all documents belonging to the same class. All reports will have their title centered and written with the same size, if the system uses the same presentation rules for the class 'report'. The presentation is not intermixed with the structure or the content of the document. It is described outside the document, within the set of presentation rules associated with the class. This set of rules is called a *presentation schema*.

Several presentation schemas can be defined for the same class of documents, allowing the user to display the document in different ways according to the task to be performed. It is thus possible to use a simple presentation schema for editing and a more sophisticated one for printing, without modifying the document itself, just by changing the presentation schema used by the system.

The presentation schema defines how each type of element defined in the structure schema is to be displayed. There are presentation rules for elements of the structure and for attributes.

In a presentation schema, several views may be defined. As in PECAN [Reiss], a *view* is a partial representation of a document. So, a table of contents is a view which collects together all section titles. The presentation schema allows any number of views to be defined, specifying, for each type of element, in which views the element is visible and how it is to be presented in those views. While editing, the user can create the views he requires, being able to destroy any view at any time.

As the layout of the document can be built from its structure and from a presentation schema, a document is stored with only its specific structure and its content. This representation is called the *external representation*.

2.3. A Flexible Structure

Structure oriented systems are often blamed for their rigidity, especially in the field of textual document manipulation. They are well accepted for editing programs, because, for a given language, programs have a fixed and well known generic structure; but the structure of documents is not so stable and it is impossible to describe all possible documents with a unique generic structure.

Grif solves this problem by accepting different generic structures for different classes of documents. In addition, these classes are not fixed; the user may specify new generic structures by writing a variety of programs, called *structure schemas*. A language has been developed for this purpose which resembles somewhat the type declaration part of Pascal.

Flexibility is also enhanced by the possibility of using different classes of objects simultaneously, for the same document. The generic structure specified in the structure schema may impose the type of certain parts of the document, but in most cases, as in a paragraph for example, the user is free to choose the type of the element: pure text, a mixture of text and formulæ, a table, or any other content.

3. Architecture

Another originality of Grif comes from its architecture. Grif's end user interface functions are separated from the processing functions. The former is a specialized software called the Mediator while the latter belongs to the Editor. The Editor checks the specific structure of documents; it elaborates them according to their generic structure and prepares their display. The Mediator takes full responsibility for the physical support; it produces pictures on the screen and manages all physical interactions.

The main reasons for separating Grif's two components are :

Device independence: Grif must be able to interact with its user by means of a standard terminal as well as on a highly sophisticated workstation. Using up-to-date graphic technology and interactive input devices it can provide a versatile user interface, but document manipulation features do not have to change with the terminal. Only the user interface is device dependent.

Customisation: Designing the dialogue for an interactive application is a complex task although designers can now be helped by tools developed for design of dialogue scenario [Wong]. By offering a general tool for physical interaction management, the Mediator allows the Editor to focus on its dialogue. Concurrently, the Mediator realizes the customisation of the user interface. It can generate a more or less verbose information exchange with the user for a single Editor command.

Man-machine interface prototyping: The Mediator is an embryonic man-machine interface package. It does not yet present all the generality to be expected for such a product but offers some interesting characteristics. Most of the existing user interface managers [Kasik, Harslem, Gosling] are very close to device functionalities, describing terminal behaviour rather than user behaviour. With these interface managers, applications usually precisely control the positions of the drawing on the screen and sometimes use virtual function keys as if they were using a virtual terminal. In Grif, exchanges are at a more logical level. The Mediator is seen as just one of the Editor's potential users; another user could be an application able to execute automatic updates in documents using the same exchange level with the Editor. Exchanges between the Mediator and an application program are based on only two notions : abstract pictures and commands.

3.1. Operation

The Editor uses document and objects structure schemas for generating the abstract representation of a document. The *abstract representation* is a tree which represents the whole document. Using presentation schemas in accordance with structure schema requirements, the Editor produces an *abstract picture* of the document. An abstract picture gives the logical layout of what the Mediator has to show. It is in fact a tree describing the arrangement of several types of units: texts, pictures, graphics and symbols. These units are the leaves of the tree. A node of an abstract picture corresponds usually to a node of an abstract representation, but occasionally several nodes are added within abstract pictures. These additional nodes correspond to presentation elements. The Mediator analyses each abstract picture and, by taking into account the physical characteristics of the device (character size, window size ...) it constructs a *set of boxes* making up the real picture, which is finally displayed.

Concurrently, the Editor defines the set of *commands* it will be able to interpret. The Mediator builds forms and menus to present these commands to the end user and returns the user's answers to the Editor.

3.2. Picture Display

A node of an abstract picture gathers together information and *presentation constraints* which define how the associated information is to be presented. The Mediator builds a *box* for each node of an abstract picture; the notion of box being the same as that used in TEX. Presentation constraints permit the calculation of the width, height and positioning of the boxes, the bodysize and style of the characters and the construction of lines.

In all cases, presentation constraints are completely device independent. So the choice of font style and size is performed by the Mediator by deduction from two logical constraints: the highlight level and the relative pointsize. In the same way, the horizontal and vertical units used are converted into physical units according to the associated relative pointsize. The construction of lines is performed by the Mediator but constraints act on their characteristics: adjustment, centering, indentation, length, vertical spacing...

Finally, the set of produced boxes is organized into a connected graph which represents all relationships between boxes (relative positions or dimensions). The connected graph allows the Mediator to update the real picture as soon as the document content is modified.

3.3. Command Display

Due to the design, the Mediator does not know about the semantics of commands. Actions as well as action parameters are commands for it, but classes of commands are defined so as to allow it to do syntactic verification. Knowing the expected answer layout, it can check the user input, react rapidly to errors and choose the right tool for data acquisition. The different classes available are menu, text, numerical value and designation of the whole or a part of an abstract picture. The Mediator also permits these different classes of commands to be intermingled, in which case it controls the sequence of data acquisition and returns command anwers when the user input is completed.

Concurrently, the Mediator itself performs text editing when it acquires command answers as well as when it updates text into documents. To do so, it predefines four commands: Copy, Delete, Insert, Undo (see figure 1) which operate on strings.

4. Interactivity

Until now, interactive structure-oriented systems have mainly been used for manipulating programs. They have been designed to be used by computer-oriented people. The structure of the program being edited is represented within the system by a tree and the user is supposed to have a good knowledge of this structure as commands are often expressed by reference to that tree. This approach cannot be used in a document manipulation system where the user is unfamiliar with such concepts. Although a rich structure is necessary for powerful processing, it is not desirable to use it systematically in the dialogue between the user and the system.

Grif is an interactive system: every user action immediately reacts on the document content and document change is directly visible to the user. Of course, the Editor takes advantage of its knowledge of the documents being handled. It knows their structure and so can conduct the user in the elaboration and modification of the document. So it offers, like syntactic editors used in programming environments, powerful commands based on structure, especially for movement, selection and creation.

If on one hand structural organisation of documents permits some manipulation, it complicates normal text manipulation. In Grif, structure manipulation does not inhibit text manipulation. The user can select a part of the document by searching for character strings, extend this selection by pointing to a character as well as by invoking a structure selection command. When the user deletes, copies, inserts or undoes within a part of the displayed picture of the document, Grif manages the right choice between manipulations done by structure and those done by text. The Mediator manipulates the text part of the document and calls the Editor for updating the structure part.

5. An Example
In this section we present an example of a document processed by Grif. For the sake of brevity, this example is a simplification of a real document. Figure 1 is a "hard-copy" of the screen that shows what the user actually sees while editing the document **Example**.

5.1. The Generic Structure
This document belongs to the class **Report**, whose generic structure is defined by the following structure schema.

```
Report = BEGIN
         Title = Text;
         Authors = LIST OF (Author = Text);
         Abstract = LIST OF (Paragraph);
         Body = LIST OF (Section =
                           BEGIN
                           Section-Title = Text;
                           Section-Body =
                                   BEGIN
                                   LIST OF (Paragraph);
                                   LIST OF (Section);
                                   END;
                           END);
         END;
Paragraph = CASE OF
                 Simple-Paragraph = LIST OF (UNIT);
                 Displayed-Formula = Math-Formula;
                 END;
```

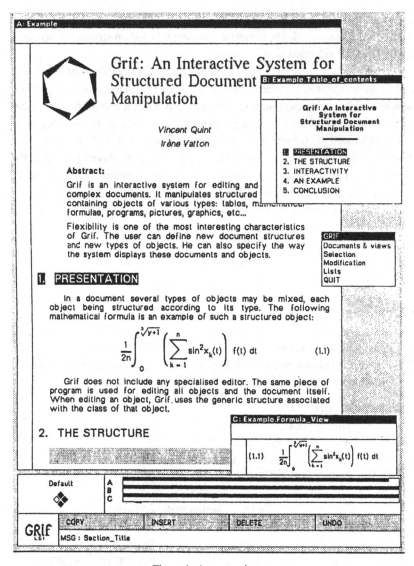

Figure 1: A screen picture

At the first level, a Report is made up of a Title, Authors, an Abstract and a Body. The Title is just Text, i.e. a character string. The element Authors is a sequence of elements Author, each one being a character string. The Abstract is a sequence of elements Paragraph. The Body is a sequence of elements Section. A Section is made up of a Section-Title (a character string) and a Section-Body. The Section-Body contains a sequence of elements Paragraph followed by a sequence of lower level elements Section. At each level, a Section has the same structure: a sequence of elements Paragraph followed by a sequence of lower level elements Section; the rule defining the structure of a Section being recursive.

A Paragraph may appear in the Abstract or in a Section. It is either a Displayed-Formula or a sequence of UNITs. A Displayed-Formula has the same structure as Math-Formula. As Math-Formula is not defined in this schema, it is assumed to be defined by another schema called Math-Formula, which defines the generic structure of mathemetical formulæ.

A UNIT is either a basic element or a structured element. Basic elements are Text (character string), Graphics (vector, rectangle, circle,...), or Pictures (bitmaps). So with this structure schema, it is possible to put a small picture within the text of a paragraph. As a UNIT may also be a structured element, it is also possible to put a formula within the text, or any other object of a class defined by another structure schema.

5.2. The Presentation

The presentation schema that has been used for editing this document contains presentation rules for each type of element defined in the structure schema. As it would be too long to show the program which defines these rules, we shall present here only some of them.

Three views are defined (figure 1), and all three have been created by the user. One view, called the *main view,* shows all elements of the document; it is always created by the system. Another view, named Table-of-contents, shows only the title of the report and the Section-Titles of the first level sections (displayed in window B). The last view, named Formula-View shows only Displayed-formulæ (displayed in window C). Different presentation rules have been specified for elements which are displayed in several views. For example, in Formula-View, Displayed-formulæ are written with smaller characters than in the main view and the formula number is not in the same place. The title of the report is centered in the Table-of-contents, and left aligned in the main view.

Several presentation elements are added by the presentation schema. These elements are related to elements of the structure and they are automatically created by the system when the element of the structure is created. As for any other element, the presentation schema defines the way to display them, but for these presentation elements it also defines their content which may be either constant or variable.

Constant elements may be any type of basic unit with a specified value. In this example three constant elements are used: the "Logo" (a Picture UNIT associated with the type Report) at the top left corner of the report, the word "Abstract:" (a Text UNIT associated with the type Abstract) at the top left corner of the abstract, and the "Horizontal-Bar" (a Graphic UNIT associated with the type Title) centered under the title, but only in the view Table-of-contents.

Two types of variable presentation elements are used in this schema: section number and formula number. The section number is associated with the type Section-Title and its value is the rank of the section in the sequence of sections it belongs to. The formula number is associated with the type Displayed-Formula. Its value is the rank of the first level section in which the formula appears, followed by the rank of the displayed formula in the section.

Even empty elements are displayed in accordance with their presentation rules. In the example, one can see the first paragraph of section 2 as a grey rectangle having the width of any other paragraph.

Presentation rules may depend on the context. In our example, rules specify that the content of a Paragraph is split into lines, that these lines are justified, and that the width of the paragraph is the width of the enclosing element. Another rule specifies that the indentation of the first line of a Paragraph is inherited from the enclosing element. A rule for the type Abstract defines the value of the indentation as zero. Therefore the first line of paragraphs is not indented in the abstract. The type Section-Body has a presentation rule specifying a positive value for this indentation. Hence the difference between paragraphs in the abstract and in the sections.

5.3. Selection

Figure 1 shows the document when the user has selected the Section-Title of the first Section. When selecting, the type of the selected element is displayed at the bottom of the editor window (e.g. Section-Title at the bottom of the screen). In addition, the selected element is displayed in reverse video in all views in which it appears (e.g. in the main view and in the Table-of-contents).

When an element of the structure is selected, all presentation elements related to it are also selected. In figure 1, a section number has been automatically created by the presentation schema, therefore it is selected when the user clicks on the word "PRESENTATION".

It is possible to select any visible element using the mouse. So, if the user wants to modify the text of the conclusion, he may select this part by clicking on the word "CONCLUSION" in the Table-of-contents; the main view displays then the beginning of the conclusion.

5.4. Editing

When creating a report, Grif automatically creates the structure of the new document according to the generic structure. Thus it creates a Title, a first Author, an Abstract containing a Paragraph and a Body with only one Section containing a Section-Title and a Section-Body (a first Paragraph and a first Section of level 2). All these elements are displayed as grey rectangles with the size and position specified in the presentation schema. For entering the text of an element, the user just has to click on its grey rectangle (its type then being displayed at the bottom of the editor window), and to type. While typing, the text is displayed according to the presentation schema: justified, or centered, and with the correct font.

In our example, when the first paragraph of section 1 is finished, the user presses a function key, 'Next', and a new Paragraph is created after the current one; this paragraph being automatically selected (the grey rectangle becomes dark). As the second paragraph will not be just text, he cannot type immediately. He clicks the command 'Insert' in the editor window and a menu is diplayed for choosing among the various possible contents of a paragraph (Simple-Paragraph or Displayed-Formula: this menu is built following the structure schema). He selects the entry 'Displayed-Formula' and an empty formula is created: a small grey rectangle centered in the window, with the number (1.1) on the right margin.

The structure schema of a formula specifies that a formula has the same structure as a mathematical expression which is a sequence of mathematical constructs. A construct is either a character string, a fraction, an integral, or a summation, etc... A fraction contains a numerator and a denominator, both being mathematical expressions. An integral contains an integration symbol (a single character) two limits (expressions) and the function to be integrated (an expression); the other constructs being defined in a similar way. This structure is very similar to that used by Edimath [Quint], therefore a formula is handled with Grif in the same way as in Edimath.

When the formula is created, a menu is displayed for selecting the type of its first construct. The user selects the entry 'Fraction'. The grey rectangle is then replaced by a small fraction bar with a grey rectangle above (the numerator) and another below (the denominator). The upper one is selected (in dark grey), the user types '1' and presses the 'End' function key which means that the numerator is finished (the 'Next' key would have created another construct within the numerator, after the character string '1'). The '1' replaces the grey numerator and the empty denominator is selected. The user types '2n' and presses 'End'. The fraction is now complete and another empty construct is created after the fraction. The 'construct' menu is displayed and the user selects 'Integral'. Four grey rectangles appear on the screen, for the integral symbol, the two limits and the function to be integrated. The user enters these elements in the same way as in the fraction. While entering the formula, the formula view is updated. The user may therefore act on either this view or the main view for editing the formula.

At any time, the user may suspend this sequential creation by clicking within any element. He can then edit this element and come back to the one he was previously creating.

6. Conclusion

Grif is implemented on a Perq running the PNX operating system, a version of UNIX. It uses all available features of the PNX window manager and its graphics primitives.

Grif is a part of a larger project, called Tigre, which aims at developing a complete environment for documents. Another important part of Tigre is the generalised data base management system [Lopez] which uses the same notion of structured documents [Bogo]. So, documents produced with Grif can be stored in the data base and their structure may be used when they are processed by the data base system.

Further developments of Grif are intended, specifically an adaptation of the Mediator for simple terminals. This will allow us to use the full flexibility of the architecture.

References

[1] André, J., Grundt, Y., Quint, V. (1985). Towards an interactive math mode in TEX. In *TEX for Scientific Documentation*, ed. D. Lucarella, pp. 79-92, Addison-Wesley.

[2] Bogo, G., Richy, H., Vatton, I. (1983). Un modèle de représentation de documents généralisés. In *Actes des journées sur la manipulation de documents*, ed. J. André, pp. 221-235, INRIA, Rennes.

[3] Chamberlin, D.D., King, J.C., Slutz, D.R., Todd, S.J.P., Wade, B.W. (1981). JANUS: An Interactive System for Document Composition. In *ACM SIGPLAN Notices*, 16, 6.

[4] Donzeau-Gouge, V., Kahn, G., Lang, B., Mélèse, B., Morcos, E. (1983). Outline of a tool for document manipulation. In *IFIP 83*, pp. 615-620, Paris, R.E.A. Mason ed., Elsevier Science Publishers B.V.

[5] Estublier, J., Krakowiak, S., Mossière, J., Rouzaud, Y. (1983). Design Principles of the Adèle Programming Environment. In *International Computing Symposium on Application Systems Development*, ACM.

[6] Furuta, R., Scofield, J., Shaw, A. (1982). Document Formatting Systems: Survey, Concepts, and Issues. *Computing Surveys*, 14, 3, pp. 417-472.

[7] Gosling, J. (1984). An Editor Based User Interface Toolkit. In *Protext I*, ed. J.J.H. Miller, Dublin, Boole Press.

[8] Gutknecht, J., and Winiger, W. (1984). Andra: The Document Preparation System of the Personal Workstation Lilith. *Software-Practice and Experience*, 14, pp. 73-100.

[9] Harslem, E., Nelson, L.E. (1982). A Retrospective on the Development of Star. In *Proceedings of the 6th International Conference on Software Engineering*, pp. 377-383, Tokyo.

[10] Hibbard, P. (1983). *User Manual for Mint - The Spice Document Preparation System*. Spice Document S153, Carnegie-Mellon University.

[11] Joloboff, V. (1983). An Interactive Graphics Editor for Document Preparation. In *Proceedings of 1983 ACM Conference on Personal and Small Computers*, pp. 45-53, San Diego.

[12] Joloboff, V., Quint, V. (1984). Two-dimensional editing, In *Proceedings of the IEEE First International Conference on Office Automation*, pp. 41-49, New Orleans.

[13] Kasik, David J. (1982) A User Interface Management System, In *Siggraph'82 Conference Proceedings*, ed. R. Daniel Bergeron, pp. 99-106, *Computer Graphics*, **16**, 3.

[14] Kernighan, B.W. (1984). The Unix Documentation Preparation Tools - A Retrospective. In *Protext I*, ed. J.J.H. Miller, Dublin, Boole Press.

[15] Knuth, D.E. (1984). *The TEXbook*, Addison-Wesley, Reading, Mass.

[16] Lopez, M., Palazzo Oliveira, J., Velez, F. (1983). The TIGRE Data Model, *Rapport de Recherche TIGRE* n.2, IMAG, Grenoble.

[17] Medina-Mora, R. (1982). *Syntax directed editing: toward integrated programming environments*, CMU-CS-82-113, Carnegie-Mellon University.

[18] Meyrowitz, N., van Dam, A. (1982). Interactive Editing Systems, *Computing Surveys*, **14**, 3, pp. 321-415.

[19] Quint, V. (1983). An interactive system for mathematical text processing, *Technology and Science of Informatics*, **2**, 3, pp. 169-179.

[20] Reid, B.K. (1980). A high-level approach to computer document production. In *Proceedings of the 7th Annual ACM Symposium on Principles of Programming Languages*, ACM SIGPLAN-SIGACT.

[21] Reiss, S.P. (1984). Graphical Program Development with PECAN Program Development Systems. In *ACM Sigplan Notices*, **19**, 5.

[22] Teitelbaum, T., Reps, T. (1981). The Cornell program synthesizer: a syntax directed programming environment. *Communications of the ACM*, **24**, 9, pp. 563-573.

[23] Wong, Peter C. S., Reid, Eric R. (1982). Flair - User Interface Dialog Design Tool, In *Siggraph'82 Conference Proceedings*, ed. R. Daniel Bergeron, *Computer Graphics*, **16**, 3, pp. 87-98.

Procedural Page Description Languages

Brian K. Reid

Stanford University

ABSTRACT

An important goal of document preparation systems is that they be device-independent, which is to say that their output can be produced on a variety of printing devices. One way of achieving that goal is to devise a device-independent page description language, which can describe precisely the appearance of a formatted page, and to produce software that prints the required image on each variety of printer. Most attempts at device-independent page description languages have failed, resulting either in schemes that are only partially device-independent or in proclamations from researchers that device independence is a bad idea [2, 4].

A new generation of procedural page description languages promises a solution. The PostScript language, and to a lesser extent the Interpress language, offers a means of describing a printed page with an executable program; the page is printed by loading the program into the printer and running it.

1. Page Description Languages

An imaging device, such as a typesetter, laser printer, or display, must have some way of knowing what image it is being asked to show. The two traditional means of providing it with that information have been to describe the image to the imager in terms of a bitmap or character map or describe the image to the imager by means of a sequence of control commands to the imager's electronics.

The bit-map or character-map schemes are the simplest and oldest. For example a line printer is provided with a character map (in this spot put the character X; in this spot put the character Y, and so forth). A CRT screen normally has a corresponding memory buffer such that each bit on the screen is tied to one bit in memory, and the screen pixel can be made light or dark by turning the bit on or off. Mapping schemes require that the dimensions and spacing of the characters or bits be identical to what the image creator wanted, or the resulting image will be rotated or scaled, perhaps even anamorphically. For example, the pixels on the IBM Personal Computer screen are rectangular rather than square, so that an image that was specified as an evenly-spaced bitmap will appear to be vertically elongated when displayed on its screen.

Schemes to describe images via commands to the controllers that generate the image are potentially more device-independent. For example, if the image is to consist of a horizontal line, then the image description can consist of the commands to move a pen to one end of the line and then swing it to the other end of the line, without needing to know the device resolution or how many pixels must be turned on between the endpoints in order to draw the line. Examples of command-stream image description include pen plotters, daisy-wheel printers, and laser printers made by Imagen [7]. Almost all current command-stream image description languages are derivatives of the XCRIBL system done in 1972 at Carnegie-Mellon [5].

Bitmap image descriptions take an enormous amount of storage space, are not device-independent, and require the program generating the images to have access to character font information so that the proper bits can be set. Furthermore, it is extremely difficult to edit or modify a bitmap image description, as for example to change a spelling error in a formed image, or to remove a component of the image and replace it by another: bitmap image descriptions are not suitable for further processing.

By contrast, command-stream image descriptions do not always have the capability of describing every possible image. For example, if the controller has no command for rotating the page or rotating a text character, then it is impossible to describe an image that includes a rotated character. The allure of bitmap image descriptions is that they are universal; the allure of command-stream image descriptions is that they are more compact, more editable, and somewhat device-independent.

Clearly an ideal image description scheme will share the universality of bitmap descriptions with the device-independence and compactness of command-stream image descriptions.

2. Procedural Page Description Languages

A procedural page description is a program, written in some graphics pro-gramming language, that, when executed, will create the intended page im-age. The idea is attributed to Warnock and Sproull, who devised it as the basis for the Interpress page description language [3].

Command-stream page description languages would appear to be ''procedural'' and in fact the descriptions that are written in these language are definitely procedures in the ordinary meaning of the word: ''move the cursor to [12,354]. Switch to boldface. Draw a 'Q'. Move right 9 units.'' The true power of a procedural page description language, however, comes from the ability to write conditionals, to define and call functions, and to perform arbitrary computations based on the value of variables stored inside the printer. I reserve the term ''procedural page description'' for languages with these properties. The ability to redefine built-in functions is valuable but not necessary.

3. Comparing procedural and nonprocedural page descriptions

Procedural descriptions are often more compact than nonprocedural descriptions of the same image, for they can take advantage of regularities in the image. For example, consider a procedural description of a piece of graph paper or a geometric grid. It can define a procedure to draw a line, then call it repeatedly in an appropriate loop. A nonprocedural description of the same image, by comparison, must have a separate item describing each line in the grid.

Procedural descriptions allow the use of abstraction and modular construction in image assembly. One can assemble a library of procedures that draw commonly-used images, and call them inside larger diagrams. Naturally the ability to achieve modularity is not a guarantee that image representations will be modular, any more than a structured programming language like Modula-2 will guarantee that the programs written in it are well-structured.

Procedural descriptions can mimic any other page-description language, simply by programming subroutines in the procedural description language that duplicate the effect of the commands in another language.

Procedural descriptions can be device-adaptive as well as device-independent, by delaying certain decisions about the appearance of he image until the specifics of the printing device are known. For example, see Figure 1, which shows four instances of the Stanford University logo in 25-point through 50-point size.

Figure 1:   Adaptive specification: increasing detail with size

All four of these logotypes are generated from the same procedural definition; notice that the detail in the outermost ring, the detail in the trunk of the tree, and the spacing between the two innermost rings changes as a function of the physical size of the logo.

It is also worth noting that procedural descriptions can be abused more easily than nonprocedural descriptions: it is possible to write bad code in any programming language, but there is often only one workable way to describe an image in a nonprocedural description scheme. PostScript printers must be on guard for infinite loops in the pictures they are printing.

4. PostScript and Interpress

There are two extant procedural page description languages, namely the aforementioned Interpress and PostScript [1]. A brief discussion of their relative histories can be found in the preface of the PostScript reference manual; a more detailed explanation is given by Reid [1, 6].

Both PostScript and Interpress assume that the printer contains an interpreter for the executable language, and that a page is printed by executing the page description program on the printer; the image is constructed as a side-effect of the program execution.

PostScript is more interesting because a complete implementation is readily available, and because a language description is widely available. The implementation of Interpress is much more limited and is not widely available; the Interpress documentation can only be obtained by special order from Xerox [3].

Therefore I shall take examples from PostScript. PostScript can do anything Interpress can do; the reverse is not true, as Interpress has a certain number of limitations not present in PostScript [6]. In general, however, the explanations and examples to follow comment on both Interpress and PostScript.

```
while input remains do
    begin
    token := nextLexeme(input);
    lexType := lexicalType(token);
    if lexType = name then
        begin
            tokenvalue := lookup(token);
            tokentype := type(tokenvalue);
            if executable(tokentype) then
                execute(tokenvalue)
            else
                push(tokenvalue)
        end;
        else push(token)
    end
end
```

Figure 2: PostScript semantics: outline of the interpreter

5. PostScript Language Details

A PostScript image description is a sequence of lexical tokens. Those tokens can be names, numbers, delimited strings, procedure bodies, array bodies, or comments. The tokens are delimited by white-space characters, and by certain other delimiter characters when a token boundary can be determined unambiguously.

When a PostScript program is presented to a printer, it is executed. That execution takes place on a stack machine, with names stored in dictionaries,

```
%!PS-Adobe-1.0
72 72 moveto    360 576 lineto
stroke copypage
newpath
200 200 moveto    300 400 lineto
0 -200 rlineto
400 200 100 180 360 arc
400 700 lineto
40 setlinewidth 1 setlinejoin 1 setlinecap
stroke copypage
72 72 translate
360 72 sub 576 72 sub atan neg 90 add rotate
/Helvetica-Bold findfont 90 scalefont setfont
70 10 moveto (etaoinshrdlu) show
```

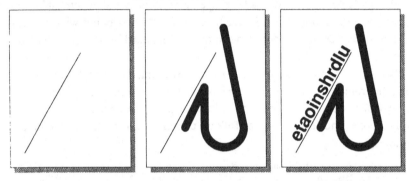

Figure 3:   PostScript code and the page images that it generates

and graphics state stored in global variables. This stack semantics makes
PostScript operators be postfix, hence the name. Figure 2 shows an approximation of the PostScript interpreter. Each page begins completely
white. Execution of imaging operators causes ink to be put in the image
buffer. Color and grayscale are achieved by changing ink color before calling
the imaging operators. All ink is opaque, even white ink, which is to say that
"image priority" is always obeyed. The imaging operators use the
interpreter's global "graphics state" variables for such information as current
position, ink color, clipping region, line-drawing parameters, halftone
parameters, font, transformation matrix, etc.

6. Some Illustrative Examples of PostScript
Further explanation best awaits some examples. Each of these figures shows
a PostScript program and a 15%-scale image of the page that it generates.
Because of space limitations in this volume, these examples are necessarily
cryptic; the reader is referred to the PostScript reference manual for further
explanation [1].

Figure 3 shows two pages and the PostScript code that generated them;
note the use of moveto, lineto, and stroke as active operators. The

```
%!PS-Adobe-1.0
newpath
100 100 moveto    400 600 lineto
100 setlinewidth 1 setlinecap stroke copypage
400 100 moveto    100 400 lineto
50 setlinewidth 0 setlinecap 0.75 setgray
stroke copypage
100 100 moveto    400 600 lineto
30 setlinewidth 1 setgray stroke
showpage
```

Figure 4:   Building up a page image from overlays of opaque inks

```
%!PS-Adobe-1.0
/xcoord  100 def    /ycoord  200 def
10 setlinewidth
/linefunc {
    newpath
    xcoord ycoord moveto
    100 100 rlineto
    stroke
    /ycoord ycoord 100 add def} def
linefunc copypage linefunc
20 setlinewidth linefunc copypage
10 setlinewidth linefunc showpage
```

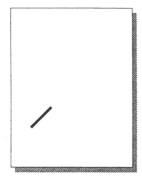  

Figure 5:   Variables, functions, and arithmetic

copypage operator is a debugging operator that prints the page buffer and then continues. The default coordinate system is in points, with the origin in the lower left corner. First it draws a thin line, using the default line thickness. Then it sets the line width to 40 points, and draws a complex curve. Finally it rotates the coordinate system so that the originally-drawn line is the *x*-axis, then displays some characters of text horizontal along that axis. Figure 4 shows the mechanism by which the page image is built up from overlays of opaque inks. It sets a very wide line width and draws a diagonal line, then sets the ink color to gray and draws a cross-line, then sets the ink color to white and re-draws the original line with a narrower width and square corners. Notice that in every case the newest "ink" covers the older inks. Figure 5 shows the use of variables, functions, and arithmetic. It defines two variables, xcoord and ycoord, then defines a function linefunc that will draw a diagonal line at that [*x,y*], then add 100 to the value of ycoord. The four calls to linefunc generate the four diagonal lines shown. Figure 6 shows the effect of coordinate system transformations on an image. It defines a function named A, which draws a 300-point letter "A" when it is called. The example calls A once, then shrinks the coordinate system anamorphically and calls it again, then rotates the coordinate system, changes to a dark gray ink, reverses the anamorphic scaling, and calls it again.

7. Capabilities of Procedural Systems

Having skimmed the basics of how a procedural page-description scheme works, let us turn our attention to some of its capabilities. The power of a procedural page-description language comes from:

- the ability to express geometric shapes in a device-independent fashion, while retaining the ability to be device-dependent if necessary,

- the ability to define and use new abstractions, and

- the ability to do "late binding" of shapes, which permits a defined operator to be used for varying effects in varying contexts.

The first of these capabilities is obvious, and was demonstrated by the Stanford-logotype example in section 3. The second of these capabilities is evident to any experienced programmer; its virtues need not be further praised. The third virtue—late binding—can best be explained with more examples. The production of the PostScript figures in this article is a good, though complex example. Consider Figure 7. It shows a small image of this page, with a drop shadow and a thin line around the outside. This figure was generated by extracting (with a text editor) one page image from the Scribe-generated PostScript file for this article, surrounding it with some redefini-

```
%!PS-Adobe-1.0
/A {
      newpath moveto
      100   300 rlineto
      100 -300 rlineto
      -50   130 rmoveto
     -100     0 rlineto
      stroke
} def

20 setlinewidth  50 50 A copypage
300 400 translate  0.5 0.25 scale
50 50 A copypage
1 2 scale -40 rotate
0.8 0.8 scale 0.5 setgray
100 -150 A
showpage
```

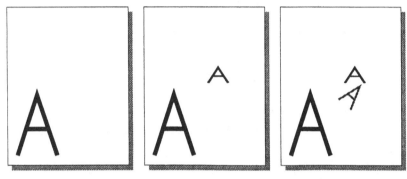

Figure 6: The effect of coordinate system transformations

tions, including it as a figure in the page, then repeating the process. Figure 8 shows those redefinitions, which change the scale factor, produce a clipping region exactly equal to the scaled page image, put a drop shadow and a frame outside that clipping region, and redefine operators that might interfere.

Figure 7: Example of late binding of PostScript code

```
%!PS-Adobe-1.0
0.15 dup scale
/mydict 100 dict def    /inch {72 mul} def
/pagepath {
    newpath
    0 0 moveto 8.5 inch 0 lineto
    8.5 inch 11 inch lineto
    0 11 inch lineto
    closepath
} def
mydict begin
    /showpage {} def
    /nextpage {grestore 9.6 72 mul 0 translate
                initclip initpage} def
    /initpage {
      gsave 0.3 inch -0.35 inch translate
      pagepath 0.8 setgray fill grestore
      pagepath gsave 1 setgray fill grestore
      0 setgray 0 setlinewidth stroke
      pagepath clip newpath gsave
    } def
    initpage
    % ---
    The PostScript page image text goes here
end
```

Figure 8: PostScript definitions for page-image figures

This example, though fanciful, demonstrates the flexibility of the procedural scheme.

The physical nesting of the diagrams is made possible by the recursive nature of the PostScript execution environment. The ability to redefine a page image to be a figure within itself comes from the ability to specify the page image in terms of late-bound names, *i.e.* as operators whose definitions can be changed. In this PostScript example, the late binding is achieved by redefining the built-in operators, though the same effect can be had, with a certain amount of discipline on the part of the user, by specifying every page in terms of user-defined functions that merely call the corresponding system function, then accomplishing the late binding by redefining those outermost functions.

This same technique can be used to advantage in many ways. A PostScript file can be wrapped in a set of definitions that will cause it to print as 2 pages per page, or as 4 pages per page, or with decorated borders, or in white letters on a black background, or with a frame for overhead projector slides. As with any other programmable system, it is limited more by imagination than by technology.

Colophon

This document was formatted with Scribe, which produced a PostScript file. That PostScript file was then appended to a PostScript header that specified a scale factor of 1.5; the resulting document was printed on an Apple LaserWriter, which has a resolution of 300 points to the inch (11.8 lines per millimeter). It was then reduced photographically by the printer in making plates, giving an effective resolution of 450 points to the inch.

References

[1] Adobe Systems, Inc., *PostScript Language Reference Manual*, Addison-Wesley, Reading, Massachusetts, 1985.

[2] Earnest, Les, "Would you want your daughter to be device-independent?", ARPANET Laser-lovers distribution, March 1985.

[3] Xerox Corporation, *Interpress Electronic Printing Standard*, Stamford, Connecticut 06904, 1984, Document number XSIS 04804

[4] Newman, William, "Press: A flexible file format for the representation of printed images", in *Actes des Journees sur la Manipulation de Documents*, Rennes, France, 5 May 1983..

[5] R. Reddy, B. Broadley, L. Erman, R. Johnson, J. Newcomer, G. Robertson, and J. Wright, "XCRIBL, a hardcopy scan line graphics system for document generation", Tech. report, Department of Computer Science, Carnegie-Mellon University, October 1972.

[6] Reid, Brian K., "PostScript and Interpress: a comparison", ARPANET Laser-lovers distribution, March 1, 1985..

[7] Ryland, Chris, Imagen Corporation, *Imprint System Manual*, 2660 Marine Way, Mountain View California 94304 USA, 1983.

A Strategy for Compressed Storage and Retrieval of Documents

P. Goyal and V. Kotamarti
Concordia University, Montreal.

Abstract
Document storage and retrieval systems should possess fast
string search capabilities. The access paths needed to
reduce the search times require substantial amounts of
storage in addition to the very large storage requirements
for the documents themselves. In this paper we investigate
a technique that supports access paths on compressed documents, so that the total storage requirements for the
access paths and the compressed documents are less than
that for the original documents.

1. Introduction

Advances in hardware technology are unlikely to keep pace with the
increasing growth of on-line document storage. In an environment
where the trend is towards local and wide area networks (there is the
promise of an interconnected society around the corner), a large
number of documents would be transmitted between nodes. Document
storage, their communication along network paths and between peripherals and processors requires, for the provision of a satisfactory
service at reasonable cost, that the documents be held more compactly
than at present. Natural language being highly redundant a suitable
encoding scheme could be utilized with any resultant compression
reducing both storage and communication cost. In an online environment
the compression and decompression schemes must not involve excessive
overheads in either time or space; since the documents would need to
be compressed only once for storage while decompressed (or retrieved)
more often, it is possible to tolerate higher levels of overhead
during the compression stage.

Document retrieval requires fast string search capabilities, and it
is usual to provide additional access paths to reduce the search
times   e.g. by providing inverted lists on words. In [Goyal83] a
scheme was proposed that made use of inverted indexes associated with
compressed documents.

In this paper we first present a survey of some compression techniques and then describe the implementation of techniques that support
both document compression and fast string search.   Some preliminary
results are also presented.

2. Document Compression
The majority of text compression techniques fall into two classes.

(i) Inverted Files : In this approach text is replaced with a string of pointers to a dictionary. Each pointer represents the segment of the text to which it points in the dictionary and is shorter than the text segment. In the partially inverted file approach only some of the text segments are replaced by pointers, and the rest of the segments remain in unencoded form. Various studies using a partially inverted file [Mayne75], equifrequent text fragments [Heaps70, Schuegraf73], phrases [Wagner73], and a combination of inverted file and dictionary [Weiss78], report compression results in the range of 25 - 50 per cent.

(ii) Variable Length Encoding : This approach is based on the minimum redundancy principle and assigns to text fragments codes whose lengths are inversely proportional to their frequency of occurrence in the text [Fano61, Huffman52]. In natural language text, the characters do not occur independently of each other, and thus strings of characters need to be chosen as symbols and a dictionary constructed to effect the coding transformation. The problem of dictionary construction, which requires some kind of statistical analysis of the data, and its effects on compression have been extensively discussed in the literature [Clare72, Cooper82, Heaps72, McCarthy73, Rubin76, Schuegraf73, Schwartz63, White67].
When constructing a dictionary a decision on the use of fixed or variable length elements, and fixed or variable length codes must be made.

(1) Fixed Length Elements, Variable Length Codes.
The best known examples of this class are the Morse and Huffman codes. Huffman codes, widely used for digital data, have the advantage that they produce a code of minimum length. As most computers work with a fixed length word, the processing of variable length bit strings generated by Huffman's method results in complicated algorithms for code manipulation.

(2) Fixed Length Elements, Fixed Length Codes.
This is a simple and common coding scheme. In computers, where the characters are mapped into fixed length binary codes, a theoretical saving of 25% would result by changing from a 8 bit to a 6 bit character representation.

(3) Variable Length Elements, Variable Length Codes.
Complete words or some convenient set of variable length strings, with known a priori probability distributions, may be selected as the elements [Heaps70, Schwartz63]. The probabilities can be found by statistical analysis, and some of these probability distributions have been shown to be stable over a period of years [Lynch73]. Maximum compression results from the use of Huffman codes, with their accompanying problem of having to process variable length bit strings.

(4) Variable Length Elements, Fixed Length Codes.
Variable length elements are stored in a table with the codes representing   the   position   of   the   associated   element   in   the   table
[Schuegraf76].   Decoding is, thus, just a simple table look up, while
compression, in common with all variable length schemes, is inefficient. N-gram encoding, is one such technique, which attempts to
convert the normal hyperbolic distribution of single letters to an
equiprobable   distribution by including frequently occurring strings
of characters in the symbol set. Equiprobability increases entropy
(or   decreases   redundancy) and it is possible to assign fixed length
codes to these equiprobable symbols such that the coding efficiency
is high [Barton73, Brack78, Clare72, Cooper80, Cooper82, Fokker74,
Goyal81, Lynch77, Lynch73].

3. Document Retrieval

Searching for a string pattern over a document text is performed not
only during edits,   but also during full- or partial document retrieval. Algorithms for speeding searches strive to reduce the number of
times a character of the text has to be examined in searching for a
string   [Boyer77].   It is also possible to devise codes (superimposed
codes or text signatures [Christodoulakis84, Faloutsos84, Harrison71,
Tharp82], and concatenation of word signatures [Tsichritzis83]) that
could be used to eliminate portions of text from such a search operation and thus reduce the number of characters that have to be examined. Some of the well known natural language databases, e.g. LEXIS,
the legal database, and STAIRS, IBM's storage and retrieval utility,
however, use inversion at the word level to provide fast access and
retrieval;   these   inverted   indexes add to the storage cost of the
documents. All of these schemes are only applicable to non-compressed
documents. Special purpose processors can also be used for fast text
retrieval [Haskin81].

[Goyal83] proposed a scheme using inverted lists on compressed
partitions of the database; the inversion is on the text fragments
(n-grams) that are used to encode the documents for compression. A
document in the database consists of compressed pages and an associated inverted index for the page.   To further save on storage, at
the expense of retrieval time, only the inverted index for each page
may be kept; the compressed pages are reconstructible from the index
entries by a simple sort operation.   The search string is similarly
mapped onto a sequence of symbols, $S = s_1 s_2 ... s_m$, from the n-gram
symbol set.   The symbols in S are used to search the inverted
indexes. This scheme may be used in conjunction with signature
schemes   [Christodoulakis84,   Faloutsos84,   Harrison71,   Tharp82,
Tsichritzis83] for further improvement in retrieval performance, with
the signatures being used to select a subset of the index pages for
searching;   compared with the original database there is little or no
storage overhead - a major concern in large document databases.

4. String Encoding and Search Technique

The search string encoding technique (Appendix A) generates all the
possible n-gram symbol sequences and also caters for unknown sequences at either or both ends of the search string. The search for
strings of type $'s_j * s_k'$, where '*' represents an unknown string

sequence of some specified length, is handled by searching for s_j and s_k such that s_k follows s_j in the document within the specified distance; s_j and s_k may themselves have unknown sequences at their front- and back-ends respectively. Distinctive symbols or commands can be used in the user interface to restrict the handling of unknown sequences to either or neither of the ends.

The string encoding technique generates a set of symbol sequences, $T = \{S_1, S_2, .., S_k, .., S_z\}$ where each S_k is a sequence of n-gram symbols, $S_k = s_1 s_2 ... s_m$.

The string search algorithm (Appendix B) identifies the string occurrence position within those pages of text in which at least one of the S_k's occur, $S_k \varepsilon T$. The sequence of codes for each S_k is searched for in the inverted index for the page, and if there is a mismatch then the search operation for that S_k is aborted and that for the subsequent code sequence S_{k+1} is initiated. If there is a match, the decompression of the complete page, the whole document or just the surrounding text (some prespecified length before and after) may then be performed.

5. Results

The symbol set given in [Cooper82] was modified, by removing some of the special characters, for use in this study; the special characters were instead coded using an escape sequence allowing for some extra n-grams to be included in the symbol set at the expense of a longer code for the special characters. The symbol set used in this study is given in Appendix C.

The compression and search schemes have so far been tested on the following four documents :

A Technical Report (from the Dept. of Computer Science)
A Pascal Program
A general, weekly news magazine article
A Computer Manual

and Table 1 gives the compression results; compression factor is defined as the compressed file size expressed as a percentage of the original file size.

Text File	File Sizes (in Bytes)		Compression factor
	Original	Compressed	
Technical report	256424	74337	28.99%
Pascal program	60315	40938	67.87%
Magazine article	11855	4115	34.71%
Computer manual	370144	173561	46.89%

Table 1. Compression results

String index		1	2	3	4	5	6	7	8
Number of code patterns		6	6	8	8	11	193	27	17
Text File									
Technical Report	T	338403	328951	473684	465885	62399	142469	59247	50337
	F	y	y	y	y	y	y	y	y
Pascal Program	T	602134	590909	889246	892410	1104724	1112170	2076769	66676
	F	n	n	n	n	n	n	n	n
Magazine Article	T	81019	81418	114168	127032	127032	129799	259353	68715
	F	n	n	n	n	n	n	n	y
Computer Manual	T	3120337	3107435	4440954	4404354	259407	328345	464236	65199
	F	n	n	n	n	y	y	y	y

T: Time taken for the string search in micro-seconds
F: Found (y/n)

Table 2.   String Search Characteristics over Partitioned Compressed Files.   The number of code patterns indicates the complexity of search.   Each code pattern is a sequence of symbols; the number of symbols depends upon the length of the search string and its makeup.   The actual search time depends upon the number of index pages scanned; these times should only be used for comparison as no optimization was carried out.

The   following strings were used in the search over   the   different compressed files :

STRING	STRING INDEX
purpose of the testing	1
purpose of the test	2
pose of the testing	3
pose of the test	4
dictionary	5
diction	6
tionary	7
ictio	8

The results from the search procedure (Table 2) indicate that trunca- tion of the search string may considerably increase the number of code patterns to be searched. Our analysis shows that most of these combinations,   within the S_k's (of T), are due to the many different codes generated for the beginnings and ends of the search string, and that,   except for both ended truncation of words (like 'diction'),   a large number of code sequences in the different S_k's are common.   An efficient algorithm would first search for these common 'core' seque- nces and thus further optimize search times.

6. Conclusions
In this paper we have demonstrated the feasibility of searching over compressed databases.   The major advantage of the scheme is that the increased search speeds require little or no storage overheads;   even faster string searches are possible if the number of indexes to be searched are reduced by the use of superimposed coding or text signa- ture schemes.

Acknowledgements
This research has been supported by a grant from NSERC, Canada.

References
[1] Barton, I.J., Lynch, M.F., Petrie, H. & Snell, M.J. (1973). Variable Length Character String Analysis of Three Data Bases, and Their Application to File Compression. In Proc. of the First Informatics Conf., pp. 154-162. London, Aslib.
[2] Boyer, R.S. & Moore, J.S. (1977). A Fast String Searching Algo- rithm, Comm. of the ACM, **20**, 10, 762-772.
[3] Brack, E.V., Cooper, D. & Lynch, M.F. (1978). The Stability of Symbol Sets Produced by Variety Generation from Bibliographic Data, Program, **12**, 2, 64-67.
[4] Christodoulakis, S. & Faloutsos, C. (1984). Design Considerations for a Message File Server, IEEE Trans. on Soft. Engg., **SE-10**, 2, 201-210.
[5] Clare, A.C., Cook, E.M. & Lynch, M.F. (1972). The Identification of Variable Length,Equifrequent Character Strings in a Natural Language Data Base, Computer J., **15**, 3, 259-262.
[6] Cooper, D., Emly, M.A., Lynch, M.F. & Yeates, A.R. (1980). Compression of Continuous Prose Texts using Variety Generation, J. Amer. Soc. for Inform. Sc., **31**, 201-207.(1980).

[7] Cooper, D. & Lynch, M.F. (1982). Text Compression Using Variable to Fixed Length Encodings, J. Amer. Soc. for Inform. Sc., **33**, 18-31.

[8] Faloutsos, C. & Christodoulakis, S. (1984). Signature Files : An Access Method for Documents and Its Analytical Performance Evaluation, ACM Trans. on Office Inf. Systems, **2**, 4, 267-288.

[9] Fano, R.M. (1961). Transmission of Information, Cambridge: MIT Press.

[10] Fokker, D.W. & Lynch, M.F. (1974). Application of the Variety Generator Approach in Searches of Personal Names in Bibliographic Data Bases. I., J. Library Autom.,**7**, 105-118.

[11] Goyal, P. (1983). Coding Methods for Text String Search on Compressed Databases, Information systems, **8**, 3, 231-233.

[12] Goyal, P. (1981). Computer Coding Processes to Aid Bibliographic Record Control and Storage, Ph.D. Thesis, University of Bradford.

[13] Harrison. M.C. (1971). Implementation of the substring test by Hashing, Commun. of the ACM, **14**, 777-779.

[14] Haskin, R.L. (1981). Special Purpose Processors for Text Retrieval, Database Engineering (IEEE), **4**, 1.

[15] Heaps, H.S. (1972). Storage Analysis of Compression Coding for Document Data Bases, INFOR, **10**, 1, 47-61.

[16] Heaps, H.S. & Thiel, L.H. (1970). Optimum Procedures for Economic Information Storage and Retrieval, Information Storage and Retrieval, **6**, 137-153.

[17] Huffman, D.A. (1952). A Method for the Construction of Minimum Redundancy Codes, Proc. IRE, **40**, 1098-1101.

[18] Lynch, M.F. (1977). Variety Generation - A Reinterpretation of Shannons Mathematical theory of Information and its Implication for Information Storage, J. Amer. Soc. for Inform. Sc., **28**, 19-25.

[19] Lynch, M.F., Petrie, J.H. & Snell, M.J. (1973). Analysis of the Microstructure of Titles in INSPEC Data Base, Information Storage and Retrieval, **9**, 331-337.

[20] Mayne, A. & James, E.B. (1975). Information Compression by Factorising Common Strings, Computer J., **18**, 157-160.

[21] McCarthy, J.P. (1973). Automatic File Compression, Proc. of Intl. Computing Symp., North Holland Publ. Co., 511-516.

[22] Rabitti, F. & Zizka, J. (1984). Evaluation of Access Methods to Text Documents in Office Systems, Proc. of the Third BCS and ACM Symp. in Information Storage and Retrieval, Cambridge, July 1984, 21-40.

[23] Rubin, F. (1976). Experiments in Text File Compression, Comm. of the ACM, **19**, 11, 617-623.

[24] Schuegraf, E,J. (1976). A Survey of Data Compression Methods for Non-Numeric Records, Canadian J. of Inform. Sc., **2**, 1, 93-105.

[25] Schuegraf, E.J. & Heaps, H.S. (1973). Selection of Equifrequent Word Fragments for Information Retrieval, Information Storage and Retrieval, **9**, 697-711.

[26] Schwartz, E.S. (1963). A Dictionary for Minimum Redundancy Encoding, J. ACM, **10**, 413-439.

[27] Tharp, A.L. & Tai, K.C. (1982). The Practicality of Text Signatures for Accelerating String Searching, Software Practice & Experience, **12**, 1, 35-44.

[28] Tsichritzis, D. & Christodoulakis, S. (1983). Message Files, ACM Trans. on Office Inform. Systems, **1**, 1, 88-98.

[29] Wagner, R.A. (1973). Common Phrases and Minimum Text Storage, Comm. of the ACM, **16**, 148-153.

[30] Weiss, S.F. & Vernor III, R.L. (1978). A Word Based Compression technique for Text Files, J. of Libr. Autom., **11**, 2, 97-105.

[31] White, H.E. (1967). Printed English Compression by Dictionary Encoding, Proc. IEEE, **3**, 390-396.

Appendix A

Algorithm STRINGCODE

1. For the search string, $A = a_1 a_2 ... a_x$, generate all possible n-gram sequences. Let A' be the substring $a_1 ... a_v$ of A where $1 < v \leq x$, and A'' be the substring $a_w ... a_x$ of A where $1 \leq w < x$.

2. Generate all possible n-grams from string ends :

   (a) From beginning of search string. Identify all n-grams having the substring A' in their last characters. If a character from the search string is not the last character of a n-gram in the symbol set, no more n-grams which are also in the symbol set can be generated.

   (b) From the End of the search string. Identify all n-grams having the substring A'' in their starting positions.

Appendix B

Algorithm STRINGSEARCH.

1. Encode the search string (e.g. using Algorithm STRINGCODE). Let there be 'm' code sequences, $T = \{S_1, .., S_m\}$.

2. Read a compressed page. If no more pages return with 'string not found' message.

3. For i = 1 to m do
   (a) Search for the code sequence S_i in the Inverted Index.

   (b) If the sequence is found return with page number and starting position of string in the compressed page.

4. Goto 2.

Appendix C

Fragment Dictionary

Current Dictionary Size is 256
All the special characters like punctuation symbols and digits are stored in separate dictionary. A shift character "@" is preceded for all the character in this separate dictionary.

	0	1	2	3	4	5	6	7	8	9
0	( )	(A)	(AN)	(AND)	(B)	(C)	(CH)	(CO)	(D)	(DE)
1	(E)	(F)	(FO)	(G)	(H)	(I)	(IN)	(IN)	(L)	(M)
2	(MA)	(N)	(O)	(OF)	(OF)	(P)	(PO)	(PR)	(R)	(RE)
3	(S)	(SE)	(ST)	(T)	(TH)	(TO)	(W)	(@)	(°)	(A)
4	(A)	(AC)	(AD)	(AG)	(AI)	(AL)	(AM)	(AN)	(AN)	(AND)
5	(AND)	(AR)	(AS)	(AT)	(ATI)	(B)	(BE)	(BO)	(BR)	(C)
6	(C)	(CA)	(CE)	(CH)	(CI)	(CO)	(COM)	(CON)	(CT)	(D)
7	(D)	(D T)	(DE)	(DI)	(DU)	(E)	(E)	(E A)	(E C)	(E 0)
8	(E P)	(E S)	(E T)	(EA)	(EC)	(ED)	(ED)	(EE)	(EL)	(EM)
9	(EN)	(ENG)	(ENT)	(ENT)	(ER)	(ER)	(ERN)	(ERS)	(ES)	(ES)
10	(ET)	(F)	(F)	(F T)	(FI)	(FO)	(G)	(G)	(GE)	(GR)
11	(H)	(H)	(HA)	(HE)	(HE)	(HI)	(HO)	(I)	(IA)	(IC)
12	(IC)	(ICA)	(ID)	(IE)	(IL)	(IN)	(IN)	(ING)	(IO)	(IR)
13	(IS)	(IST)	(IT)	(J)	(K)	(K)	(L)	(L)	(LA)	(LAN)
14	(LE)	(LI)	(LL)	(LO)	(LY)	(M)	(M)	(MA)	(ME)	(MEN)
15	(MI)	(MO)	(MP)	(N)	(N)	(N A)	(N T)	(NA)	(NAL)	(NC)
16	(ND)	(ND T)	(NE)	(NG)	(NG)	(NI)	(NO)	(NS)	(NS)	(NT)
17	(NT)	(O)	(O)	(OC)	(OD)	(OF)	(OG)	(OL)	(OM)	(ON)
18	(ON)	(OO)	(OP)	(OR)	(OR)	(ORT)	(OT)	(OU)	(P)	(PA)
19	(PE)	(PH)	(PL)	(PO)	(PR)	(PRO)	(Q)	(R)	(R)	(RA)
20	(RD)	(RE)	(RI)	(RN)	(RO)	(RS)	(RT)	(RU)	(RY)	(S)
21	(S)	(S A)	(S I)	(S 0)	(SC)	(SE)	(SH)	(SI)	(SO)	(SP)
22	(SS)	(ST)	(SU)	(T)	(T)	(TA)	(TE)	(TER)	(TH)	(TH)
23	(THE)	(THE)	(TI)	(TIO)	(TO)	(TO)	(TR)	(TRA)	(TS)	(TU)
24	(U)	(UC)	(UN)	(UR)	(US)	(UT)	(V)	(VR)	(VI)	(W)
25	(WE)	(X)	(Y)	(Y)	(Y 0)	(Z)				

CONCEPT BROWSER:
a System for Interactive Creation
of Dynamic Documentation

U. Corda

TLD System LTD. Torrance, California.

G. Facchetti

Ing. C. Olivetti & C. S.p.A. Ivrea, Italy.

ABSTRACT

In this paper, a system for interactive creation and browsing of dynamic documents is described. The Concept Browser allows the user to create a semantic network of interrelated concepts and interactively navigate through the network. Outlines and printed documents can be automatically generated from the network of concepts. The Concept Browser has been designed and implemented in a Smalltalk programming environment. An interactive, window-based user interface is provided that allows the user to browse through and modify the network of concepts.

Possible applications for the Concept Browser are in the areas of on line documentation, tutorial systems, document preparation systems and electronic books.

1. Introduction

The traditional method of storing information in a printed, linear form as it is done with conventional books has been demonstrated to be inadequate both to represent the complexity of information and to offer quick and flexible access to it [8].

The personal computer appears to be the ideal tool to satisfy these requirements, but a simple computer-based transcription of traditional books is not the best way of taking advantage of the new functionalities offered by computers.

The purpose of this article is to describe one experiment in the design of a documentation system that can take advantage of the flexible data structures and advanced user interface provided by a Smalltalk programming environment.

A semantic network was chosen as the best way of representing the complexity of information ([4],[6]) instead of a more traditional tree structure [5].

The way semantic networks are used in the Concept Browser is different from the one adopted by Artificial Intelligence systems [1]. The purpose of the semantic networks of the Concept Browser is to amplify the user intelligence, not to substitute computer intelligence for human intelligence [7]. Therefore, processing of the semantic network is done by the user himself. The main role played by the computer is in providing a user-friendly, interactive interface that can be easily learnt and used.

2. The user interface

Since the system has been implemented in a Smalltalk ([2],[3]) programming environment, the general ideas about the user interface and the basic tools used to implement it are directly derived from the Smalltalk user interface itself.

The Concept Browser user interface consists of two different types of browsers (a browser is a multi-window structure intended to give users access to different pieces of interrelated information).

In the following description we will refer to fig. 1, where a typical screen the Concept Browser presents to its users is shown. We refer to the small browser on the lower left by the name of "List Browser". It is composed of two windows. The smaller one, on the left, contains the list of all the different dynamic documents available in the system. If one entry in the list is selected, a short description of the contents of the corresponding dynamic document is displayed in the window on the right. A pop-up menu, associated to the left window, provides commands for defining new dynamic documents and for removing existing ones. The real Concept Browser is the bigger browser on the right in fig. 1. This is the main dynamic document interface that lets the user enter the concepts that constitute the document and browse through them.

Let us consider this second browser in deeper detail. The window on the top contains the name of the current concept. This is the concept that is being created or examined; it belongs to the network of concepts which constitutes the dynamic document. The text associated with this concept appears in the window just below.

The window labelled 'link types' contains the list of the different types of links that connect the current concept to other concepts in the network. Possible link types are 'related concepts', 'dependent concepts', 'parent concepts', etc. The Concept Browser provides a short list of general-purpose, predefined link types, but the user is allowed to invent and use new ones. When a link type is selected, a list of the network concepts

Current Concept
Description Window

Current Concept
Name Window

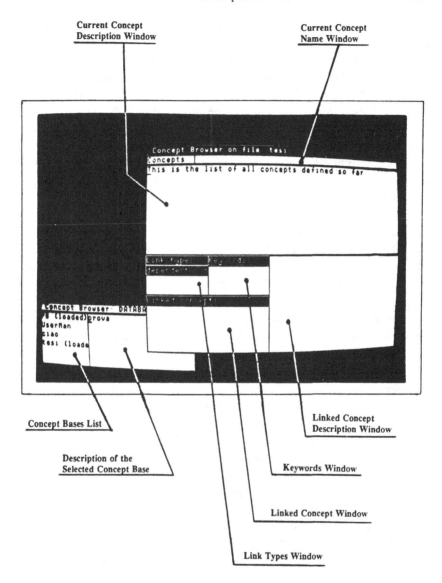

Concept Bases List

Description of the
Selected Concept Base

Linked Concept
Description Window

Keywords Window

Linked Concept Window

Link Types Window

Figure 1: A typical screen presented to a user of the Concept Browser

connected to the current concept through the selected link type is presented in the 'linked concepts' window. This way, a "topological" information regarding the current concept is obtained.

The 'keywords' window contains a list of keywords associated with the current concept. The choice of the keywords is completely left to the user. If one of these keywords is selected, the list of all the other concepts that share the same keyword appears in the 'linked concepts' window. This way, information about the "logic" connections in the network is obtained.

Finally, selecting a concept in the 'linked concepts' window causes the text associated with this concept to be displayed in the window on the lower right.

3. Creating and modifying the network of concepts

The Concept Browser user interface provides a set of interactive tools that help the user in the process of defining the concepts that the dynamic document is composed of and establishing different types of relationships between these concepts.

From this point of view, the Concept Browser can be seen as a generalised type of editor that is capable of handling a semantic network of concepts.

3.1. How to create a new concept

New concepts can be inserted in the network in two different ways.

The name of the concept may be entered in the top window and then a description of it may follow in the window below.

A new concept can also be created using the 'add' command that appears in a pop up menu associated with the 'linked concepts' window. A prompter (a pop up window with a prompt message and a subwindow to hold the reply text) asks the name of the concept. The new concept is created and linked to the top window concept through a link of the type currently selected in the 'link types' window. A description of the new concept may then be entered in the 'selected linked concept description' window.

Once a concept has been created, its name can be changed selecting a menu command provided by the top window.

Also, the concept description can be edited using the window editor inherited from the Smalltalk environment. The modified text is then automatically reformatted within the window where it is displayed.

3.2. How to add and remove links

A new link between two concepts can be added at any time. In order to do that the user must set the current concept (the concept defined in the top window) to be the concept that the link comes from (links have a direction associated with them), and select in the 'link types' window the link type that is to be assigned to the new link. Then the 'add' command should be activated from the pop-up menu appearing in the 'linked concepts' window. A prompter is displayed that asks the name of the second concept. After this information has been provided, the new link is built and the second concept appears in the list of concepts linked to the current concept. Now, two situations are possible: either the second concept already exists, and in this case only a new link is created, or the concept just introduced is a new one, and then also a new node is added to the semantic network. In the latter case the user may, as usual, select this new concept and write its description into one of the concept-description windows. All this has the aim to guarantee the maximum flexibility to the Concept Browser.

For some link types that are supposed to be frequently used, a second link is automatically created in the opposite direction (for instance, if the link type is 'dependent concepts', a link of type 'parent concepts' is also created that links the second concept to the first one). The user is asked to confirm the creation of this second link.

Existing links can also be removed in a manner similar to creating a new link. Instead of selecting 'add', the 'remove' command from the pop up menu in the 'linked concepts' window is selected. Once the link is removed, the second concept is also removed from the list of concepts linked to the current concept (however, the second concept may remain linked to the current one by link types different from the selected one).

3.3. Defining keywords

A list of keywords can be associated with any concept. The concept must be selected as the current one. Then the 'add' command must be activated using the pop-up menu defined for the 'keywords' window. The user is prompted for the new keyword name. Following the user response, the 'keywords' window is redisplayed containing the newly added keyword.

An existing keyword can also be removed from a concept using the 'remove' entry of the pop up menu.

3.4. Additional network modification tools

To help with some complex network operations such as splitting or joining two concepts, a command associated with the top window menu creates a new window that contains a list of all the links entering the current concept together with the concept each link comes from.

This information, together with the list of the outward links provided by the 'linked concepts' window, gives a complete representation of the environment that exists around the current concept. The user can then decide whether these links are to be removed or instead redirected towards different concepts.

4. Navigating through the network of concepts

The network structure we have chosen for the organization of information in the Concept Browser has the advantage of being a powerful and flexible tool. On the other hand, it lacks the hierarchical structure that makes tree or linear structures (e.g., books) easily decomposable and easy to "order" (in the sense that it is immediate to understand "what" must be read before "what"). In a data structure as generalised as a network can be, there is no logically predefined path the user has to follow in order to extract the information he is interested in (think of the opposite case, the purely linear approach provided by a traditional book).

Browsing in a network is more like exploring an unknown geographical region, trying to follow the most promising routes. Concept names and descriptions, links and keywords provide the indications the user can consult during his navigation. As a matter of fact, the user who enters a network of concepts for the first time, possibly searching for information regarding an unknown argument, may have great difficulty in finding a reasonable and "propedeutical" path.

The next sections illustrate the various tools the Concept Browser furnishes to let experts as well as unskilled users to do their best with it.

4.1. How to find an entry point

Finding an initial concept from which to begin browsing might be a non-trivial task, unless the user already knows the name of the concept he is interested in (in this case, typing the name of the concept in the top window is enough to establish this concept as the starting point).

To solve this information-retrieval problem, different strategies can be adopted, each one supported by a particular Concept Browser feature.

In the following, we shall provide some examples, considering one of the first concept bases we built using the Concept Browser: the set of rules of the popular game "Monopoly". In that base we created concepts named "introduction", "number of players", "prison", "bank tasks" and so on, connected by links of type "dependent concepts", "preceding knowedge", "hints to beginners"

Returning to the general information-retrieval problem, let us say that the user might try to look for a concept whose name is similar to the one he has in mind. To do this, the special concept called 'Concepts' can be set as the current concept in the top window. Selecting the link type 'dependent concepts', an alphabetically sorted list of all the concepts defined in the network appears in the 'linked concepts' window. The user can then look at this list for any name that might give him a hint, or he can select the 'search' command, provided by the pop up menu, that performs a search through the list looking for a specified string or substring (this method is similar to looking at the table of contents of a book).

So, the user interested in Monopoly may look at the list of "chapters" of the rules, and choose the one which seems to give the answers he is searching for. Otherwise, if he needs general information about, say, the bank, he can "search" all the concepts whose name contains the string "bank".

A different approach is to use a keyword to identify one or more concepts which share that keyword. In a way similar to the one described before, selecting the special concept 'Concepts' causes the list of all the keywords defined in the network to be displayed in the 'keywords' window. Again, the 'search' command can be used to find an entire keyword or a keyword substring. Once a good keyword is identified, a list of all the concepts that declare this keyword can be displayed in the 'linked concepts' window (this approach is similar to looking at the subject index of a book).

In our example, the keyword "dices" links (in a logical sense) the concepts "how to begin", "prison" and "conducting the game".

However, if also this method fails, a full text search can be requested on all the concept texts contained in the network. This way, a group of concepts is found that might have something to do with the subject the user is interested in. This is the most general inquiry method, used by somebody who knows exactly what he wants, but has little or no knowledge about the network.

4.2. *Following the links*

Given a certain concept as the current one (the one defined in the top window), the user can explore the network area that is close to it. To do so, all the user has to do is to follow the links. For instance, selecting the link type 'related concepts' gives a list of all the concepts that are linked to the current concept through that type of link and are therefore likely to provide information closely related to the current concept. Selecting the link type 'dependent concepts' returns a list of concepts that are intended to give more details about the subject the current concept talks about. And so on, with any other link type the user has defined.

This way, our playful user, positioned on the concept "introduction to the game", selecting the link type "dependent concepts" will see the list "number of players", "dowry" and "game preparation" to appear in the linked concepts window. These concepts are a refinement of the arguments considered in the current concept.

Once this list of concepts logically related to the current one is identified, the description of one particular concept in the list can be visualised in the 'selected linked concept description' window. If any of these concepts looks interesting enough to deserve further examination, it can be moved to the top window and made the current concept (using the 'browse' command from the pop up menu of the 'linked concepts' window). All the windows of the Concept Browser are updated to reflect the status of the new current concept. This action corresponds to a move in the network of concepts.

At this point, the entire process can be repeated with the new current concept.

4.3. Keywords as special link types
For any concept defined in the top window (the current concept), the 'keywords' window provides a list of the keywords associated with this concept. If one of these keywords is selected, a list of all the concepts that share the same keyword is displayed in the 'linked concepts' window.

Keywords can then be thought of as implicit links connecting concepts together and therefore they can be used to move around through the network of concepts.

Once a list of concepts has been derived in the 'linked concepts' window via a keyword selection, the mechanism to make any of these concepts the current one is identical to the one used with explicit links.

4.4. Moving back and forth along a path
The user can decide that the path he is following is not fruitful and that he wants to back up to some concept he has already examined before. Or he just wants to look again at some previously selected concept before continuing browsing new concepts. This problem convinced us to introduce one of the features we consider most interesting of the Concept

Browser: the path walked by the user is memorised and, in case, shown in a menu-like form, to allow the repositioning on already visited nodes.

The main menu commands 'next', 'previous' and 'show path' help the user with this kind of requests. 'previous' and 'next' allow the user to move back and forth along the path already followed. 'show path' displays a list of the concepts in the path along with the link type or keyword that determined each single step; selecting an item in the list makes this concept the current one.

Moreover (and here is the idea), the concept base creator, or a particularly expert reader, can build one or more useful (in some sense) paths, give them a name (evoking the kind of knowledge the path itself may furnish), and store them for subsequent use. Naive users will then find a guide, to the exploration of the base, surely superior to the one provided by traditional tools like tables of contents and subject indexes.

In our Monopoly concept base, for example, two paths have been memorised. The first, called "general description", is an introductory overview of the game. The second, called "the Monopoly hacker", walks through concepts giving precious hints about how to propose other players ways to become bankrupt without making them aware of it.

4.5. Opening multiple browsers on the same dynamic document
The Concept Browser allows the user to open more than one browser on the same dynamic document, offering in this way simultaneous views on different parts of the document. With this mechanism the reader can pursue several lines of thought or view a given object at several levels of detail.

5. Creating a traditional document
The Concept Browser can also be used to create more traditional types of documents, that is documents that are mainly used in printed form (articles, books, etc.).

Even though this kind of document only requires a linear browsing through the static printed representation, the use of the Concept Browser encourages a modular approach to the document preparation phase. The final document is obtained through the composition of self consistent single modules that represent chapters or sections. In this way better control can be reached over the process of 'debugging' the single pieces and of defining the overall organization of the entire document.

5.1. Defining chapters and sections
Due to the restricted type of browsing required by a traditional document,

a full network structure is not necessary to link concepts (chapters, sections, etc.) together: a tree will do. The general mechanisms used to create the network are still valid. Only, the link types used must be chosen in such a way that a parent-child relationship is established between concepts (for example, the link type 'dependent concepts' might be used).

This way, a concept defining a document chapter may be created and then linked through a 'dependent concepts' link to a series of concepts representing sections of that chapter. These dependent concepts can be ordered in a particular sequence chosen by the user; this same sequence will be used when linearizing the tree into a printed document.

Even though a static kind of document is being created, the process of preparing the document can still be highly dynamic. A framework of chapters and sections can be defined before text has been entered for them (top down approach). This framework can easily be restructured during document composition. Also, parts of the document can be written before knowing exactly where they are going to be placed in the document; adding a new link will suffice to insert the new part in a specific position (bottom up approach).

All these functionalities make the Concept Browser a particularly flexible tool, allowing the user to organise the construction of the concept base in the way he feels better.

To give the user an idea of what the document will look like in its printed form, the 'outline' command is provided that opens a new window containing the document outline, with chapters and sections properly indented and numbered.

5.2. Producing a printed document

Once the document is complete, a printed representation of the document itself can be produced using the 'print doc' command in the top window pop up menu.

This utility does a walk of the tree that represents the document, starting from the current node (usually the top node) and going down the hierarchy. Each concept name appears as a chapter or section name, followed by the associated text and then by the sequence of concepts directly dependent on that concept (it is a depth first tree walk).

By default the link type 'dependent concepts' is used to determine the tree structure, but the user can specify other types of links. This way, a tree structure can also be extracted from a dynamic document organised as a more general network structure. Also, several different printed documents can be obtained from the same dynamic document starting from different nodes and following different links (generality and flexibility of use are again the inspirers of these features).

5.3. *Making a dynamic document out of a traditional one*

The tree representing a traditional document can always be augmented with non-hierarchical link types and transformed into a dynamic document. As an example, consider this article, which has been prepared using the Concept Browser. The same information it contains could be used to provide online help to the user of the Concept Browser itself. If we now add new link types like 'related concepts' and a series of appropriate keywords to the article, we get a dynamic document to which browsing strategies other than the purely linear one suggested by the printed form can be applied (for instance, looking only at the concepts that deal with a specific subject like the user interface).

6. Additional applications

Due to the characteristics of dynamic browsing and user-friendly, interactive interface, the Concept Browser can be used to implement an electronic book or to provide on-line documentation.

As we have seen in previous sections, since a browsing path can be saved and then "played back" again, the user can create a particular path which can be used later as a tutorial about a subject contained in the dynamic document. The student would only have to load the path and follow it using the commands 'next', 'previous' and 'show path'.

Finally, the Concept Browser could also be used to create and edit generic semantic networks: this way, its application fields become all fields where semantic networks are or may be used.

7. Implementation

Four new Smalltalk classes have been defined to implement the Concept Browser.

The class 'Concept' generates the concepts of the network, with instance variables for the concept name, concept text, list of keywords and list of links (the concept text is actually a pointer to a location within a text file).

The class 'ConceptLink' generates instances that group together links of the same type originating from one concept. Its instance variables are the link type and an OrderedCollection of Concepts.

Another two classes handle the user interface.

The data base associated with a particular dynamic document consists of two Smalltalk dictionaries (that is, sets of couples "name --> value"). One of them contains entries of the type "conceptName --> concept" to retrieve all the contents of a concept starting from its name: remember that the user selects a concept name, but the Concept Browser shows its description text, the list of link types and the list of keywords associated with it.

The other dictionary has entries of type "keyword --> setOfConcepts", to find all the concepts sharing a given (user-selected) keyword. This is redundant information, because this list might be obtained running over the whole concept base, selecting the concepts containing the keyword. However, typical waiting times, for the user, induced by this method advise to use the solution we adopted.

Memory-occupancy criteria have influenced the management of the various data bases the Concept Browser can handle. In particular, we have to load the information necessary to access a concept base only when the user opens a Concept Browser on that base. Subsequently, the user may decide to close the browser without discarding the concept base: the close operation causes a reduction of the system load, and the keeping in memory of the base accelerates possible future reopenings of browsers on the same base.

8. Conclusions

The Concept Browser appears to be a flexible tool to organise information in a non traditional way. Instead of using a hierarchical approach, a more generalised network data structure represents the connections between different pieces of information.

The window-based user interface and the path mechanism seem to be adequate tools for the user to traverse the data structure. Great effort was put, into the development of the tool, to guarantee the maximum flexibility and generality of use to different types of users (together with a user-friendly interface, which was our first target).

As it can be seen, both the naive user, who enters a concept base for the first time, and the expert one, who knows "where" to search for "what", find suitable facilities. The former may look at concept names or at the keywords defined, or possibly load one of the predefined paths and just use the "next" entry of the main menu. The latter may simply type the name of the desired concept in the concept-name window, and read its contents in the window below.

Nobody is asked to be an expert, and nobody is forced to follow heavy enquiry procedures.

Further study is required to understand what kind of discipline should be imposed on the creator of the network. In fact, proper choice of link types and keywords, together with a good partitioning of the entire information into manageable pieces, might greatly improve the browsing process.

References

[1] Feigenbaum. *The handbook of Artificial Intelligence.*

[2] Goldberg, A. (1984). *Smalltalk-80. The Interactive Programming Environment.* Addison-Wesley.

[3] Goldberg, A., Robson, D. (1983). *Smalltalk-80, the Language and its Implementation.* Addison-Wesley.

[4] Knuth, D.E. (1984). *Literate programming* .
The Computer Journal,vol.27,no.2.

[5] Leclerc, Y., Zucker, S.W., Leclerc, D. (1982).
A browsing approach to documentation. Computer, June 1982.

[6] Shapiro, E (1984). *Text databases.* Byte, October 1984.

[7] Wegner, P. (1984). *Perspectives on capital intensive software technology.* International conference on advanced personal computer technology, Capri 1984.

[8] Weyer, S.A. *Searching information in a dynamic book.* Xerox PARC Report number SCG-82-1.

An Integrated, but not Exact-Representation, Editor/Formatter

Richard Furuta

*University of Maryland**

ABSTRACT

Integrated Editor/Formatters merge the document editing and formatting functions into a unified, interactive system. A common type of Integrated Editor/Formatter, the Exact-representation Editor/Formatter (also known as WYSIWYG), presents an interactive representation of the document that is identical to the printed document. Another powerful metaphor applied to documents has been to describe the document as abstract objects— to describe the document's logical structure, not its physical makeup. The goal of the research reported here is to merge the flexibility found in the abstract object-oriented approach with the naturalness of document manipulation provided by the Exact-representation Editor/Formatters. A tree-based model of documents that allows a variety of document objects as leaves (e.g., text, tables, and mathematical equations) has been defined. I suggest a template-oriented mechanism for manipulating the document and have implemented a prototype that illustrates the mechanism. Further work has concentrated on handling user operations on arbitrary, contiguous portions of the display.

1. Motivation and Goals of the Research

The world of text formatters can be divided into two parts.[1] In one group are the *pure formatters*, which convert a document description, prepared by a separate editing system, into a formatted document suitable for display on an appropriate hardware device. In the other group are the *Integrated Editor/Formatters*, which merge the editing and the formatting functions into one unified, interactive system—documents are created, viewed, and revised without leaving the editor/formatter.

---

*This work was carried out at the University of Washington. This paper is a summary and condensation of [Fur86]. I thank Alan Shaw and Pierre MacKay for their advice and assistance.

[1] We have given more complete definitions of this terminology in [FSS82].

A powerful metaphor applied in the pure formatter domain has been to view the document as consisting of abstract objects [Rei80, Uni84, Lam85]. The system's user describes the document's logical structure instead of its physical makeup, and therefore can concentrate on specifying the document's content. The document description can be used more flexibly since the description of the document's contents and structure is separated from definition of its appearance. Consistent, wholesale modification of the appearance of the document's objects can be made without change to the document's description. Similarly, the document's text can be used in different contexts without requiring change.

A powerful metaphor applied in the Integrated Editor/Formatter domain has been to present the interactive representation of the document as identical to the paper representation, maintaining all the fonts, sizes, and spacings in both forms [Lam78, SIKV82, App84]. I call an editor/formatter of this type an *Exact-representation Editor/Formatter*. Much of the popularity of such editor/formatters is due to the naturalness of the editing process—the representations and manipulations that take place are similar to those that are used with paper documents. A negative factor, however, is the inflexibility of the description—others have called these editor/formatters "What you see is what you get" systems. Brian Kernighan's well known retort was to describe them instead as "What you see is *all* you've got" systems.

The overall goal of my research is the design of an Integrated Editor/Formatter that merges the naturalness of document manipulation provided by an Exact-representation Editor/Formatters with the flexibility inherent in an abstract object representation. To achieve this, the abstract objects and their semantic relationships must be displayed in a way consistent with their concrete representation on paper and manipulation of the abstract objects should be carried out through manipulation of this concrete representation. As a consequence, the design avoids interactive operations that operate on hidden data structures or in which the target of an operation is not directly connected to the context in which the operation is issued. This rules out, for example, a system that shows a paper-like representation of the document on the display but in which the operations are traditional tree-traversal commands, phrased in terms of an underlying (and invisible) tree structure.

2. The Model of Documents

A document consists of abstract objects, hierarchically related to each other. A wide variety of leaf object types are desirable and necessary at the lowest level of the hierarchy; for example, objects containing textual material, tabular material, mathematical formulæ, line drawings, or scanned images (bits). Additionally, these lowest-level objects may interact with each other—for example, tabular objects may contain textual or mathematical objects within the individual entries of the table.

A tree structure provides an attractive approximation of the object relationships. However, the tree representation cannot adequately model the wide variety of structures found at the leaves. A tree is not powerful enough in some cases: tables are not naturally tree structured because the entries in the table have multiple parents (row and column). In other cases, a tree representation is awkward because it is *too* powerful: paragraph text is most naturally treated as a string of characters.

For this reason, a hybrid structure, the **tnt**, is used to model the document.

The highest level structure of a **tnt** is an ordered tree. The relationships between objects in the tree can be and are represented and constrained by a context-free grammar. The objects found in this higher level structure are said to be in the *strict tree* portion of the **tnt**.

At the "leaves" of the strict tree portion are instances of the various *tree blocks*. An arbitrary structure is found within a tree block— the only requirement is that it be possible to define a representation-independent ordering between the components located within the tree block. The structures within the tree blocks collectively make up the *free structure* portion of the **tnt**.

There is exactly one kind of structure in the strict tree portion of the **tnt** but there may be many different kinds of structures in the free structure portion. The terminating nodes of any particular free structure may be defined to be either *atoms* or *transition nodes* (or both). Atoms are actual terminating points in the **tnt**. A transition node is a terminating point for the structure that contains it and also a root for an enclosed strict tree structure. Thus, a **tnt** is built from alternating structures—first the strict tree, then a tree block enclosing a free structure, and then perhaps a transition node that leads to another strict tree. This alternation is reflected in the term "**tnt**," which stands for "strict t̲ree—n̲ot strict t̲ree."[2]

---

[2]All objects are ordered with respect to each other in a **tnt**. When the relationships between two document objects cannot be constrained in this manner, as is the case with floating figures and footnotes, the objects are placed in separate **tnts**, which are related to each other by a linking scheme. [Fur86] discusses the forest of **tnts** in more detail. The discussion in this paper is limited to the processing of a single **tnt**.

Looking at the **tnt** from the bottom up, it can be seen that the basic building blocks of the document are the tree blocks. These tree blocks are related to one another through the hierarchical relationships expressed by the structure of the strict tree. These hierarchical relationships differ between document classes and are what distinguish different document classes, for example the document class that defines a document divided into sections and the document class that describes a business letter. The *same* tree blocks can be used in each of the different document classes.

My document model is derived from one defined by Shaw [Sha80, FSS82].[3] Other researchers have independently developed similar document models. A partial list includes Borkin and Prager's work [BP80], Peels, et al.'s COBATEF [PJN85], and Quint and Vatton's GRIF [QV86].

2.1.   Internal and External Representations

The **tnt** is the *internal representation* of the document. A system that processes a document does so by mapping between the internal representation and one or more external representations. Each mapping may be either unidirectional or bidirectional.

External representations are put to many uses in a document processing system. An external representation that is modified interactively presents the document to the user of the system and allows modifications to be made to the document. An interactive representation could be highly oriented to the appearance that the document would take if it were to be printed on paper, in which case the interface probably would resemble that of the Exact-representation systems, or the representation could be highly oriented to manipulation of abstract objects.

Also of use are external representations that present condensed or symbolic versions of the document, for example, the document in outline (or table of contents) form or the document as a picture of a tree. When the summary representation is bidirectional, manipulations on it can be used to alter and restructure large parts of the document or can be used to move about quickly in the document.

File-oriented external representations are also desirable. For example in this work, a bidirectional external representation, called the "storage representation," is provided to allow documents to be saved and restored

---

[3]Another document model, also based on Shaw's work, has been defined by Kimura and Shaw [KS84, Kim84]. In Kimura and Shaw's model, the document is represented by a single homogeneous structure. In my model, the representation of the document is through a heterogeneous collection of structures.

```
<document>        = article-title authors (<paragraph>|<section>)+
<section>         = section-id section-title (<paragraph>|<section>)+
<paragraph>       = [text-block|tbl-block|eqn-block|<itemized-list>|
                    <enum-list>|<quotation>]+
<itemized-list>   = <i-item>+
<i-item>          = item-marker <paragraph>+
<enum-list>       = <e-item>+
<e-item>          = enum-marker <paragraph>+
<quotation>       = <paragraph>+

<tbl-entry>       = <paragraph>+
```

Figure 1: The grammar describing a sectioned document

across sessions. A useful unidirectional class of file-oriented representations are the "formatter representations," which serve as *input* to a batch-oriented formatter such as TEX, Scribe, or **troff**.

The relaxation of the constraints imposed by exact-representation allows the specification of different external representations for specific purposes. For example, a interactive representation need not incorporate pagination, thereby simplifying its design considerably. However, a paginated representation of the document still can be obtained through a formatter representation.

3. A Prototype System

A central part of this work has been the design and development of a prototype system, sketching the means for manipulating the **tnt**. Three external representations are included in the prototype: a storage representation, a formatter representation,[4] and an interactive representation.

The interactive representation will be the topic of the remainder of this paper.

3.1. The Grammar and Augmentations

The syntax of the context-free grammar that defines the **tnt** is slightly modified from the BNF to allow the prototype's interactive representation to be driven directly from the grammar.

A terminal in the grammar is further classified as being either user-defined terminal or system-defined terminal, respectively representing

---

[4]The formatter representation is driven by translation tables and the table to produce LATEX input has been designed and is being tested.

information supplied by the system's user and information generated by the system. In the grammar of Figure 1, for example, `text-block` is a user-defined terminal representing a block of text and *section-id* is a system-defined terminal representing the number associated with a document's section.

Each nonterminal must appear on the left hand side of exactly one grammar production. The right hand side of the production rule consists of a sequence of *components* where each component is either a grammar terminal, a grammar nonterminal or a *group*. A group is a set of grammar elements, where each element is either a grammar terminal or grammar nonterminal. When the production is expanded, exactly one of the elements contained within the group will be present in the expansion. Syntactically the group is bracketed and the elements of the group are separated from one another with the "|" symbol.

It has been convenient to provide two categories of groups in the grammar description, called *choose one* and *choose all*. The distinction was made to help direct the way in which the prototype interactive representation displays the unexpanded elements from the group. Choose one is used when the user of the system is expected in general to choose only one of the alternatives presented within the group. Choose all is used when the user of the system is expected to want to use all the alternatives presented within the group.

Choose one groups are syntactically identified in a production by being enclosed in square brackets. Choose all groups are enclosed parentheses.

Each of the components of the right hand side may be single (present in the expansion only once), starred (present zero or more times), or plussed (present one or more times). Note that the elements of a group cannot be starred or plussed.

3.2. The Prototypical User Interface

The intention in the prototypical user interface is not to provide an "exact representation" of the document as it would appear on paper but a "sufficient representation" that gives a good intuitive feeling for what the elements are of the document but that does not necessarily indicate what the exact details of the placement of these elements will be in other representations.

The approach taken in the prototypical user interface is to provide a template-driven system for creation and modification of a document, directed by and constrained by the grammar defined above. Manipulation

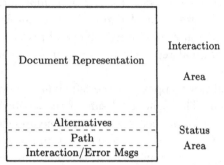

Figure 2: The overall layout of the interactive representation's window.

involves a *family* of editors. One, called the *generalized manipulator*, is used for altering the strict tree portion of the **tnt**. A separate, specialized, editor is provided for each of the classes of user-defined terminals.

3.2.1.   *The Generalized Manipulator*

The generalized manipulator presents the elements of the grammar through *templates*. A template consists of a *button* and an indication of what the template represents. When the button is *selected*, it expands. In the case of a nonterminal, the expansion is another set of buttons indicating the expansion of that nonterminal, enclosed in a box that represents the expanded nonterminal itself. When the element is a user-defined terminal, the expansion presents the specialized editor for that particular type of terminal. System-defined terminals cannot be selected—the system expands them when they are present, generating their values as needed.

The placement of buttons and the placement of the expansion of buttons resembles that the object would take if placed onto a hard copy medium. The intention is to help indicate the semantics of the object by representing its appearance.

When the button corresponding to a user-defined terminal is selected, a window is opened to allow editing of the terminal's contents. Initially, the window corresponds in size and position to the button being expanded. As the information is edited, the window grows temporarily obscuring the display of adjacent objects. When the editing is complete, the information is put into the **tnt** and the **tnt**'s display is adjusted.

The grammar augmentations aid in the generic manipulation of the **tnt**. When a choose all group is displayed, a button is presented for each of its alternatives. When a choose one group is shown, only one of the alternatives is shown. In both cases, the *transform* operation

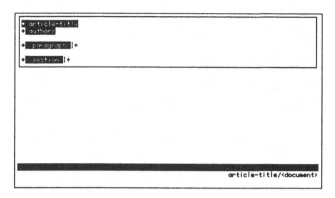

Figure 3: The initial display on creation of a new sectioned document.

allows the element associated with the button to be changed to another alternative from the group.

If a selected element can be replicated (starred or plussed in the grammar) or if it is an element in a group that can be replicated, selecting it causes new buttons to be inserted before and after the expansion, permitting further specification of elements of that type.

The opposite of expanding a button is collapsing a subtree into a button. Selecting this button restores the contents that have been hidden by the collapse. The button's display also includes a brief summary of the collapsed objects' contents.

Figure 2 shows the overall arrangement of the interactive display of the tnt. The display is divided into two major areas: the Interaction Area and the Status Area. The Interaction Area contains the templates described above. The Status Area subdivides into three parts. The topmost shows the "alternatives." When a button representing an element from a group is the current selection, this area shows what it could be transformed into. The second part of the Status Area is the "path," which shows the nodes between the root and the current position. The third part shows "interaction and error messages." When the prototype needs additional information from the system's user, it poses its queries in this area. When an error occurs, the explanation of what happened is posted here.

The prototype has been implemented using an 80 column by 24 row terminal. Figure 3 shows the initial display that would result when the prototype was started with the <document> as described by the grammar previously shown in Figure 1. The four buttons correspond

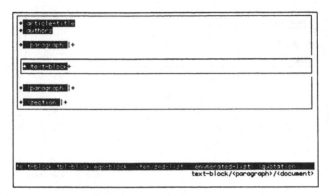

Figure 4: After selection of a `<paragraph>` button.

to the elements on the right hand side of the production. The "|+" following the `<paragraph>` and `<section>` buttons indicates that the elements are in an or list and are plussed. Since `<paragraph>` and `<section>` are in a choose all group, both alternatives are shown.

In Figure 4, the cursor has been moved to the `<paragraph>` button and the button selected. Replacement buttons for new `<paragraph>`s have been inserted before and after the expansion. Since the **text-block** in the `<paragraph>`'s expansion is in a choose one group, only one representative selection is shown. The available alternatives are shown in the status area.

In Figure 5, the **text-block** has been selected, activating the specialized editor for text blocks. Again, replacement buttons have been inserted before and after the expansion.[5]

Figure 6 shows the final state. The text block editor has exited, inserting the contents into the **tnt** and returning control to the generalized manipulator.

3.2.2. *Specialized Editors for User-defined Terminals*
The specialized editors correspond to the various kinds of **tnt** tree blocks and are invoked by the strict tree's generalized editor. In turn, some of the specialized editors may invoke another instance of the generalized editor to manipulate a strict tree rooted within their data structure.

Three specialized editors are defined in the prototype implementation: a text block editor, a table block editor, and an equation block editor.

---

[5]The replacement buttons here are known as *ellipsis* buttons and are used because the original element was a member of a choose one group.

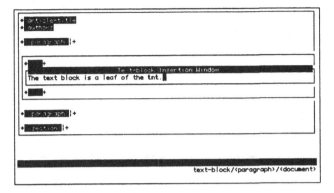

Figure 5: In the specialized editor for text blocks.

The text block editor: The text block editor is perhaps the simplest of the prototype's specialized editors. A text block is modeled as an unbroken string of characters and represents the text of a paragraph or of a substantial part of a paragraph. The text block editor presents this string as a sequence of lines. The editor's operations alter the position of the cursor and insert and delete characters relative to the cursor. The displayed lines are continuously adjusted as characters are added to or deleted from the string. The text block editor also supports font face changes (the provided font faces are roman, italic, bold, and default).

The table block editor: The table block editor is used to create and modify the *structure* of the table and not the *contents*. The table block is modeled as a set of *skeleton nodes* placed into a two-dimensional structure of rows and columns. A skeleton node is in exactly one row and in one column. A table is a set of rectangular *entries*, each of which occupies one or more adjacent skeleton nodes.[6]

The table entries are strict trees, each rooted in a `<tbl-entry>`. Therefore, manipulations on the contents of the table are carried out by invoking a new instance of the generalized manipulator on the entry's tree.

The table block editor provides commands to modify the structure of the table by adding, deleting, and moving rows and columns, commands to create and break up "spans" of skeleton nodes, thereby associating entries with multiple skeleton nodes, and a command that transfers control to the new instance of the generalized manipulator.

---

[6]A similar model of tables can be found in work by Biggerstaff, Endres, and Forman [BEF84], and indeed in that provided by Unix's **tbl** table processor [Les76].

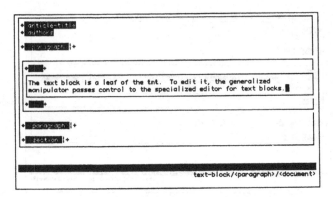

Figure 6: After exiting the text block editor.

The equation block editor: The equation block editor differs from the other editors in that it uses keywords to direct its actions. Input resembles **eqn** or TeX input strings [KC75, Knu84] but the resulting structures are displayed while they are being entered. Characters are placed at the current position as they are entered from the keyboard. The system also provides positioning commands, which are allowed to roam across the partially specified equation changing the current position within the equation.

The equation description is a set of lists of elements. Each element in the list is either a terminal (a character or a special symbol) or an *entry record*. Entry records point to additional lists related to each other by the physical grid of Figure 7.

An empty list is displayed as an isolated button (without any attached identifiers). Hence in the equation domain, buttons indicate the places where it is possible to place material.

As characters are entered, keywords are detected and acted on. Keywords fall into two main classifications. The first are those that represent special symbols not present on the keyboard. For example, the sequence "**sum**" causes a large summation sign to replace the string on the display and in the data structure. "+-" or "-+" produce the "$\pm$" symbol, and similar key mappings produce "$\geq$", and "$\leq$".

The second class of keywords are those that modify the data structure, generally creating new lists that can then be inserted into. The **over** keyword inserts an "over" node (for a fraction) into the equation list. The "over" node has two empty lists, representing the numerator and the denominator of the fraction separated by horizontal bar the

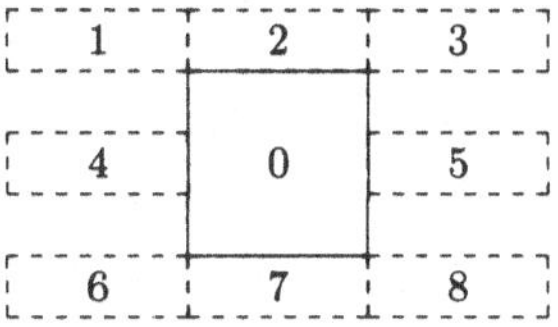

Figure 7: The grid that constrains equation element placement.

width of which is the same as the width of the widest of the two lists.
sup and sub take the preceding token and convert it into a "superscript" or "subscript" node that contains an empty list representing the
superscript or subscript.

The equation block editor is largely table driven. In particular, the
keywords are defined in a table and the translations and graphical representations for the special symbol keywords are defined solely by table.

3.3. Region-oriented Manipulation

A goal of this research is to allow concrete-oriented manipulations of
the document and the region commands are one of the means provided
for this purpose. Region commands are carried out on an arbitrary
contiguous region of the display. The selection of the region on which
the command will operate can be made using a combination of cursor-
oriented selections and tree-oriented selections.

In cursor-oriented selection, the cursor is initially positioned at one
end or the other of the selection and cursor motions cause the selection
to expand or contract. With tree-oriented selection, the selection is
increased to encompass the parent of a node.

A postfix command notation is used: the region selection is made
first and then the command is specified. Region commands provide the
means to copy, delete, and move parts of the document, as well as to
set the region's font.

A region may span across different structure contexts. When this
occurs, the system converts the operation into a sequence of operations
each within a single context through the use of heuristics. After the
actions have been carried out, a routine that analyzes the tree based on
the grammar is called to fix up the tree and the display.

4. Conclusions

An important pedagogical distinction within this work has been the
distinction of the Exact-representation Editor/Formatters from the Integrated Editor/Formatters. The focus in this work has been to examine Integrated Editor/Formatters that are not also Exact-representation

Editor/Formatters. One lesson learned from TEX is that high-quality document formatting benefits from use of algorithms that may be quite expensive computationally in the worst case. Developing an Integrated but not Exact-representation Editor/Formatter allows the presentation of information in a form that can be quickly recognized by its appearance while using algorithms more suited to interactive manipulation.

Also important has been the separation of the document model into a single internal representation and multiple external representations. Scribe alters the appearance of the objects in a document to best suit the intended output device. In essence, this use of multiple external representations is a generalization of that concept.

The separation of the **tnt** into the strict tree and the tree block objects allows definition of different document types while providing a consistent means for their manipulation. The basic building blocks (the tree blocks) are the same across the different document types. Generic operations on the strict tree allow manipulation of the document type's objects. The tree/non-tree/tree/... relationships in the **tnt** extend this consistency.

Interestingly, the framework that allows the multiple editors and tree blocks to co-exist makes it relatively easy to add new block object types to the **tnt** and to change the definition of the existing block object types. As such, it resembles the Unix pipe concept, which allows the easy interconnection of separate cooperating programs.

The region-oriented commands demonstrate that it is possible to allow concrete-like manipulations of a document represented as abstract, hierarchically structured objects without requiring that the system's user manipulate a hidden data structure.

The prototype is far from being a production system and its display, limited by the standard terminal, is quite coarse. It has, however, served as a useful testbed for investigation and implementation of the algorithms that allow the system to generate a display and allow document manipulation based on a grammatical description. A project of particular interest will be to translate the techniques developed here into the environment provided by bitmapped displays with attached pointing devices.

References

[App84] *MacWrite*. Apple Computer, Inc., 1984.

[BEF84] Ted J. Biggerstaff, D. Mac Endres, and Ira R. Forman. TABLE: Object oriented editing of complex structures. In *Proceedings—International Conference on Software Engineering*, pages 334–345, IEEE

Computer Society, 1984.

[BP80] S. A. Borkin and J. M. Prager. *Some issues in the design of an editor-formatter for structured documents.* Technical Report, IBM Cambridge Scientific Center, November 1980.

[FSS82] Richard Furuta, Jeffrey Scofield, and Alan Shaw. Document formatting systems: Survey, concepts, and issues. *Computing Surveys,* 14(3):417–472, September 1982.

[Fur86] Richard Furuta. *An Integrated, but not Exact-Representation, Editor/Formatter.* Ph.D. dissertation, University of Washington, Department of Computer Science, Seattle, WA, 1986. In preparation.

[KC75] Brian W. Kernighan and Lorinda L. Cherry. A system for typesetting mathematics. *Communications of the ACM,* 18(3):151–157, March 1975.

[Kim84] Gary Dean Kimura. *A Structure Editor and Model for Abstract Document Objects.* Ph.D. dissertation, University of Washington, Department of Computer Science, Seattle, WA, 1984.

[Knu84] Donald E. Knuth. *The TEXbook.* Addison-Wesley, 1984.

[KS84] Gary D. Kimura and Alan C. Shaw. The structure of abstract document objects. *Proceedings of the Second ACM-SIGOA Conference on Office Information Systems, SIGOA Newsletter,* 5(1–2):161–169, June 1984.

[Lam78] Butler W. Lampson. Bravo manual. In B. W. Lampson and E. A. Taft, editors, *Alto User's Handbook,* Computer Science Laboratory, Xerox Palo Alto Research Center, November 1978.

[Lam85] Leslie Lamport. *LATEX: A Document Preparation System.* Addison-Wesley, 1985.

[Les76] M. E. Lesk. *Tbl—A program to format tables.* Computer Science Technical Report 49, Bell Laboratories, Murray Hill, N.J., September 1976.

[PJN85] Arno J. H. M. Peels, Norbert J. M. Janssen, and Wop Nawijn. Document architecture and text formatting. *ACM Transactions on Office Information Systems,* 3(4):347–369, October 1985.

[QV86] Vincent Quint and Iréne Vatton. GRIF: An interactive system for structured document manipulation. In *Proceedings of the International Conference on Text Processing and Document Manipulation,* April 1986. This volume.

[Rei80] Brian K. Reid. *Scribe: A Document Specification Language and its Compiler.* Ph.D. dissertation, Carnegie-Mellon University Computer Science Department, Pittsburgh, PA, October 1980.

[Sha80] Alan C. Shaw. *A Model for Document Preparation Systems.* Technical Report 80-04-02, University of Washington, Department of Computer Science, Seattle, WA, April 1980.

[SIKV82] David Canfield Smith, Charles Irby, Ralph Kimball, and Bill Verplank. Designing the Star user interface. *Byte,* 7(4):242–282, April 1982.

[Uni84] Unilogic, Ltd. *Scribe Introductory User's Manual.* Unilogic, Ltd., Pittsburgh, fourth edition, April 1984.

An Annotated Bibliography on Document Processing

J.C. van Vliet, J.B. Warmer

Centre for Mathematics and Computer Science, Amsterdam

The scope of this bibliography, though given in the title, might be further pinned down by means of the following list of topics **not** covered:
- (digital) typography;
- electronic publishing;
- text editing;
- user interfaces;
- writing aids, such as spelling checkers;
- hyphenation;
- computer graphics;
- text retrieval;
- office automation;
- multi-media documents;
- special inputmedia, such as tablets;
- specific problems for non-latin script.

Obviously, the border lines are not sharp; papers on interactive text processing systems generally do say something about user interfaces and/or text editing, etc. Also, a few important papers, such as [Meyrowitz82] on text editing, were included. The emphasis is on papers published after 1975. But again, a few oldies, such as [Tesler73], have been retained.

Following the bibliography, a rather global cross-reference index is given. This index contains names of well-known systems such as Troff, TEX, Scribe, and some important recurring topics.

Readers are encouraged to provide us with comments and/or suggestions for additions, so that we may regularly update the bibliography.

The bibliography has been prepared with the help of Refer [Lesk79a]. The details hereof had better not be revealed. The early assistance of Ger-Jan Hofman, and many helpful comments by Heather Brown and Jacques André are gratefully acknowledged.

[Achubue81] J. O. Achubue, "On the Line Breaking Problem in Text Formatting," in: *[SIGPLAN81]*, pp. 117-122, 1981.

This paper presents and discusses solutions to the line breaking problem.

[Aderet84] A. Aderet and P. J. Hoffman, "Mnemonic Strategies in Word Processing Systems," *SIGOA*, no. 5.1-2, pp. 188-198, 1984.

The usability of character mnemonics is discussed and several issues involved in its use as effective design concept are highlighted in the context of word processing tasks.

[Allen81] T. Allen et al, "PEN: A Hierarchical Document Editor," in: *[SIGPLAN81]*, pp. 74-81, 1981.

PEN is an interactive system supporting the preparation of manuscripts containing significant mathematical notation.

[Anderson75] R. O. Anderson and R. E. Griswold, *ACOLYTE, a document formatting program*, University of Arizona, Department of Computer Science, 1975.

A nroff-like system writtem in SNOBOL4.

[André82] J. André, "Bibliographie Analytique sur les Manipulation des Textes," *Technique et Science Informatique*, no. 1.5, pp. 445-455, 1982.

Bibliography on text processing.

[Appelt85] W. Appelt, "Hohe Druckqualität mit Laserdruckern und dem Textformatierungssystem TEX," *Der GMD-Spiegel*, no. 15.1, pp. 27-31, 1985.

With TEX, the GMD offers its writers a 'comfortable' environment.

[Beach83] R. Beach and M. Stone, "Graphical style: towards High Quality Illustrations," *Computer Graphics*, no. 17.3, pp. 127-135, 1983.

Describes a prototype system that uses a set of graphical style rules to define guidelines for illustrations. These can be used to control a uniform "look" over a set of illustrations.

[Beatty79] J. C. Beatty et al, "An Interactive Documentation System," in: *Siggraph '79*, B. W. Pollack (ed.), ACM, 1979.

Possibilities include mathematics and 2D-graphics. A variety of (color) output devices, such as offset reproduction masters, color slides and viewgraphs are supported.

[Becker84] J. D. Becker, "Multilingual Word Processing," *Scientific American*, no. 251.1, pp. 82-93, July 1984.

A word-processor is described for multilingual text, which may involve multi-directional text in many languages including Russian, Greek, Japanese, Chinese, Korean, Arabic, and Hebrew. The system is interactive and runs on a high-resolution Xerox Star workstation.

[Benoliel78] J. Benoliel and H. Manuguerra, "Mise en page et impression automatiques des textes fondees sur la reconnaissance de leur structure," PhD Thesis, Université de Nice, 1978.

describes a document preparation system which is based on recognizing the syntactic structure of a document.

[Bentley84] J. L. Bentley and B. W. Kernighan, "GRAP — A Language for Typesetting Graphs, Tutorial and user manual," Computer Science Technical Report 114, Bell Laboratories, 1984.

GRAP is a language for describing plots of data. It is a preprocessor that works with PIC and Troff.

[Berns69] G. M. Berns, "Description of FORMAT, a Text-Processing Program," *Communications of the ACM*, no. 12.3, pp. 141-146, 1969.

An early influential system for the IBM S/360. Commands are embedded within the text, and an escape character is used to switch from text to command mode.

[Biggerstaff84] T. J. Biggerstaff et al, "Table: Object Oriented Editing of Complex Structures," in: *Proceedings 7th International Conference on Software Engineering*, pp. 334-345, IEEE, 1984.

In the context of text and table objects, this research explores a Smalltalk-like, object oriented architecture for editors of such complex structures.

[Blomberg84] L. Blomberg et al, "A New Approach to Text and Image Processing," *IEEE Computer Graphics and Applications*, no. 4.7, pp. 12-22, 1984.

The user interface of a system for page make up is described. It uses a 'simulated desktop' to envision the different elements (text and graphics) that can be manipulated along the page.

[Borkin78] S. A. Borkin and J. M. Prager, "Some Issues in the design of an Editor-Formatter for Structured Documents," Technical Report, IBM Cambridge Scientific Center, 1978.

[Buchmann84] C. Buchmann and D. M. Berry, "Ditroff/Ffortid, An adaption of the Unix Ditroff for Formatting Bidirectional Text," in: *The 4th Jeruzalem Conference on Information Technology (JCIT) Proceedings*, pp. 1-6, IPA, 1984.

A collection of pre- and postprocessors to Unix Ditroff, which permits formatting text involving a mixture of languages written from left to right and from right to left.

[Burkhart80] H. Burkhart and J. Nievergelt, "Structure-oriented editors," *Berichte des Instituts fur Informatik*, no. 38, ETH Zurich, 1980.

Gives design principles for structure editors, including editors for document preparation.

[Burns76] J. C. Burns, "The evolving market for word processing and typesetting systems," in: *AFIPS 45*, pp. 617-623, 1976.

Describes industry installations and gives forecasts. Suggests an evolution which will link word-proceccing, publishing, editing and data processing.

[Canzii84] G. Canzii et al, "A scientific document delivery system," *Electronic Publishing Review*, no. 4.2, pp. 135-143, 1984.

Outlines the general architecture, and discusses technical issues of a scientific document delivery system.

[Chamberlin81] D. C. Chamberlin et al, "JANUS: An Interactive System for Document Composition," in: *[SIGPLAN81]*, pp. 82-91, 1981.

Architecture of a proposed system, intended to provide support for authors of complex documents. The system uses two displays; markup is by high level 'descriptive' tags.

[Chamberlin82] D. C. Chamberlin et al, "JANUS: an Interactive Document Formatter based on Declarative Tags," *IBM System Journal*, no. 21.3, pp. 250-271, 1982.

See [Chamberlin81].

[Coulouris76] G. F. Coulouris et al, "The design and Implementation of an Interactive Document Editor," *Software — Practice and Experience*, vol. 6, pp. 271-279, 1976.

A system designed to combine the editing and formatting power of a text editor with the simplicity and immediacy of a typewriter, meant for simple alphanumeric displays.

[Coutaz84] J. Coutaz, "The box, A layout Abstraction For User Interface Toolkits," CMU-CS-84-167, Carnegie-Mellon University, 1984.

The box can be considered as a high level input and output logical device, which automatically formats the screen-view of an object.

[Dam70] A. van Dam and D. E. Rice, "Computers and Publishing: writing, Editing and Printing," in: *Advances in Computers 10*, F. L. Alt and M. Rubinoff (ed.), pp. 145-174, Academic Press, 1970.

Concentrates on computer-assisted online writing and editing.

[Day83] R. A. Day, "Typesetting Mathematics on Multi-Acces Systems," *Software — Practice and Experience*, vol. 13, pp. 131-138, 1983.

Describes a system for typesetting mathematics on conventional multi-access systems using standard, ready-available peripherals.

[Donzeau-Gouge83] V. Donzeau-Gouge et al, "Outline of a tool for document manipulation," in: *IFIP83*, R. E. A. Manson (ed.), pp. 615-629, North-Holland, 1983.

Gives an account of MENTOR, a general system for the manipulation of formal documents of various kinds.

[Doster84] W. Doster and R. Oed, "Word Processing with On-line Script Recognition," *IEEE Micro*, no. 4.5, pp. 36-43, 1984.

Adding a graphics tablet, a stylus, and special software to a personal computer system enables its users to edit text with simple, handwritten commands.

[Feiner81] S. Feiner et al, "An Integrated system for Creating and Presenting Complex Computer-Based Documents," *ACM Computer Graphics*, no. 15.3, pp. 181-189, 1981.

Describes an experimental sytem in which pictures and text can be combined on a high resolution display.

[Furuta82] R. Furuta et al, "Document formatting Systems: Survey, Concepts, and Issues," *ACM Computing Surveys*, no. 14.3, pp. 417-472, September 1982.

This excellent paper describes and evaluates several representative and seminal systems, and discusses some issues relevant to future systems. The emphasis is on topics related to the specification of document formats.

[Furuta85] R. Furuta and P. A. Mackay, "Two TEX Implementations for the IBM PC," *Dr. Dobb's Journal*, pp. 80-91, sep 1985.

Discusses MicroTEX and PCTEX.

[Ganzinger85] H. Ganzinger and W. Willmertinger, "FOAM: A Two-Level Approach to Text Formatting on a Micro-computersystem," *Software — Practice and Experience*, vol. 15, pp. 327-341, 1985.

The system accepts descriptions of text and document classes together with formatting styles for text components. From the description, a specific instance of a formatter is generated.

[Gehringer80] E. F. Gehringer and S. R. Vegdahl, "LETTER: A system for Personalizing Processed Text," *ACM Sigsmall Newsletter*, no. 6.2, pp. 199-205, 1980.

LETTER provides a high-level language for creating multiple versions of a document.

[Gibson85] D. R. Gibson and D. A. Duce, "GKS graphics and text processing," *Computer Graphics Forum*, no. 4, pp. 259-270, 1985.

> Discussion of a Troff preprocessor which translates GKS metafiles to PIC's language.

[Goldfarb81] C. F. Goldfarb, "A Generalized Approach to Document Markup," in: *[SIGPLAN81]*, pp. 68-73, 1981.

> In GML, the user marks up a document with mnemonic tags. The specific layout is determined by the formatting program. GML is a predecessor to SGML (see [ISO85a]).

[Good81a] M. Good, "An Ease of Use Evaluation of an Integrated Editor and Formatter," LCS TR-266, M.I.T., 1981.

> In this report the results of a controlled experiment, in which computer-naive office workers were taught Etude's use, are presented. See also [Hammer81]. Contains an annotated bibliography on human factors.

[Good81b] M. Good, "Etude and the Folklore of User Interface Design," in: *[SIGPLAN81]*, pp. 34-43, 1981.

> In this paper the principles are shown that underlie the design of the Etude text processing system.

[Gutknecht84] J. Gutknecht and W. Winiger, "Andra: The Document Preparation System of the Personal Workstation Lilith," *Software — Practice and Experience*, vol. 14, pp. 73-100, 1984.

> A more-or-less WYSIWYG system, inspired by the Bravo editor.

[Gutknecht85] J. Gutknecht, "Concepts of the text editor Lara," *Communications of the ACM*, no. 28.9, pp. 942-960, 1985.

> Lara is the successor of Andra [Gutknecht84]. Lara does not depend on a 'style' file, but layout attributes may be copied from one place on the display to another.

[Hammer81] M. Hammer et al, "The Implementation of Etude, An Integrated and Interactive Document Preparation System," in: *[SIGPLAN81]*, pp. 137-146, 1981.

> Etude is an experimental text processing system that is being developed in order to formulate and evaluate new approaches in the design of user interfaces.

[Hansson81] H. Hansson and J. Steensgaard-Madsen, "Document Preparation Systems," *Software — Practice and Experience*, vol. 11, pp. 983-997, 1981.

> Gives an introduction to programs used to prepare the layout of a text. It presents a suitable terminology for the description of documents, and describes the basic characteristics of phototypesetters.

[Hibbard84] P. Hibbard, *Mint Reference Manual,* Carnegie-Mellon University, 1984.

> Mint provides for an interactive layout facility tailored to document preparation needs, which supports heterogeneous data.

[Horak83] W. Horak, "Interchanging mixed text-image documents in the office environment," *Computers & Graphics,* no. 7.1, pp. 13-29, 1983.

> Discusses existing document communication services, techniques for the interchange of mixed text-image documents, and an experimental text-image workstation.

[Horak84a] W. Horak, "Concepts of the Document Interchange Protocol for the Telematic Services — CCITT Draft Recommendation S.a.," *Computer Networks,* no. 8, pp. 175-185, 1984.

> An overvieuw of Draft Recommendation S.a., intended for the interchange of mixed text/image documents.

[Horak84b] W. Horak and G. Krönert, "An Object-Oriented Office Document Architecture Model for Processing and Interchange of Documents," *SIGOA,* no. 5.1-2, pp. 152-160, 1984.

> Discusses the standardization work of ECMA TC2 on ODA and ODIF.

[Horak85] W. Horak, "Office document Architecture and Office Document Interchange formats: Current status of International Standardization.," *IEEE Computer,* no. 18.10, pp. 50-60, 1985.

> Discusses the architectural model, the underlying processing model, and the principles of the interchange formats of ECMA 101 and ISO drafts, known as ODA and ODIF.

[ISO85a] ISO, "Information processing — Text and office systems — Standard Generalized markup Language (SGML)," Draft international Standard ISO/DIS 8879, 1985.

> Specifies a language for document representation. See also [Goldfarb81].

[ISO85b] ISO, "Text Preparation and Interchange — Text and Office Systems," DP 8613 ISO/TC97/SC18/WG3, 1985.

> A proposed multi-party standard. Part 2 describes the Office Document Architecture (ODA); Part 5 the Interchange Formats (ODIF).

[Ilson80] R. Ilson, "An integrated Approach to Formatted Document Production," LCS TR-253, M.I.T., 1980.

> Discusses characteristics and details of the implementation and characteristics of Etude, an interactive text processing system. See also [Hammer81].

[Irving84] R. H. Irving, "An approach to assessment of Text Handling

Systems," *SIGOA*, no. 5.1-2, pp. 181-187, 1984.

> Describes an initial framework for assessing the productivity of text processing centres and discusses results from a field trial.

[Jochum81] G. Jochum and W. Willmertinger, "A tool for developing text processing sytems: Translator Writing Systems," TUM-I8103, TU Munchen, Institut fur Informatik, 1981.

> With the help of TWS, editing and formatting programs can be generated in a formal and also simple manner.

[Joloboff83] V. Joloboff, "An Interactive Graphics Editor for Document Preparation," *SIGPC Notices*, no. 6.6, pp. 45-53, 1983.

> This paper describes an interactive graphics editor for designing illustrations to be inserted in documents.

[Kernighan75] B. W. Kernighan and L. L. Cherry, "A System for Typesetting Mathematics," *Communications of the ACM*, no. 18.3, pp. 151-157, 1975.

> EQN is a program for typesetting mathematics on UNIX. The EQN language was designed to be easy to use by people who know neither mathematics nor typesetting. EQN works as a preprocessor to Troff.

[Kernighan78] B. W. Kernighan et al, "Document Preparation," *The Bell System Technical Journal*, no. 57.6, pp. 2115-2135, 1978.

> An overview of Troff and its preprocessors.

[Kernighan79a] B. W. Kernighan, "A TROFF Tutorial," in: *UNIX Programmers Manual 7th edition*, vol. 2A, pp. 237-250, Bell Laboratories, 1979.

> An introduction to the most basic use of Troff. It presents just enough information to enable the user to do simple formatting tasks, and to make incremental changes to existing packages of Troff commands.

[Kernighan79b] B. W. Kernighan and L. L. Cherry, "Typesetting Mathematics — User's Guide," in: *UNIX Programmers Manual 7th edition*, vol. 2A, pp. 151-161, Bell Laboratories, 1979.

> User's guide to EQN. See also [Kernighan75].

[Kernighan81] B. W. Kernighan, "A Typesetter-independent TROFF," Computer Science Technical Report 97, Bell Laboratories, 1981.

> Describes the conversion of Troff to deal with a wide class of typesetters.

[Kernighan82a] B. W. Kernighan, "PIC — A language for typesetting graphics," *Software — Practice and Experience*, vol. 12, pp. 1-21, 1982.

> PIC is a language for drawing simple figures on a typesetter. The basic ob-

jects in PIC are boxes, circles, ellipses, lines, arrows, arcs, spline curves and text. These may be placed anywhere, at positions specified absolutely or in terms of previous objects. It is implemented as a preprocessor to Troff.

[Kernighan82b] B. W. Kernighan and M. E. Lesk, "Unix Document Preparation," in: *[Nievergelt82]*, pp. 1-20, 1982.

A revised version of [Kernighan78].

[Kernighan84a] B. W. Kernighan, "PIC — A graphics language for typesetting," Computer Science Technical report 116, Bell Laboratories, 1984.

The PIC manual as of December 1984; see also [Kernighan81].

[Kernighan84b] B. W. Kernighan, "The UNIX Document Preparation Tools — A Retrospective," in: *[Miller84b]*, pp. 12-25, 1984.

An overview of the UNIX tools for document preparation.

[Kernighan85] B. W. Kernighan, "Recent Work in Unix Document Preparation Tools," in: *Proceedings EUUG85*, Copenhagen, 1985.

Describes GRAP, a preprocessor to Troff for typesetting graphs, and enhancements to PIC that permit the creation of more complex figures. See also [Bentley84].

[Kimura84a] G. D. Kimura, "A Structure Editor and Model for Abstract Document Objects," TR 87-07-04, Department of Computer Science, University of Washington, 1984.

This dissertation presents an expressive model that is suitable for paper and electronic documents, and a designs of an editor that is based on a graph-like structure.

[Kimura84b] G. D. Kimura and A. C. Shaw, "The Structure of Abstract Document Objects," *SIGOA*, no. 5.1-2, pp. 161-169, 1984.

The principal concepts are the notions of abstract and concrete objects, hierarchical composition of objects, sharing of components and reference links.

[King84] P. R. King, "W-p: a prototype text-processor and document formatter," in: *[Miller84b]*, pp. 161-172, 1984.

An interactive, 'what you see is close to what you get', system whose commands are high-level and serve to define the hierarchical composition of a document.

[Knuth79] D. E. Knuth, *T_EX and Metafont: new Directions in Typesetting*, Digital Press, 1979.

Part I is a reprint of 'Mathematical Typography' (Bulletin AMS, March 1979, Vol 1.2, pp 337-372), which discusses both the typography of mathematics and the use of mathematics in typography. Part II is a hand-book of TEX, woefully out of date. Part III discusses METAFONT, a system for alphabet design.

[Knuth81] D. E. Knuth and M. F. Plass, "Breaking Paragraphs into Lines," *Software — Practice and Experience*, vol. 11, pp. 1119-1184, 1981.

Detailed discussion of TEX's linebreaking algorithm, based on the concepts 'boxes', 'glue' and 'penalties'.

[Knuth84] D.E. Knuth, *The TEXbook*, Addison-Wesley, 1984.

The definitive guide to the use of TEX, written by the system's creator.

[Kowarski83] I. Kowarski and C. Michaud, "Midoc, a microcompuer system for the management of structured documents," in: *IFIP83*, pp. 567-572, 1983.

Describes Midoc, a system in which documents may be parametered, and are provided with a user-defined logical tree structure.

[Lamport85] L. Lamport, *LATEX: A Document Preparation System*, Addison-Wesley, 1985.

[Lampson78] B. W. Lampson, "Bravo Manual," in: *Alto User's Handbook*, B. W. Lampson and E. A. Taft (ed.), Xerox PARC, 1978.

Bravo is an integrated text editor/formatter which influenced the design of the Star user interface. See also [Smith82a].

[Lerner83] R. G. Lerner et al, "Primary Publication Systems and Scientific Text Processing," in: *Annual Review of Information Science and Technology*, M. E. Williams (ed.), vol. 18, pp. 127-149, 1983.

This article discusses a number of text preparation systems including the Unix tools and TEX, different output and storage devices used in text processing systems, and some possible future developments.

[Lesk77] M. E. Lesk and B. W. Kernighan, "Computer typesetting of technical journals on UNIX," in: *AFIPS46*, pp. 879-888, 1977.

Describes an experiment in which Troff is evaluated by measuring use of computer and economic resources when typesetting (technical) manuscripts.

[Lesk79a] M. E. Lesk, "Some Applications of Inverted Indexes on the UNIX system," in: *UNIX Programmers Manual 7th edition*, vol. 2A, pp. 189-201, Bell Laboratories, 1979.

The second part of this paper discusses refer, a preprocessor to Troff to extract references from databases or files.

[Lesk79b] M. E. Lesk, "TBL — A Program to Format Tables," in:

UNIX Programmers Manual 7th edition, vol. 2A, pp. 163-180, Bell Laboratories, 1979.

> TBL is a preprocessor to Troff which makes even fairly complex tables easy to specify and enter.

[Levison83] M. Levison, "Editing Mathematical Formulae," *Software — Practice and Experience*, vol. 13, pp. 189-195, 1983.

> An editor which allows the user to create and modify a formula by manipulating a pictorial representation on a display.

[Lippman85] A. Lippman et al, "Color word processing," *IEEE Computer Graphics and Applications*, pp. 41-46, June 1985.

> Addresses incorporation of color into word processing systems as a cognitive aid.

[Lucarella85] D. Lucarella, *Proceedings of the first European Conference on TEX for Scientific Documentation.*, Addison-Wesley, 1985.

> Contains 18 papers discussoing various aspects of TEX and METAFONT.

[Meyrowitz82] N. Meyrowitz and A. van Dam, "Interactive Editing Systems, part I, II," *ACM Computing Surveys*, no. 14.3, pp. 321-415, 1982.

> Part I provides a comprehensive and systematic view of the features of typical editing systems. Part II is a survey which presents numerous examples of systems in both the academic and commercial arenas.

[Miller84a] J. J. H. Miller (Ed.), *An Introduction to Text Processing Systems*, Boole Press, 1984.

> Provides, for a non-specialist audience, an introduction to computer-aided text processing (mainly TEX and Troff).

[Miller84b] J. J. H. Miller (Ed.), *Protext I Conference Proceedings*, Boole Press, 1984.

> Proceedings of the First International Conference on Text Processing Systems (29 papers).

[Mooney82] J. D. Mooney, "MFS: A Modular Text Formatting System," in: *AFIPS 1982 National Computer Conference Proceedings*, H. L. Morgan (ed.), pp. 529-535, 1982.

> This paper presents the design goals and architecture of the Modular Formatting System. MFS applies to formatters the principles of separation of functions. A small kernel forms the basis of a family of formatting systems.

[Mudur79] S. P. Mudur et al, "Design of Software for Text Processing," *Software — Practice and Experience*, vol. 9, pp. 312-323, 1979.

> Favourable features of text processing systems are: flexible style

specifications, economical proof generation, multilingual text input, device independence, and portability. A system designed on the basis of such considerations is briefly described.

[Nemeth85] K. Nemeth, "Principles of Document Interchange Protocol for CCITT Telematic Services," *IEEE Communications Magazine*, no. 23.3, pp. 23-28, March 1985.

Descibes the CCITT Document Interchange Protocol.

[Nievergelt82] J. Nievergelt et al (Ed.), *Document Preparation Systems,* North-Holland, 1982.

A snapshot of representative developments in the field of computer aids to document preparation, dissemination, storage and retrieval.

[Noot83] H. Noot, "Structured Text Formatting," *Software — Practice and Experience*, vol. 13, pp. 79-94, 1983.

An abstract format machine is presented which can be 'microprogrammed' to yield (structured) document formatters. Its language contains constructs for the manipulation of blocks of text.

[Ossanna79] J. F. Ossanna, "NROFF/TROFF user's manual," in: *UNIX Programmers Manual 7th edition*, vol. 2A, pp. 203-236, Bell Laboratories, 1979.

This manual contains a description of all the basic functions incorporated in Nroff and Troff. Some examples are given of how to define commands using the basic functions as primitives.

[Plass81] M. F. Plass, "Optimal Pagination Techniques for Automatic Typesetting Systems," Report STAN-CS-81-870, PhD Thesis Stanford University, 1981.

Discusses techniques for optimal placement of figures, displays and the like. The model is based on the one used in TEX.

[Plass82] M. F. Plass and D. E. Knuth, "Choosing better line breaks," in: *[Nievergelt82]*, pp. 221-242, 1982.

Considers a new approach to the problems of dividing a paragraph into lines. The method considers the paragraph as a whole, and is based on the concepts 'boxes', 'glue' and 'kerfs'. Implemented in TEX. See also [Knuth81].

[POSTSCRIPT85a] POSTSCRIPT, *POSTSCRIPT Language Reference Manual,* Adobe Systems Incorporated, Addison-Wesley, 1985.

Postscript is an interpretative programming language to describe the appearance of text, images and graphic material on printed pages.

[POSTSCRIPT85b] POSTSCRIPT, *POSTSCRIPT Language Tutorial*

and Cookbook, Adobe Systems Incorporated, Addison-Wesley, 1985.

Another book on POSTSCRIPT, see also [POSTSCRIPT85a].

[Pringle79] A. Pringle et al, "Aspects of Quality in the Design and Production of Text," in: *Siggraph '79,* B. W. Pollack (ed.), pp. 63-70, ACM, 1979.

Addresses quality aspects of a letter design system, high quality television transmission of text, and presentation of tabular text.

[Quint82] V. Quint, "An Interactive System for Editing Mathematical Documents," in: *Integrated Interactive Computing Systems,* P. Degano and E. Sandewall (ed.), pp. 153-165, North-Holland, 1982.

Describes Edimath, a syntax-directed interactive system for manipulating mathematical formulae.

[Quint83] V. Quint, "An interactive system for mathematical textprocessing," *Technology and Science of Informatics,* no. 2.3, pp. 169-179, 1983.

See [Quint82].

[Quint84] V. Quint, "Interactive Editing of Mathematics," in: *[Miller84b],* pp. 55-68, 1984.

See [Quint82].

[Reid80a] B. K. Reid, "A High-Level Approach to Computer Document Formatting," *POPL ACM,* no. 7, pp. 24-31, 1980.

An overview of Scribe. The user indicates the structure of a document in his text, while layout directives are collected in a database with document types.

[Reid80b] B. K. Reid and J. H. Walker, *Scribe Introductory User's Manual, 3rd ed.,* Unilogic, Pittsburgh, 1980.

Scribe's manual. See also [Reid80a].

[Reid80c] B. K. Reid, "Scribe: A Document Specification Language and its Compiler," CMU-CS-81-100, Carnegie-Mellon University, 1980.

Describes the design of a 'formatter' in which the separation of form and content is achieved. See also [Reid80a].

[Reid81] B. K. Reid and D. R. Hanson, "An annotated bibliography of background material on text manipulation," in: *[SIGPLAN81],* pp. 157-160, 1981.

A small bibliography listing classic or important work.

[Reid84] J. K. Reid and M. J. Hopper, "TSSD: A Typesetting System for Scientific Documents," in: *[Miller84b]*, pp. 216-221, 1984.

> Describes TSSD's high-level descriptive command language and some of the design aims.

[Saltzer65] J. Saltzer, "Manuscript typing and editing: TYPESET, RUN-OFF," in: *The Compatible Time-Sharing System: A programmer's guide,* , P. A. Crisman (ed.), section AH.9.01, 2nd edition, MIT , 1965.

> An early influential system, having distinct command and text lines. Differentiation is by a special character in column one. A predecessor of Troff.

[Seybold82] J. W. Seybold, "Document Preparation Systems and Commercial Typesetting," in: *[Nievergelt82]*, pp. 243-264, 1982.

> The development of methods of photocomposition is described and the history of the use of computer programs for the production of typeset output is traced.

[Shaw80] A. C. Shaw, "A model for document preparation systems," Technical Report 80-04-02, Department of Computer Science, University of Washington, Seattle, 1980.

[SIGPLAN81] SIGPLAN, "Proceedings of the ACM SIGPLAN SIGOA Symposium on Text Manipulation," *SIGPLAN Notices*, no. 16.6, 1981.

> Contains 20 papers and a bibliography; some of these are mentioned separately.

[Smith82a] D. C. Smith et al, "Designing the Star User Interface," *BYTE*, pp. 242-282, feb 1982.

> The Star user interface differs from that of other office computer systems by its emphasis on graphics, its adherence to a metaphor of a physical office, and its rigorous application of a small set of design principles.

[Smith82b] D. C. Smith et al, "The Star User Interface: an Overview," in: *AFIPS 1982 National Computer Conference Proceedings*, H. L. Morgan (ed.), pp. 515-528, AFIPS, 1982.

> See [Smith82a].

[Spivak83a] M. Spivak, *The Joy of TEX*, American Mathematical Society, 1983.

> 'A Gourmet guide to Typesetting Technical Text by Computer'. Gives an introduction to typesetting mathematical documents using TEX80. Includes a summary of A_MS-TEX for TEX82.

[Spivak83b] M. Spivak, "Summary of A_MS-TEX," *TUGboat*, no. 4.2, pp. 103-126, 1983.

A brief summary of $A_{\mathcal{M}}S$-T_EX as written for T_EX82.

[Strömfors81] O. Strömfors and L. Jonesjö, "The implementation and experiences of a structure-oriented text editor," in: *[SIGPLAN81]*, pp. 22-27, 1981.

> Describes a prototype structure-oriented text editor (ED3) providing a uniform interface to text, pictures and formatted database records.

[Sundblad84] Y. Sundblad, "Computer Based Tools for Skilled Page Make-up Work," in: *[Miller84b]*, pp. 227-233, 1984.

> Describes requirements for good functionality and good quality of page make-up work using graphic workstations. The approach is tool- and object-oriented, 'What you see is what you have got'.

[Tesler73] L. Tesler, "PUB, The document compiler," Stanford Artificial Intelligence Project, Operating Note 70, 1973.

> An advanced text justifier and page formatter. PUB's formatting language is similar to RUNOFF. Provides a number of ALGOL-like features, most notably block-structuring.

[TUGboat] TUGboat, TUG, P.O.Box 9506, Providence, RI 02940.

> Newsletter of the T_EX Users Group, published irregularly since 1980.

[Verges-Escuin73] J. C. Verges-Escuin and J. P. Verjus, "Reconnaissance automatique des structures des textes en vue de l'edition," *RAIRO*, no. B-2, pp. 85-120, 1973.

> A rather early paper describing syntax-directed editing of documents.

[Walker81] J. H. Walker, "The Document Editor: A Support Environment for Preparing Technical documents," in: *[SIGPLAN81]*, pp. 44-50, 1981.

> Describes a research effort into identifying the requirements for an interactive environment for editing complex documents, and an initial implementation.

[Williams83] G. Williams, "The Lisa Computer System," *BYTE*, pp. 33-50, feb 1983.

> Discusses Lisa, including its document processing.

[Williams84] G. Williams, "The Apple Macintosh Computer," *BYTE*, pp. 30-54, feb 1984.

> A general description of the Macintosh, including its word-processing capabilities.

[Witten82] I. H. Witten et al, "On the power of Traps and Diversions in a document Preparation Language," *Software — Practice and Experi-*

ence, vol. 12, pp. 1119-1131, 1982.

> Considers figure placement, setting text in arbitrary shapes, and balancing final columns in multi-column layout. Discusses nroff-solutions for these problems.

[Woodman84] M. Woodman, "Formatting Syntactically Nested Documents," in: *[Miller84b]*, pp. 240-246, 1984.

> Documents belong to a generic class (e.g. text, Pascal program) within which a variety of types may exist (e.g. reports, memos). A syntactic description of a document type drives the formatting system.

[Wyk80] C. J. van Wyk, "A Language for typesetting Graphics," PhD Thesis, Stanford, 1980.

> Presents IDEAL, and the principles that motivate the form of IDEAL. See also [Wyk81a].

[Wyk81a] C. J. van Wyk, "A Graphics Typesetting Language," in: *[SIGPLAN81]*, pp. 99-107, 1981.

> Presents IDEAL, a language in which two-dimensional figures can be expressed. The language is intended to work with existing text-formatting systems so that text and figures can be typeset at the same time. Another preprocessor to Troff.

[Wyk81b] C. J. van Wyk, "IDEAL User's Manual," Computing Science Technical report 103, Bell Laboratories, 1981.

> Describes how to use the existing implementation of IDEAL. See also [Wyk81a].

[Yankelovich85] N. Yankelovich et al, "Reading and writing the electronic book," *IEEE Computer*, no. 18.10, pp. 15-30, 1985.

> Outlines the capabilities that electronic document systems should possess, and describes four document systems developed or under development at Brown University.

Cross-reference index

bibliography :
> [André82] [Reid81]

Etude :
> [Good81a] [Good81b] [Hammer81] [Ilson80]

formatting :
> [Anderson75] [Berns69] [Furuta82] [Mooney82] [Noot83] [Reid80c] [Saltzer65] [Tesler73]

IDEAL :
> [Wyk80] [Wyk81a] [Wyk81b]

interchange :
> [Horak83] [Horak84a] [Horak84b] [Horak85] [ISO85b] [Nemeth85]

line-breaking :
> [Achubue81] [Knuth81] [Plass82]

mathematics :
> [Allen81] [Day83] [Kernighan75] [Kernighan79b] [Knuth79] [Levison83]
> [Quint82] [Quint83] [Quint84]

miscellaneous :
> [Aderet84] [Beatty79] [Becker84] [Biggerstaff84] [Burns76] [Canzii84]
> [Chamberlin81] [Chamberlin82] [Coulouris76] [Doster84] [Gehringer80]
> [Irving84] [Jochum81] [Lampson78] [Lippman85] [Mudur79] [Plass81]
> [POSTSCRIPT85a] [POSTSCRIPT85b] [Pringle79] [Reid84] [Shaw80]
> [Sundblad84] [Walker81] [Williams83] [Williams84] [Witten82]
> [Yankelovich85]

overview :
> [Dam70] [Furuta82] [Hansson81] [Lerner83] [Meyrowitz82]
> [Nievergelt82] [Seybold82]

PIC :
> [Kernighan82a] [Kernighan84a] [Kernighan85]

pictures :
> [Beach83] [Bentley84] [Feiner81] [Gibson85] [Joloboff83]
> [Kernighan82a] [Kernighan84a] [Kernighan85] [Wyk80] [Wyk81a]
> [Wyk81b]

proceedings :
> [Lucarella85] [Miller84a] [Miller84b] [SIGPLAN81]

Scribe :
> [Reid80a] [Reid80b] [Reid80c]

SGML :
> [Goldfarb81] [ISO85a]

standards :
> [Horak84a] [Horak84b] [Horak85] [ISO85a] [ISO85b] [Nemeth85]

structured documents :
> [Allen81] [Benoliel78] [Borkin78] [Burkhart80] [Donzeau-Gouge83]
> [Ganzinger85] [Hibbard84] [Kimura84a] [Kimura84b] [Kowarski83]
> [Reid80a] [Strömfors81] [Verges-Escuin73] [Woodman84]

TEX :
> [Appelt85] [Furuta85] [Knuth79] [Knuth81] [Knuth84] [Lamport85]
> [Lucarella85] [Plass82] [Spivak83a] [Spivak83b] [TUGboat]

troff :
> [Bentley84] [Buchmann84] [Gibson85] [Kernighan75] [Kernighan78]
> [Kernighan79a] [Kernighan79b] [Kernighan81] [Kernighan82a]
> [Kernighan82b] [Kernighan84a] [Kernighan84b] [Kernighan85] [Lesk77]
> [Lesk79a] [Lesk79b] [Ossanna79] [Wyk81a]

user-interfaces :
> [Blomberg84] [Coutaz84] [Good81a] [Good81b] [Smith82a] [Smith82b]

WYSIWYG :
> [Gutknecht84] [Gutknecht85] [King84]

Systems used

C. Bigelow (p 1), composed in Lucida typefaces, formatted with TeX82 on a VAX11/730 under VAX/VMS, printed on an Imagen 8/300 laser printer.

R.J. Beach (p 18), formatted with Tioga in the Cedar environment on a high-performance workstation, the Interpress 3.0 master was printed on an experimental high-resolution laser platemaker.

P.J. Brown (p 34), Troff with ms-macros, using a Canon LBP-10.

V.A. Burrill (p 43), Troff on a PDP11/44, printed on a Versatec V-80 phototypesetter; screens by MacPaint.

E.J. Yannakoudakis (p 65), RX 860 word processor linked to XVC2E Xenotron make-up screen, printed on Linotron 101 typesetter.

R. Hamlet (p 78), Device-independent Troff on a VAX 11/780, printed on an Imagen 8/300 laser printer (and reduced before printed).

M. Nanard (p 90), prepared using the Biostation whith an HP-Laserjet.

V. Joloboff (p 107), Sroff on a VAX under UNIX, printed on a Digital LN01 laser printer.

M.H. Kay (p 125), prepared on ICL DRS 8801 word processor using COMPOSE, printed on Visutek Scantext typesetter; diagrams on Apple Macintosh.

D.D. Cowan (p 140), LaTeX on a VAX 780 (UNIX 4.2), printed on an Imagen 300 laser printer.

B. Gowan (p 171), ditroff on VAX11/780, printed on a Harris 7500 typesetter.

C.Y. Suen (p 178), homegrown system on a VAX 11/780, printed on a Versatec printer, 200 dots/inch.

V. Quint (p 200), typeset using Sroff (homegrown) on a VAX 11/780, printed on a Digital LN01 laser printer.

B. K. Reid (p 214), used Scribe and PostScript, printed on an Apple LaserWriter, and later reduced.

P. Goyal (p 224), homegrown program, running on a CYBER 835, printed on a XEROX 2700II laser printer.

U. Corda (p 233), Troff on a SUN running UNIX and producing PostScript, printed on an Apple LaserWriter.

R. Furuta (p 246), LaTeX on a VAX running UNIX, set on an Alphatype.

J.C. van Vliet (p 260), ditroff on a VAX11/780, printed on a Harris 7500 typesetter.